Northwestern University
Studies in *Phenomenology &*
Existential Philosophy

The Visible and the Invisible

Maurice Merleau-Ponty

Edited by Claude Lefort

Translated by Alphonso Lingis

The Visible and the Invisible

FOLLOWED BY WORKING NOTES

NORTHWESTERN UNIVERSITY PRESS

1968   EVANSTON

Originally published in French under the title
Le Visible et l'invisible
Copyright © 1964, Editions Gallimard

Copyright © 1968 by Northwestern University Press
Library of Congress Catalog Card Number: 68–31025
All rights reserved
Manufactured in the United States of America

Permission has been granted to quote from Jean-Paul Sartre,
Being and Nothingness,
translated by Hazel E. Barnes (New York: The Philosophical
Library, 1956).

Contents

Editor's Foreword

HOWEVER EXPECTED it may sometimes be, the death of a relative or a friend opens an abyss before us. How much more so when it comes absolutely unannounced, when it can be ascribed neither to illness, nor to age, nor to a visible concourse of circumstances, when, moreover, he who dies is so alive that habitually we had come to relate our thoughts to his, to seek in him the strength we lacked, and to count him among the truest witnesses of our undertakings. Such was the sudden death of Maurice Merleau-Ponty, and such was his personality, that all those who were bound to him by friendship knew the bitter truth of this affliction by the shock it sent into their lives. But now they have yet to hear the silence of a voice which, though it had always come to them charged with personal accents, seemed to them to have always spoken and to be destined to speak always.

It is a strange silence to which the interrupted conversation abandons us—where we forget the death of the writer only to return to it by another route. The work has come to an end, and, simply because everything in it is said, we are suddenly confronted with it. The term has come too soon, we think, but this regret does not affect the evidence that the work is born the moment it is closed. From now on it is what it says and nothing more, a complete word that refers only to itself, rests only on itself, and from which the memory of its origin fades away. The writer has disappeared; henceforth we read his work. To it—no longer to him—we turn with expectation. A profound change: for we doubt not that attention and patience will suffice for the meaning the work bears inscribed in itself to come to us. Now xii / THE VISIBLE AND THE INVISIBLE

everything induces this meaning, even the ideas we would judge most contestable, since in their own way they also teach us the truth of the discourse. Yesterday we still thought the writer was only responding to the questions we put to ourselves, or formulating those that arose from our common situation in the world. The things at the end of his look were the same as those we saw or could see from our place. His experience was, to be sure, singular, but it developed within the same horizons as our own, nourished itself with the same refusal of ancient truths and the same uncertainty of the future. Whatever was the prestige he enjoyed in our eyes, we knew well that his function invested him with no power, that he only took the risk of naming what in the present had no name, that the route was blazed under his steps as it opens under our own when we set out to advance. Thus we discovered his writings with the astonishment due to all that is new, without ever throwing off our reserve before what we admired most, so little sure were we of what thought they would bring or what consequences they would develop within us, and aware that the author himself did not know how far he would have to go. Without being his equal, we were close to him, because we were subject to the same rhythm of the world, participating in the same time, equally without support. Now that the work owes nothing more to its author, a new distance is established between it and us, and we become another reader. Not that our power to criticize will be diminished. It is possible that we will detect uncertainties, lacunae, discordances, even contradictions; in any case, the variety of the ideas and their genesis are palpable to us: for example, we measure the difference that separates the last writings from the early works. But the critique does not cast doubt on the existence of the work; it is still a means of rejoining it, for this very movement, these divergencies, these contradictions we observe belong to it as its own. The obscurity in which the work remains is no less essential than the luminous passages where its intention appears unveiled. More generally, there is nothing in the work that does not bespeak it and manifest its identity—what it states and what it passes over in silence, the content of its propositions and its style, the frank way it has to proceed to its goal, and its detours or its digressions. Everything that solicits the attention indicates a route that leads to it and is equally an overture to what it is.

Whence comes this shift of the reader's gaze, upon the disappearance of the writer? It is that, metamorphosed now into a work, the sole function of the writer's experience is no longer to render intelligible the reality before which it takes form. Doubtless the work remains a mediator—we seek in it a way of access to the present and past world, learn from it the measure of our own task of knowledge—but the peculiarity of this mediator is that it henceforth is a part of the world to which it leads. The work from which the writer has withdrawn has become a work among others, a part of our cultural milieu, and contributes to situate us in relation to it, since it finds its meaning only within the horizons of that culture and thus renders it present to us while drawing for us a singular figure of it. It is a thing that exists by itself, which, to be sure, would be nothing had it not its origin in the writer and would fall into oblivion if the reader ceased to interest himself in it; yet nevertheless the work does not depend entirely on either—both writer and reader also depend on it, inasmuch as it is true that the memory of what the writer was will survive only through the work and that men will discover the work only on condition that they let themselves be guided by it toward the domain of thought in which it once settled. And as we question after him this thing that has conquered a space of its own in the spiritual universe the writer questioned, it connects up to that spiritual universe in a thousand ways, radiating in all the directions of the past and the future, finally acquiring its true meaning only when it is acknowledged to be a modulation of a thought without origin nor term, an articulation within a discourse perpetually recommenced. The work therefore lives on the outside. Like things of nature, like facts of history, it is a being of the outside, awakening the same astonishment, requiring the same attention, the same exploration of the gaze, promising by its sole presence a meaning of an order other than the significations contained in its statements. It does not belong to the world like the rest, since it exists only in order to name what is and the bond that attaches us to what is. But, in naming, it exchanges its own presence for that of the things, borrows from them their objectivity: it imprints itself in what it expresses. We are compelled to see the world in it only because in the moment it converts all things into things thought, the thought compounds itself with the things, ballasts itself with their weight, lets itself be caught up in their movement, their duration, their exteriority, and appropriates them to itself only by breaking with its own origins. Such a rupture is no doubt evinced by every work as soon as it is written but is not completely consummated until the thinker is no longer there. For, from then on, the events that marked his life, those of his personal history—the private history that the reader always knows something about, for the writer most discreet about himself never entirely succeeds in dissimulating it, or the history of his activities, his discoveries, his contentions with his contemporaries—and those of the public history, whose effects we undergo while they cede to it the efficacity we attributed to them, cease orientating our gaze and pass into the state of anecdotal references, to give place to the reality of the work which retains from them only their meaning. Deprived of their former figure and their former power, they are inscribed in a new temporality and come to serve a new history; metamorphosed into their meaning, they henceforth sustain an enigmatic correspondence with other events we know likewise to live in the depths of the past; changed into general powers, they hold under their dominion a domain of being to which neither dates nor places are assignable with precision.

Thus the withdrawal of the things from the world accompanies the withdrawal of him who thinks them, and the work exists completely only in virtue of this double absence, when, all things having become thoughts and all thoughts having become things, it suddenly seems to draw the whole of being to itself and to become, by itself alone, a source of meaning.

It is therefore not saying much to say that the work survives the writer, that, when its incompletion will be forgotten, we will know only the plenitude of its meaning. This plenitude is *de jure*. The work alone seems to have a positive existence, for, even though its fate be suspended on the decision of future readers to let it speak, at least each time they will turn to it, it will come to interpose itself, as on the first day, between him who reads and the world to which he is present, compelling him to question that world in it and to relate his own thoughts to what it is.

Such is the fascination the finished work exercises on its reader that for a moment it renders vain all recrimination of the death of the writer. The writer disappears just when he was preparing for new beginnings, and the creation is interrupted, forever beneath the expression it announced, from which it was to draw its final justification. But, whatever be the consternation of him who considers the absurd denouement—of him, in particular, to whom is given the sad privilege of entering the room where the writer worked, of measuring with his gaze the abandoned labor, the notes, the plans, the drafts which bear everywhere the palpable trace of a thought in effervescence, on the verge of finding its form—it is still associated with the memory of the man to whom, suddenly, to pursue his task was forbidden. Once this memory fades, it will be of little importance—one persuades oneself—to know when the author died, in what circumstances, and whether or not he still had the power to continue. For just as we cannot imagine, as we have no need to imagine, the movements of thought that accompany his creation, his interior disorder, his hesitations, the endeavors in which he gets bogged down and from which he returns after efforts spent in pure waste, the stammerings among which his language takes form, neither can we find in the ultimate defeat in which his enterprise sinks the matter for a reflection on his work.

But what does it mean that a work becomes foreign to the conditions of its creation? Do we not have to understand that it is beyond completion as well as incompletion? And, indeed, how could a work ever be completed, in the ordinary sense of that word? To think that it were, one would have to suppose that its meaning were rigorously determined, that it one day would have been able to acquire, by the statement of certain propositions, such a coherence that any new word would have become superfluous; one would have to see in it a long chain of demonstrations destined to reach its term in a final proof. But the power we recognize in the work to solicit the reflection of future readers indefinitely, to join into one same interrogation the questions they put to the work and those that arise out of their own experience would forthwith become unintelligible. A completed work would be a work which the author would have entirely mastered and which, for this very reason, the reader would have only to take possession of in his turn; it would have, consequently, through all those who read it but one sole reader. Then we could not say that it would remain present to men, despite the time passed by since the moment of its creation; not because the truths discovered should cease to be valid as such, but because, fixed once and for all in operations of cognition that could always be repeated, they would constitute a simple acquisition to which it would be useless to return.

The work, we said, fascinates; the moment the author disappears, it detaches us from him and compels us to see it as future readers will see it—but that does not mean that it has gained a definite identity outside of time. Far from withdrawing from our time, and from all time, it invades the field of the past and of the future under our eyes; it is present beforehand in what is not yet, and the meaning of this presence is in part hidden from us. We have no doubt that it will speak when we will no longer be there to hear it—as the works of the past remotely distant from their author and their first readers continue to speak—and we know likewise that others will read in it what we are not in a position to read, that the most well-founded interpretations will not exhaust its meaning. The new time it initiates, if it be different from the time of *real* history, is not foreign to it, for at every moment it exists in the triple dimension of present, past, and future, and, if it remains the same, it remains always in expectation of its own meaning. It is not only its image that is renewed; it itself endures, for it duration is essential, since it is made to accept the test of the changes of the world and of the thought of the others. Only from this point of view has it a positive existence—not because it is what it is once and for all, but because it provides for thought indefinitely, it will never be wanting to whomever questions it, and tomorrow as yesterday it will be involved with our relations with the world.

Whether the writer's labor seems to have come to its term or not is, therefore, of little importance: as soon as we are confronted with the work, we are faced with the same indetermination; and the more we penetrate into its domain, the more our knowledge increases, and the less we are capable of putting a limit to our questions. In the end we have to admit that we communicate with it only by reason of this indetermination. We truly welcome what thought it gives only because this gift has no name, because it does not sovereignly dispose of its own thoughts but remains under the dominion of the meaning it wishes to transmit.

We have then to reconsider the fate of the work. We thought we had exchanged the misfortune of the interrupted creation for the security and repose of the accomplished work. In it we found plenitude of meaning and solidity of being. It is true that its presence is reassuring, since it has no limits, since it rightfully has its place among the works of the past and radiates as far as it pleases us to imagine in the direction of the future, since the very idea that it could one day fade out from the memory of men does not change the certitude that so long as literature will convey an interrogation of our relation with the world it will remain a living guidemark. Yet this presence presents an enigma, for the work evokes an attention to itself only to render palpable a certain impossibility of being. The work gives a singular figure to this impossibility but does not overcome it. It is essential to the work that it bear witness to it, remaining separated from itself as it remains separated from the world whose meaning it wishes to capture.

Thus again we discover death in the work, because its power is bound to its final impotency, because all the routes it opens and will always keep open are and will be without issue. In vain we try to brush aside the menace of this death: we imagine that what the work could not say others will say in the future, but what it has not said belongs properly to it, and the thoughts it awakens will be inscribed only far from it in a new work, by virtue of a new beginning. The meaning it dispenses always remains in suspense; the circle it traces circumscribes a certain void or a certain absence.

Such is, perhaps, the reason for our confusion before the uncompleted work; it brutally confronts us with an essential ambiguity from which more often than not we prefer to turn away. What is disconcerting is not that the last part of the discourse has been taken from us or that the goal the writer was approaching will be henceforth inaccessible (since it is a fact that that goal will never be attained); it is that we have discovered necessity inscribed in the work—the underlying movement by which it installs itself in speech so as to open itself to an inexhaustible commentary of the world, its advent to an order of existence in which it seems established for always—and that, in the same moment, this obscure decree which cuts it short of its intention throws it back to the *de facto* frontiers of its expression and suddenly makes doubt arise as to the legitimacy of its undertaking. We can, to be sure, convince ourselves that the uncertainty to which it abandons us motivates and supports our questioning concerning the world, that it still speaks when it is silent by the power it has to designate what is and what will always be beyond the expressible; yet the fact remains that it was destined for the incessant unveiling of meaning, that all its truth was in that disclosure, and that it could not be terminated without the veil enshrouding it in its turn, and without its ways being lost in the dark.

He to whom these thoughts come is the less disposed to forget them before Maurice Merleau-Ponty's last writing as he knows that they were Merleau-Ponty's own thoughts, and he is still learning from him to see where they lead him. If we reread, for example, "The Philosopher and His Shadow," "Indirect Language and the Voices of Silence," the texts written for *Les Philosophes célèbres,* or if we simply read the pages he left us after his death, we will see that he constantly questioned himself about the essence of the philosophical work. It was already a problem for him to understand the strange bond that connected his enterprise with that of his predecessors. Better than anyone, he has brought into the open the ambiguity of a relation that at the same time opens us and closes us to the truth of what was thought by another, disclosing the profusion of meaning behind us and simultaneously revealing an impassable distance from the present to the past in which the meaning of the philosophical tradition dies away and there arises the exigency to take up again in solitude, without exterior support, the labor of expression. And how could the questions he put to himself before the past have ceased to solicit him when he turned to the future of philosophy and sought to measure the import of his own words? It was the same thing to admit that, however rich in meaning they were, the works of the past were never entirely decipherable and did not deliver us from the necessity of thinking the world as if it had to be thought for the first time, and to admit to those who would come after us the right to see, in their turn, with a new view or, at least, to bear the center of the philosophical interrogation *elsewhere.* At the same time he contested the idea that the philosopher's enterprise had ever coincided with the construction of the system, and, for the same motive, he refused to raise his own experience to the absolute and seek in it the law of every possible experience. He was convinced that the work remains a source of meaning only because, in his own time, the writer was able to think what the present had provided for his thought. He believed that it is in taking possession anew of the former present that we communicate with it, but that this communication is always impeded, necessitated as we are in our turn to conceive all things from the point of view at which we are. He was equally convinced of the legitimacy of his own research, of his power, certainly, to speak for others who would know nothing of his situation, but he was convinced also of his impotency to make that which gave his value to his questions and which depended essentially on his idea of the truth be maintained henceforth in the same light. Thus, he thought, our labor of expression rejoins that of the others only by ways we do not master, and we must always doubt that they come to seek in it what we seek in a movement that seems to us to be the very movement of philosophical truth. And, to be sure, such a doubt never destroyed in his mind the idea of a unity of philosophy. It is precisely because philosophy is, in his eyes, continual questioning, that it each time enjoins us to presuppose nothing, to neglect the acquired, and to run the risk of opening a route that leads nowhere. By virtue of the same necessity, each undertaking presents itself as irremediably solitary, yet akin to all those that have preceded it and will follow it. There is indeed, therefore, in spite of the appearances, a great conversation which develops, within which the words of each merge, for if they never compose a history articulated logically, at least they are caught up in the same thrust of language and destined to the same meaning. But the certitude that such a conversation sustains us could not efface the frontiers between the works and assure us of being true to it when we discover in our experience the summons to thought. The ambiguity is never settled, since at no moment can we detach completely the interrogation from the works in which it has found its form, since it is in penetrating into their enclosure that we are truly initiated into it, and since finally to question by ourselves is still to speak, to find the measure of our search in a language. Thus we always run up against the fact of the work and its obscurity, and all our questions concerning the world, those we think we discover by reading our predecessors and those we think we draw from ourselves, turn out necessarily to be doubled by a question regarding the *being* of language and of the work: a question that does not nullify the conviction that meaning is given to us, but which increases at the same time as that conviction, since the foundation of this meaning and the relation of the work with what is remain obscure.

That we should, now that Merleau-Ponty is dead, look at his work as one work among others, as he himself looked and taught us to look at the work of the others, is in a sense of no help to us. It is not because he does not permit himself to reduce meaning to the thought the world provides him in the present and marks out in advance the place of our freedom that we can more easily assume it, determine what his task was, and what would be our own within philosophy. When the constitutive paradox of the work becomes palpable to us (the fact that it wants to name being as such and confesses that it repeats in its own being the enigma with which it is confronted, that it lays claim to the *whole* of interrogation without being able to do better than to open a route whose direction is for the others forever uncertain) and when the ambiguity of our relation with it is revealed (that is, that we learn to think in it and, in our inability to take possession of its domain, have to bear our thoughts *elsewhere*) our indecision only increases. But perhaps in recalling these questions, which were those of our philosopher, we are better disposed to receive his thought, in particular the last writing he was only able to begin, to weigh the event of this last beginning in which his enterprise was to find its term, and to understand how the meaning of his discourse is attested in the being of his work.

At the time of his death, Merleau-Ponty was preparing a work, *The Visible and the Invisible,* of which only the first part was written. It bears witness to his effort to give a new expression to his thought. A reading of some of the essays reassembled in *Signs,* the preface he wrote for them, and "The Eye and the Mind," all works that belong to the last period of his life, suffice to convince oneself that, far from constituting the definitive state of his philosophy, his first works, justly celebrated, had only laid down the foundations of his enterprise and created in him the necessity to go further.[1] But *The Visible and the Invisible* was to bring fully into the open the route traversed since the double critique of idealism and empiricism had brought him to a

1. *Signs,* trans. Richard C. McCleary (Evanston, Ill., 1964); "The Eye and the Mind," trans. Carleton Dallery, in *The Primacy of Perception,* ed. James M. Edie (Evanston, Ill., 1964).

new continent. In the pages that remain for us and the working notes that accompany them, the intention becomes manifest to take up again the early analyses of the thing, the body, the relation between the seer and the visible, in order to dissipate their ambiguity and in order to show that they acquire their full meaning only outside of a psychological interpretation, when they are enveloped in a new ontology. It alone can now ground their legitimacy, as it alone will permit a connection of the criticisms addressed to the philosophy of reflection, dialectics, and phenomenology—criticisms hitherto dispersed and apparently tributary of the empirical descriptions—by disclosing the impossibility of further maintaining the *point of view of consciousness*.

When Merleau-Ponty undertakes this labor, he no doubt judges that he has his work before him, not behind him. He does not think of complementing or correcting his previous writings, making them more accessible to the public, or simply defending them against the attacks made against them as if they had in his eyes a defined identity. What he has already done counts only inasmuch as he discovers in it the finality of a task; his *acquisitions* have value only because they give the capacity to continue, which can be exercised only at the cost of an overturning of the prior work, its reorganization according to new dimensions. The certainty that his first attempts were not vain comes to him only from the necessity to which they commit him to turn back to them in order to think them through and do justice to what they demand.

To be sure, the reader could not entirely share this sentiment. For him, the things said have a weight that binds the writer to them and draws us to them. When he reads the first works of Merleau-Ponty, he discovers what is already *a* philosophy. While they do awaken in him a thousand questions which dispose him to await the continuation, and even while this expectancy situates him, as we said, in the same time as that of the author, still he perceives ideas, if not theses, of whose consistency he has no doubt. With these ideas he will henceforth confront the writer's words, to seek their confirmation, or, on the contrary, variations, even to see a repudiation. But, for the writer, the *said* weighs with another weight; it institutes a muffled pressure on speaking, it is what he must take charge of, what he will always have to count on—nowise a positive reality. The ideas he has behind himself are hollow, the more efficacious in that they lack all the thought they call for, and it is this very determined void that supports his enterprise. And, no doubt, nothing can make the writer's perspective coincide with that of the reader, for their illusion arises from complementary motives. As has often been observed, the one cannot see what he writes and writes because he does not see, while the other can only see. The work which the author cannot look at is in his eyes as if it did not exist, and it is always in writing that he seeks to ascertain what it is to be, while, when addressed to our reader's view, the work tempts us to consider it as a thing among others, a thing that is since it is perceived, and of which only its properties have yet to be known. This distance from one perspective to the other suddenly increases infinitely with the death of the philosopher, for it is his whole work that is converted into something said and henceforth gives itself out with the appearance of an object. Even when, upon reading his personal papers, we discover the image of his future work which he formed for himself, it does not unsettle our certitude of being before a work; and the last writing—in spite of its incompletion—furnishes again the occasion to size up that work, particularly inasmuch as it dispenses final information about its nature. And yet upon discovering this last writing our illusion wavers. Natural as it appears to us to seek in it, if not the final meaning, at least what will give their final meaning to the antecedent works, still it is equally difficult to recognize this completion under the strokes of an introduction where the questions multiply, where the answers are always deferred, where the thought constantly depends on a future discourse, henceforth prohibited.

And, in fact, such is the function of the hundred and fifty manuscript pages to which *The Visible and the Invisible* is reduced: to introduce. The intention is to direct the reader toward a domain which his habits of thought do not make immediately accessible to him. It is a question, in particular, of persuading him that the fundamental concepts of modern philosophy—for example, the distinctions between subject and object, essence and fact, being and nothingness, the notions of consciousness, image, thing, which are in constant use—already implicate a singular interpretation of the world and cannot lay claim to special dignity when our intention is precisely to go back to face our experience, in order to seek in it the birth of meaning. The author endeavors to state first why it has become necessary to start anew, why we can no longer think within the framework of the former systems, nor even build on the ground in which we see them, different as they are in their orientation, to be enrooted. He calls for an examination of our condition such as it is before science and philosophy compose a translation of it according to the exigencies of their respective languages, and before we come to forget that they themselves have to account for their own origin. But this examination is not presented, it is only announced; only some guidemarks give an indication of what would be a description of experience faithful to the experience. The very form of the discourse is a caution. Constant reservations, allusions to what will be said later, the conditional form forbid enclosing the thought in the present statements. When the time comes, the writer is in effect saying, the true meaning of the exposition will disclose itself; the argument, he adds, would be more extensive were he not in a hurry to indicate first the main lines of his research. It would be wrong to take these precautions to be artifices; the pages left us have to be read as the author wished them to be read, with the thought that all that is said here is still provisional, and, since our waiting for the continuation cannot be satisfied, it is necessary to read them as they are, bound up with the missing pages: however strong may be our inclination to seek in the present field of discourse a meaning that suffices to itself, we cannot ignore the void it bears in its center. The work is the more lacunate in that it takes form before us only to designate what has become impossible for it to say. And no doubt the first justice to be done to it is to see it as it presents itself, to know the state of privation in which it puts us, to measure the loss it makes palpable, to know, finally, that this loss cannot be made good, and that no one could give expression to what has remained for it inexpressible.

But perhaps we err yet more seriously if, thus convincing ourselves that the first part of *The Visible and the Invisible* has the value of an introduction, we would wish to conclude that it does not reach the essential. That would already be a failure to recognize the nature of the work of thought, for in it the initiation is always decisive, the truth of the itinerary is always anticipated in the first step. Even more, at a moment of discourse there is created a relation between what has been said and what is not yet said, which doubles every statement and brings to birth, beyond the succession of the ideas, a depth of meaning in which they coexist, prove to be consubstantial, and, without ceasing to be inscribed in time, are imprinted simultaneously in one same field—so that, once this dimension is opened, we are put in the presence of the work, and the work survives the amputation inflicted on it by fate. But, in this particular case, it would be especially a failure to recognize the intention of the writer, who, from the start of his work, strives to render palpable the bond between all the questions of philosophy, their reciprocal implication, the necessity of the interrogation whence they proceed, and, far from devoting himself to preliminary considerations, assembles in a first draft most of the themes he means to stir up again and again in the continuation. This first part does not offer us, for example, the exposition of a method: it contains rather a caution against what is commonly called method, that is, against undertaking to define an order of demonstration that would be valid of itself, independently of an effective development of thought. It demands that the meaning emerge from the description of experience and of the difficulties it harbors as soon as we want to think it in terms of the categories of the past philosophy—or think it, in general. It does not wish to state a principle or principles that would permit the reconstructing of experience but proposes to explore it in all directions, at the same time questioning our relation with the world as we think we live it naïvely as well as the cultural environment in which this relation is inscribed and acquires a determined status. But, for this project to take form, we must already have sized up our situation; we must (and this is indeed the task Merleau-Ponty assigns himself in the beginning) examine the movement that inclines us to give our adherence to things and to one another and the ambiguities to which it exposes us: why it is irresistible, and why, as soon as we wish to think it out, it transforms itself into an enigma. We must confront what the writer calls our "perceptual faith" with the truths of science, discover that this science, which appears to sovereignly dispose of its object inasmuch as it constructs it from its definitions and in conformity with its ideal of measurement, is unable to elucidate the experience of the world from which, without saying so, it draws, and, finally, that when in its operations it comes upon the trace of an involvement in the real of the subject of knowledge, it proves to be as unable as is the common consciousness to give it a status. Finally we must traverse again the route of reflection which is that of modern philosophy—at whose term all the problems appear solved, since thought doubles now the perceptual life over its whole extension and bears into it the principle for a discrimination between the true and the false, the real and the imaginary —and see in what conditions this "solution" is reached, at the cost of what mutilation our situation is converted into a simple object of knowledge, our body into a thing like any other, perception into the thought of perceiving, speech into pure signification, by what artifices the philosopher succeeds in dissimulating to himself his inherence in the world, in history, and in language.

This first elucidation already implies a reciprocating motion between the description of experience and the critique of philosophical knowing, not that we ought to denounce the errors of theory in face of what is, but because, far from rejecting the past philosophy so as to edify a new system on a *tabula rasa*, we learn *in it* to see better, and, taking over its enterprise, seeking only to carry it out all the way, we clarify our own situation starting from what thought it gives us about the world. Thus we are cast into the middle of the research, already occupied in plowing the field of our questions, articulating them in relation to each other, and discovering the necessity that commands them, when we thought we were only beginning to move.

In a sense, there is indeed a beginning, but in another sense this image is misleading. For it is at the same time true that the author calls for a new start and that he nevertheless refuses to search for a point of origin that would permit the tracing out of the way of absolute knowledge. Perhaps in this his enterprise differs most profoundly from that of his predecessors. He was so convinced of the impossibility of philosophy establishing itself as a pure source of meaning that he wished first to denounce its illusion. Thus, in the first drafts for an introduction, he started with the observation that we cannot find an origin in God, in nature, or in man, that such attempts in fact converge in the myth of a total explicitation of the world, of a complete adequation between thought and being, which nowise takes into account our insertion in the being of which we speak; that, moreover, this myth no longer sustains any fruitful research in our time, and that to dissipate it is not to fall back into scepticism and irrationalism but is to know for the first time the truth of our situation. This is an idea so constant in him that we find it again expressed in the last working note, written two months before his death:

> [My plan] must be presented without any compromise with *humanism,* nor moreover with *naturalism,* nor finally with theology—Precisely what has to be done is to show that philosophy can no longer think according to this cleavage: God, man, creatures—which was Spinoza's division (p. 274).

If there is need of a recommencement, it is therefore in a wholly new sense. It is not a matter of clearing out ruins in order to lay a new foundation; it is rather a matter of recognizing that, whatever we may say about being, we inhabit it with our whole selves, our labor of expression is still an installation in it, finally our interrogation is, for the same reason, without origin and without termination, since our questions always arise from older questions and since no answer can dissipate the mystery of our relation with being.

Kafka already said that the things presented themselves to him "not by their roots, but by some point or other situated toward the middle of them." He doubtless said it to express his distress, but the philosopher who frees himself from the myth of the "root" resolutely accepts being situated in this midst and having to start from this "some point or other." This restraint is the sign of his attachment, and it is because he submits to it that the hope is given him of progressing from one domain to another, in the interior labyrinth where the frontiers of the visible fade, where every question about nature leads to a question about history, every question of this kind to a question about the philosophy of nature or of history, every question about being to a question about language. In such an enterprise one can see stages but cannot distinguish the preparations from the exploration itself. Speaking of his research, Merleau-Ponty says in one place that it is an "ascent on the spot"; very often he sees it describe a circle, bringing him to pass by the same stopping points again and again. Whatever the image is, it prevents us from thinking that we would not be at grips with the essential from the beginning. On the contrary, we have to admit that the introduction is the first traversing of the circle and that, brought to its term, the work would not thereby have exceeded the limits or terminated the movement, inasmuch as it is certain that it is in *these* limits, by *this* movement that it discovers its power of expression.

Thus it is at the same time true that the hundred and fifty manuscript pages to which *The Visible and the Invisible* is now reduced comprise its beginning and still present themselves to us as an introduction, and that they are more than that, bearing the meaning of the work and calling upon us to discover it in them; that the continuation of the work would have been something very different from the illustration or commentary of the ideas stated in the first part, and that the first part anticipates the continuation, permits us to evoke it.

But perhaps this paradox would surprise us less if we saw how it is founded in the language of the work, in the labor of writing such as the writer conceived it. It is a noteworthy fact that should we wish to reconstitute the principal articulations of the work he was preparing, we would find it materially impossible to do so. To be sure, numerous working notes, early drafts, some rare indications of an outline of extreme brevity, all of which do not agree among themselves, give an indication of the amplitude of his research. But to know that it was to return at length to the problem of perception and in particular to devote a good deal of space to the recent works on experimental and Gestalt psychology, that the analysis of the concept of nature would have required a description of the human organism, animal behavior, and the examination of the phenomena of evolution, that these studies themselves would have commanded the critique of what the author called the "complex of Western philosophy," that this critique, in its turn, was to result in a new conception of history and of the nature-history relationship, and that finally (and this is the least dubious of all the hypotheses) the work was to conclude with a reflection on language and that particular form of language which is the philosophical discourse, returning thus at its term to the mystery of its origin—this yet leaves us ignorant of the route that would have been followed, the order of the stages, or the revolutions of the thought. How then could one think that Merleau-Ponty's reluctance to draw up plans, to prepare with schemata what he intended to say, and to hold himself to his projects was a matter of temperament? The truth is indeed rather that his experience as a man philosophizing coincided with his experience as a writer, prevented him from dominating his own work, as he for whom meaning can be once entirely possessed imagines he dominates his work. In this sense, he would have to test it in the writing. Convinced that there is no privileged point whence nature, history, and being itself are unveiled, or, as he says so often, that high-altitude thinking detaches us from the truth of our situation, it was necessary at the same time that he forego the illusion of seeing his own work as a spectacle, oblige himself to make his way in semi-obscurity in order to discover the interior connection of his questions, and fully comply with what demands to be said here and now without ever giving himself over to the security of a meaning already traced out, already thought. Thus it is in the end for one sole and same reason that we are led to seek in what is written the essence of the work and prevented from imagining the sequence of the discourse as the simple prolongation of its beginning. The language of the philosopher teaches us a necessity that is not logical but ontological, such that we find in it more than a meaning, a meaning of meaning, and, as soon as it is wanting, we lose contact with what gave depth, movement, and life to the ideas. Attentive as we should be to the word of the writer, allowing it all its resonances in the space it inhabits, we are accordingly forbidden to cross the limits of this space and violate the zone of silence that envelops it. It is this speech and this silence that must be heard together—this silence which succeeds the speech, which is not nothing since it still depends on the speech and henceforth sustains it.

Merleau-Ponty already was meditating on the relation between speech and silence; in a note he writes:

> There would be needed a silence that envelops the speech anew, after one has come to recognize that speech enveloped the alleged silence of the psychological coincidence. What will this silence be? As the reduction finally is not for Husserl a transcendental immanence, but the disclosing of the *Weltthesis*, this silence will *not be the contrary* of language (p. 179).

Thus we were to understand that speech is between two silences: it gives expression to an experience that is mute and ignorant of its own meaning, but only in order to make that experience appear in its purity; it does not break our contact with the things, but it draws us from our state of confusion with all things only in order to awaken us to the truth of their presence and to render palpable their relief and the tie that binds us to them. At least such is the speech that speaks in conformity with its essence and, where philosophical discourse is concerned, that does not cede to the vertigo of eloquence, does not wish to suffice to itself or close in upon itself and upon its sense, but opens upon and leads to the outside. But if speech, which is born from silence, can seek its conclusion in silence and make that silence not be its contrary, this is because between experience and language there is, in principle, exchange; it is because experience is not something one could coincide with, because it bears a transcendence, since already, in itself, it is differentiation, articulation, structuration, and because in some way it calls for language; it is because language is also experience, because there is, as Merleau-Ponty writes so well, a *being* of language in which the enigma of being is repeated, because beyond the movement of the pure significations there remains the silent mass of the discourse, that which is not of the order of the sayable, and because the greatest merit of expression is to disclose this continuous passage from the word to being and from being to the word, or this double openness of the one upon the other. To think through this exchange is no doubt what *The Visible and the Invisible* was to devote itself to, at the end. But it is disconcerting to find it evoked in the last lines, in the writer's last words. Merleau-Ponty writes:

> In a sense the whole of philosophy, as Husserl says, consists in restoring a power to signify, a birth of meaning, or a wild meaning, an expression of experience by experience, which in particular clarifies the special domain of language. And, in a sense, as Valéry said, language is everything, since it is the voice of no one, since it is the very voice of the things, the waves, and the forests. And what we have to understand is that there is no dialectical reversal from one of these views to the other; we do not have to reassemble them into a synthesis: they are two aspects of the reversibility which is ultimate truth (p. 155).

That chance seals the book on *ultimate truth*, that the book, still far from the term it aimed at, yet closes on a thought that is its prefiguration—in this the reader will not fail to see a sign— the trace of an admonition, as it were, that the work, in the absence of the man, was able to receive. But this sign could not make us forget the meaning, and we must also recognize that what is said here, at the last moment, clarifies the problem of the philosophical work—of the work in general, and of this one we are reading. For in it is disclosed the reversibility of experience and language. It is because it brings or claims to bring the task of expression to its furthest limits, because it wishes to gather up the truth of experience such as it is before it is put into words, and, simultaneously, because it wishes to concentrate and exhaust in it all the powers of speech, that it discovers the impossibility of remaining in either intention, sees its movement reverse itself in both directions, and is finally obliged to declare this indetermination, which constitutes its existence. The reversibility of which the philosopher speaks is set forth before he names it in the form of his work. Better: in naming it he only expresses faithfully the meaning of his undertaking. For if it is not vain, it presupposes that we cannot find an absolute in experience nor make of language an absolute, that that anonymous power we call experience or language is not a positive reality that would suffice to itself alone, that there is in being a sort of need for speech and in speech a sort of need for being, indissociable from one another, that to speak and to live are equally the source of questions, and that these questions refer to one another. Thus the "ultimate truth" upon which *The Visible and the Invisible* comes to an end is also that from which the work draws its origin: this truth does not constitute a stopping point; it does not give rest to thought; it rather designates the point of passage which is for the work that of its continued foundation.

We asked: how are we to understand the silence that follows the word? But if we can do so, it is because the word never abolished the silence, that at each moment it leads beyond itself and forbids us to fall back to the limits of the immediately given meaning. The final silence is only made of those silences reassembled; it extends beyond the discourse because it constantly served as its ground. Hence it is one and the same thing to hear this discourse and this silence, to know where to stop at the frontier of the *said,* and to recognize that there is no frontier between language and the world.

Still it is true that if *The Visible and the Invisible* gives us the ability to listen, it is because the questions we put before the work and its incompletion rejoin those the author put to himself when he obliged himself to write in such a way that a termination of his enterprise (let us not say a sudden and unforeseeable cessation of speech) was not contrary to it, a termination, whatever it would be, that was to be not only a termination, but was also to signify the absence of any termination. At a given moment he himself indicates the meaning of this task, when, in the course of the work, he asks what philosophical expression can be:

> . . . the words most charged with philosophy are not necessarily those that contain what they say, but rather those that most energetically open upon being, because they more closely convey the life of the whole and make our habitual evidences vibrate until they disjoin. Hence it is a question whether philosophy as the reconquest of brute or wild being can be accomplished by the resources of the eloquent language, or whether it would not be necessary for philosophy to use language in a way that takes from it its power of immediate or direct signification in order to equal it with what it wishes all the same to say (pp. 102–3).

An enigmatic passage, no doubt. The answer does not accompany the question. It is not said what would be a work that would deprive itself of the resources of the eloquent language, what would be, to recall a formula used by the author in another circumstance, an "indirect language" of philosophy. We know only that he constantly claimed for it an original mode of expression and by no means thought of substituting for it the language of art or of poetry. However, when we read the writer, this confidence is clarified, for it turns out that his own words do not contain what they say, that their meaning always overflows immediate or direct signification, and that finally their power to open upon being is bound to the force of interrogation that animates them. Should we not understand that the philosophical language is precisely the interrogative language? If that cannot be affirmed in positive terms, it is because no formula can make understood what interrogation is. Merleau-Ponty can indeed, on several occasions, name it, say what it is not—the statement of questions which, like all the questions of cognition, are to disappear before answers—and why it is indefinitely renewed on contact with our experience. Yet every definition would turn us from it by making us forget that it is in life and in language that it unfolds itself, or, better, that it is only life and language, this life and this language, assumed. To do justice to inquiry, it is not enough for the philosopher to declare that it is interminable, that man is never done with asking questions about his situation in the world, for, true as that may be, such an idea is too general to have consistency. He must also effectively conduct the questioning, provide a route for it, act in such a way that, in the work, the answers aroused by the questions nowhere terminate the reflection, that the passage from one domain of experience to another is always preserved, that meaning unveils itself in our impossibility to remain in any place, that the whole discourse is as one sole sentence where one can distinguish, certainly, moments, articulations, and pauses, but whose content, in each proposition, is never dissociable from the total movement.

And in fact, from start to finish, *The Visible and the Invisible* is an endeavor to keep the questioning open: not an exercise of a methodic and deliberate doubt from which the subject would draw the illusion of detaching himself from all things and which would prepare the reinstatement of a thought sure of its rights, but the continuous exploration of our perceptual life and of our life of knowledge; not the negation of the common certitudes, the destruction of our faith in the existence of the things and of the others, but the adherence to these certitudes, to this faith, to the extent that the very insistence to espouse them discloses that they are indissociably certitude and incertitude, faith and non-faith; a passage as it were through opinion in order to rejoin the ambiguities it harbors; not a refutation of the theories of philosophers, but a return to what was at their origin in order to discover that they lead beyond the answers they gave; an interrogation, finally, which constantly relates to itself, does not lose sight of the condition of the questioner, knows it is caught up in being while it devotes itself to its expression.

If philosophy finds by this language the means to "equal what it wishes all the same to say," it is because the secret of our temporality is expressed by that of the work, because the work teaches us to recognize the continuity, the indivision of an experience where each moment is caught up with all the others in the same propulsion of time, and, simultaneously, to recognize the movement that prevents the fixing of the meaning of the thing, visible or invisible, and makes arise indefinitely, beyond the present given, the latent content of the world.

But when the work reaches this self-consciousness, when it knows that it is and is only the place of interrogation, does it not then silently correspond with its term? For he who goes all the way to the end of interrogation can only discover and make us discover the contingency of speech. It is one same thing, for him, to confront the obscure region from which his thoughts arise and that in which they are destined to undo themselves. And it is one same thing for us to read everywhere the signs of its presence and to feel its imminent absence. The true interrogation is a frequenting of death, and we are not surprised that the philosopher who rarely names it has nonetheless such great power, in his last writing, to turn us toward it.

CLAUDE LEFORT

Editorial Note

Maurice Merleau-Ponty died on May 3, 1961. A manuscript was found among his papers which contained the first part of a work whose composition he had begun two years earlier. It is entitled *The Visible and the Invisible*. We have found no trace of this title before March, 1959. Before then notes concerning this project bear the reference "Being and Meaning," or "Genealogy of the True," or, lastly, "The Origin of Truth."

The Manuscript

The manuscript consists of a hundred and fifty large pages covered with a dense handwriting, bearing copious corrections. The text covers both sides of the page.

The date March, 1959 figures on the first page, and page 83 is dated June 1, 1959. Apparently the author composed a hundred and ten pages between spring and summer of the same year; then in the autumn of the following year he returned to the composition of his text, setting aside the last eight pages (pp. 103–10) which would have begun a second chapter. The date November, 1960 is written on the second page 103, above the title "Interrogation and Intuition."

Structure of the Work

Outlines for the work are few and do not agree exactly with one another. It is certain that the author was recasting his project during the course of its execution. We can, however, presume that the work would have been of considerable length and that the text we possess constitutes only its first part, which was intended to serve as an introduction.[1]

Here are the few schemata we found:

a) March, 1959 (written at the head of the manuscript):
Part I. Being and World
Chap.   I.   Reflection and interrogation.
Chap. II. Preobjective being: the solipsist world.
Chap. III. Preobjective being: intercorporeity.
Chap. IV. Preobjective being: the inter-world (*l'entremonde*).
Chap. V. Classical ontology and modern ontology.
Part II. Nature.
Part III. *Logos*.

b) May, 1960 (in a note on the first page):
Being and World.
Part I:

The vertical world   or   the interrogative being
     mute   brute
                               wild
Part II will be: Wild being and classical ontology.

(and on the second page:)
Chap.   I.   The flesh of the present or the *"there is."*
Chap. II. The plot (*tracé*) of time, the movement of ontogenesis.
Chap. III. The body, the natural light, and the word.
Chap. IV. The chiasm.
Chap. V. The inter-world and Being.
             World and Being.

c) May, 1960 (in a note):
I. Being and World
Part I: The vertical World or wild Being.
Part II: Wild Being and classical ontology.
   Nature
   Man
   God.

1. Cf. Editor's Foreword.

Conclusion: the fundamental thought—Passage to the differentiations of wild Being. Nature—*logos* history.

> cultivated being.
> The *Erzeugung*.

II. *Physis* and *Logos*.

d) October, 1960 (in a note):
I. Being and World.
Part I: Reflection and interrogation.
Part II: The vertical world and wild Being.
Part III: Wild Being and classical ontology.

e) November, 1960 (in a note):
I. The visible and nature.
1. Philosophical interrogation.
2. The visible.
3. The world of silence.
4. The visible and ontology (wild Being).
II. The word and the invisible.

f) (Undated, but probably of November or December, 1960, in a note:)
I. The visible and nature.
Philosophical interrogation:
interrogation and reflection;
interrogation and dialectic;
interrogation and intuition (what I am doing at the moment).
The visible.
Nature.
Classical ontology and modern ontology.
II. The invisible and *logos*.

These few indications do not permit us to imagine what the work would have been in its matter and in its form. The reader will form a better idea of it when he reads the working notes we are publishing after the text. But at least we can make use of the outlines in order to discern more clearly the organization of the manuscript itself.

For should we follow only the divisions marked out in the text, we would have to confine ourselves to mentioning a Part

One: "Being and World," and a first chapter: "Reflection and Interrogation," while all the other sections would be parallel, all being equally preceded in the notes by the sign §. But note *f*), which confirms and completes the preceding note and which has the interest of having been written at the same time as the chapter "Interrogation and Intuition" (the author specifies: "what I am doing at the moment"), shows that we cannot retain this division. For the title of the first part, "Being and World," has been abandoned and replaced by "The Visible and Nature," the sections preceded by the sign § have been regrouped in terms of their meaning, and it becomes clear that the last two sections do not have the same function as the prior ones.

We have therefore decided to restructure the text according to the last indications left by the author. We have first distinguished three chapters, setting them under the heading "Philosophical Interrogation." The first chapter, "Reflection and Interrogation," with three subdivisions, covers the critique of the perceptual faith, scientism, and the philosophy of reflection (*la philosophie réflexive*). The second, "Interrogation and Dialectic," divided into two parts, consists of the analysis of Sartrean thought and an elucidation of the relations between dialectics and interrogation. The third, "Interrogation and Intuition," contains essentially the critique of Phenomenology.

There remains the problem of situating the last section entitled "The Intertwining—the Chiasm," which note *f*) does not mention. We could make it either the final chapter of "Philosophical Interrogation" or the first chapter of the announced Part Two: "The Visible." Either decision, we believe, can be justified by serious arguments. But in the absence of express indication by the author, the arguments would never appear decisive. In this situation, we have preferred to adopt the solution that involved the least intervention on our part—that is, to let this chapter follow the others.

STATE OF THE TEXT

THE MANUSCRIPT of *The Visible and the Invisible* was worked over at length, as its numerous erasures and corrections show. Yet we cannot suppose that it had reached its definitive state. Certain repetitions would no doubt have been eliminated; perhaps the manuscript would have been recast even more broadly. In particular, the definitiveness of the beginning of the text is open to doubt, since a note evokes the possibility of a new arrangement of the exposition. The author writes:

> Perhaps redo pages 1–13, grouping together: 1. the certitudes (the thing) (the other) (the truth); 2. the incertitudes (the Pyrrhonian difficulties, the contradictions of thematization); 3. one can neither accept the antitheses, nor confine oneself to materialized certitudes→passage to reflection.

On the other hand, we note that the author twice uses the same text of Paul Claudel (cf. below, pp. 103 and 121) without advising the reader of this repetition. The function of the citation in the two passages is such that a broad recasting would have been necessary.

THE WORKING NOTES

WE HAVE THOUGHT IT WELL to include after the text of *The Visible and the Invisible* a certain number of working notes which clarify its meaning. The author was in the habit of jotting down ideas on paper, ordinarily without concerning himself with style nor even obliging himself to compose complete sentences. These notes, which sometimes contain but a few lines and sometimes extend over several pages, constitute drafts for developments that figure in the first part of the work or would have figured in its continuation. From the end of the year 1958 on, they were as a rule dated and labeled.

It was neither possible nor desirable to publish all of them. Their mass would have overshadowed the text, and moreover a good number of them were to be excluded either because they were too elliptical or because they had no direct bearing on the subject of the research.

As soon as a selection proved to be necessary, it posed some problems of interpretation, and we feared lest our judgment be mistaken. But, rather than renounce the project, we have taken on the risk of making a choice among them, convinced as we were that by reason of the variety of the themes taken up, the quality of the reflection, the abrupt but always rigorous expression of the thought, these notes could render the philosopher's work palpable to the reader.

EDITING OF THE MANUSCRIPT AND THE NOTES

AS FAR AS THE EDITING of the manuscript is concerned, we have limited ourselves in the text to clarifying the punctuation, in concern for facilitating its reading. But in the working notes we have transcribed the text without modification, so as to leave to the expression its first movement.[2]

Wherever we could, we have furnished the references the working notes required or completed those of the author.

When it was necessary to introduce or restore a term in order to give a sentence its meaning, we have put it between brackets and added an explanatory note at the bottom of the page.

Illegible or doubtful terms are indicated in the course of the text in the following way:

illegible: [?]
uncertain: [truth?].

2. In the English translation, too, we have attempted in the text to remain as faithful to the French as possible, though alterations in punctuation and wording have been made when necessary for clarity. The Working Notes, however, are reproduced exactly as they appeared in the French edition.

French words are given in parentheses when it is helpful to include them. Footnotes of the author, the editor, and the translator are numbered consecutively within each chapter; notes written by the editor or the translator are identified to distinguish them from those of Merleau-Ponty. Merleau-Ponty's marginal comments are preceded by an asterisk.

In the Working Notes, short dashes are used as standard punctuation and long dashes are used to separate sentences or quasi-sentences.

A number of mistakes in the French edition have been corrected upon consultation with M. Lefort.—A.L.

Translator's Preface

The Visible and the Invisible was to be MERLEAU-PONTY's phenomenological ontology. It required both a phenomenological inquiry into "the origin of truth" and a philosophy of Nature—of the "wild," uncultivated, preobjective Nature. Most of the manuscript his death interrupted is devoted to a critical examination of Kantian, Husserlian, Bergsonian, and Sartrean method; but one extraordinary constructive chapter—that entitled "The Intertwining—the Chiasm"—introduces the new concepts with which to explore the production of visibility and "the metaphysical structure of our flesh." This manuscript that we now present to the English-speaking public, along with a collection of Merleau-Ponty's working notes, prepares for an ontology of Nature and of truth that shall now come only from its readers. Each reader will find in the range of this thought his own motives to assume and discoveries to appropriate; perhaps this preface may aid him by indicating the central argument that was already forged in the work Merleau-Ponty leaves us.

METHODS

WHAT IS A VISIBLE THING? What is it that makes the visible a thing? And what is the visibility of the thing? These were the questions of a phenomenology of perception; across its long chapters devoted to the critical examination first of the philosophy interwoven in scientific research, then of transcendental philosophy, dialectical philosophy, and intuitionist philosophy, these are also the questions that command The Visible *and the Invisible.* To endeavor once more to renew these questions is not simply the coquetry that, in fact only provisionally, tries to make seem questionable visibility itself, that is, the very clarity, the very patency of the real. "If the philosopher questions and hence feigns ignorance of the world and of the vision of the world which are operative and take form continually within him, he does so precisely in order to make them speak, because he believes in them and expects from them all his future science." [1]

Empiricism was a sort of disbelief in the things, an underestimation of the coherence of the things. The sensible thing is not simply a "wandering troop of sensations" (p. 123); it holds together of itself and can be recognized when it returns. Intellectualism is the recognition of this immanent unity of the things: the constituent moments of the thing are not simply contingently contiguous to one another; they are internally, intentionally, or meaningfully related to one another. Only thus can sensuous data announce or manifest a thing—or, at least, that internal principle, that essence, by which it is one thing and by which it is recognizable. In the midst of the sensuous experience there is an intuition of an essence, a sense, a signification. The sensible thing is the place where the invisible is captured in the visible.

But can we really *understand* this conjuncture? How is this compound of the visible and the invisible possible, without undermining all our positive conceptions of what it means to be visible and what it means to be invisibly? How can there be a compound of the visible with the invisible, if to be invisible is to be essence or signification, to exist in universality, in intemporal and aspatial ideality, and if to be visible is to be opaque quale, existing in the here and the now, and in itself, without transcendence, "a message at the same time indecipherable and evident, which one has or has not received, but of which, if one has received it, one knows all there is to know, and about which in the end there is nothing to say" (p. 131)?

To seriously show how the sensible thing exists between the absolute opacity of the sensuous quale and the absolute transparency of the essence, between the particular and the universal, it would be necessary to show a sensible matter which, in its very

1. See below, p. 4. Hereafter all page references to *The Visible and the Invisible* will be placed in parentheses directly following the quotation.

manner of occupying space and time, presides over space and time. It would be necessary to show a sense that is sensuous and a sensible matter that transcends itself, that is dimensional. But transcendental philosophy, dialectical philosophy, and intuitionist philosophy have rather endeavored to compose the sensible thing with our unreformed ideas of the visible and the invisible.

Thus the philosophy of reflection seeks an intrinsic understanding of the conjuncture of the visible and the invisible in the thing by exhibiting its constitution in a signifying act of the understanding. The transcendental reflection shows how the sense that is intuited is constituted in an act transcending the sense-data. It understands the sense-data to be to the essence in the sensible thing in the relation of sign to signified; then the understanding that constitutes the signified meaning *ipso facto* constitutes the sense-data as signs.

But the reflective analysis thus gives us the explanation of how there is constituted not the coherence and cohesion—the very matter or *flesh*—of the visible, but a pure *passage* from the sign to the signified, from the particular to the universal, from the order of opaque qualia to the order of limpid ideality. The visible thing is not this passage; its coherence is a cohesion, and it makes visible and not only comprehensible a depth of latent being.

It is the claim of the philosophy of negativity [2] that it alone rigorously and radically grounds a method of direct scrutiny of the sensible thing itself. It is a philosophy not of reflection but of vision (pp. 75 ff, 99 ff), and it renounces in principle every attempt to reconstruct the thing out of constitutive mental acts. It declares that the sole contribution of the seer is to provide—by auto-nihilation—the clearing, the void, the free space in which the thing can be posited and op-posed to the seer, that is, exhibit itself in its own positivity and ob-jectivity. The negativity of the seer and the invisibility of the eyes are essential, for visibility occurs as the event of a clearing in which the light plays, about which a system of faces of the world phosphoresce.

The description of the being of the thing as massive plenitude, absolute positivity, self-identity, objectivity, is the result of this thought that posits the thing upon the ground of the nothingness provided by the non-being of the seer. This method "describes our factual situation with more penetration than had

2. Cf. Sartre.

ever before been done—and yet one retains the impression that this situation is being surveyed from above, and indeed it is . . ." (p. 87). For the analysis does not begin with the sensible thing itself in its own visibility, arising in relief in a field of latent being spread out in distance and in horizons surrounding and even enveloping the seer; rather the analysis is commanded by the meaning of being and the meaning of nothingness. But the concepts of pure Being and pure Nothingness are *constructa*, they are idealizations, and their meaning is held before the thought only because it is fixed in the positivity of language (p. 88). "Is not the experience of the thing and of the world precisely the ground that we need in order to think nothingness in any way whatever?" (p. 162)

And in fact in seeking to make the openness upon being absolute, the philosophy of negativity makes it unintelligible. If the seer is nothingness, the visible forthwith occupies this void with absolute plenitude and positivity. The absolute ontological distance from nothingness to being produces an absolute presence of being to nothingness. But our openness upon being is not this absolute proximity; openness in being occurs in the form of a world, that is, a field, a topography, where nothing visible shows itself without therewith hiding most of itself, and hiding more of the visible behind itself. What makes the visible an openness is this essential explorability, this depth and horizon-structure; to make of openness a "lake of nothingness" is to over-positivize the visible (pp. 67–68, 76–77) and make unintelligible what is being in degrees, in distance, in depth, and in difference.

And if the openness in being is a horizon-structure and not the production of void, then the seer and the visible need no longer be ontological opposites; the horizon includes the seer,[3] and the world remains horizon because "he who sees is of it and is in it" (p. 100). "The relation between what I see and I who see is not one of immediate or frontal contradiction; the things attract my look, my gaze caresses the things, it espouses their

3. "No more than are the sky or the earth is the horizon a collection of things held together, or a class name, or a logical possibility of conception, or a system of 'potentiality of consciousness': it is a new type of being, a being by porosity, pregnancy, or generality, and he before whom the horizon opens is caught up, included within it" (pp. 148–49).

contours and their reliefs, between it and them we catch sight of a complicity" (p. 76).

The extended critique of the philosophy of negativity, that is, of Sartre, may seem to occupy inordinately Merleau-Ponty's attention in the manuscript we have before us.[4] But in fact the strange failure of the philosophy of negativity to produce an account of the visible is decisive for Merleau-Ponty's own conception of philosophy. "The real is to be described, and not constructed or constituted," the Preface to the *Phenomenology of Perception* had explained, with simplicity.[5] But the philosophy that wanted only to empty out the subject of all constitutive power, to make of it a pure openness upon the thing, nonetheless deforms the thing and does not describe it. Positivism was not yet overcome when the *Phenomenology of Perception* showed that the sensible field cannot be reduced to the objective, as empiricism, as well as its intellectualist compensation, supposed; the positivist preconception of being recurs even in the philosophy of negativity, which, indeed, is its radical vindication (pp. 98–99). It is because the primordial sensible being lies definitively at a distance and is not a pure positivity that would come to obturate the gaze that philosophy cannot be pure intuition, pure openness. "The sensible is precisely that medium in which there can be *being* without it having to be posited; the sensible appearance of the sensible, the silent persuasion of the sensible is Being's unique way of manifesting itself without becoming positivity, without ceasing to be ambiguous and transcendent" (p. 214). Philosophy then is and remains interrogation [6]—"but

4. Merleau-Ponty here takes pains to correct some of the defects of his earlier reading of *Being and Nothingness* (cf. *Les Aventures de la dialectique* [Paris, 1955], Chap. V): the ontology of Sartre makes of the subject not a "nothingness in general," an unqualified spontaneity, a self-transparent constitutive freedom, but rather "determinate nothingness," qualified and replete with qualities, opaque to itself, lost in the things; what I *am* is a body and a situation (cf. especially pp. 52–57).

5. *Phénoménologie de la perception* (Paris, 1945), p. iv. [English translation by Colin Smith, *Phenomenology of Perception* (New York and London, 1962), p. x.]

6. Questioning is not an attitude first made possible on the judicative level with the inversion and negation that would come, into the untroubled positivity of the silent world, with language and grammar. On the contrary, "it is not only philosophy, it is first the gaze that questions the things" (p. 103).

neither expects nor receives an answer in the ordinary sense, because it is not the disclosing of a variable or of an unknown invariant that will satisfy this question, and *because the existing world exists in the interrogative mode*" (p. 103; italics added).

These conclusions are reinforced in the criticisms Merleau-Ponty addresses to intuitionist philosophy—Husserlian or Bergsonian. The one seeking an adequate apprehension of the essence, the other seeking the immediate presence of existence, in both cases being as horizon is excluded from consideration in advance: "These are two positivisms" (p. 127).

Philosophy conceived as essential insight is proclaimed to be a return to the things themselves. To study the thing itself would be to study *what it is,* that is, what structure the thing necessarily realizes when it is this thing. If the philosophy of negativity sought to intuit the thing against the abyss of nothingness, the philosophy of essences seeks to intuit the real as it is borne upon the positive structure of the possible. The intuition of this structure would bring the mind into possession of the essence as the pure ideal possibility which the existing thing accomplishes, or specifies, in a moment of time and at a spot of space.

In fact the "intuition" of essences is produced out of an imaginary variation performed on the primal topography of the visible. Precisely Being is visible as a theme for variation because the visible itself is not *in* time and *in* space, but not outside of them either, since it is what in the present announces and harbors an immense latent content of the past, the future, and the elsewhere (p. 114). The visible being that *occupies* the present does so then not with a plenary positivity, but with pregnancy and latency, caught up in "a system of equivalencies, a *Logos* of lines, lights, colors, reliefs, masses, a conceptless presentation of universal Being." [7] This *Logos* is not the system of positive essences which will be produced from it by abstraction; and the visible it articulates by segregation, modulation, gradation, is not a multiplicity of individual facts each occupying a time and a place in a plenary and univocal fashion—which will be drawn from it by counter-abstraction.

But if the "intuition" of essences is in fact a second operation which aims to put the mind in plenary possession of the ideality

7. *L'Oeil et l'esprit* (Paris, 1964), p. 71. [English translation by Carleton Dallery, *The Primacy of Perception* (Evanston, Ill., 1964), p. 182.]

at the origin of the real, the Bergsonian intuition which seeks to come back into the immediate presence of the factual existences is equally second and expresses an equally positivist nostalgia for being. Being is occultated across the very spatio-temporal spread of its apparition, that is true; but what we need then to come into contact with its full spread is not a method of undoing the distances to achieve immediate presence and coincidence with it, but rather the "idea of proximity through distance, of intuition as auscultation or palpation in depth" (p. 128). We should need the theory of the Being that *is* in dehiscence. "The immediate is at the horizon, and must be thought as such; it is only by remaining at the distance that it remains itself" (p. 123).

THE VISIBLE

NOT AN ASSEMBLAGE OF PARTICULARS each univocally occupying its *hic et nunc*, not a wandering troop of sensations nor a system constituted by ephemeral judgments (p. 123), not a set of objects whose being is fixed in the norms for objectivity, the visible is a landscape, a topography yet to be explored, uncultivated being still, *wild being* still. "True philosophy is to learn again to see the world" [8]—and yet how sophisticated is the phenomenological naïveté! Already the phenomenology of perception could be elaborated only across the conflict of intellectualism and empiricism; [9] now the new vision of the visible and the invisible is acquired not by avoiding the false paths of the philosophy of reflection, dialectical philosophy, and intuitionist philosophy, but rather by pursuing those very paths further still. There "we catch sight of the necessity of another operation besides the conversion to reflection, more fundamental than it, of a sort of *hyper-reflection* that would also take itself and the changes it introduces into the spectacle into account" (p. 38); likewise if the dialectic is "unstable" (p. 92), it is a *hyper-dialectic* we need, which recognizes that the statement of positive theses and negative antitheses does not yet yield a dialectical

8. *Phénoménologie de la perception*, p. xvi. [Eng. trans., p. xx.]
9. Cf. J.-B. Pontalis, "Note sur le problème de l'inconscient chez Merleau-Ponty," in *Les Temps modernes*, No. 184–85 (Numéro spécial, 1961), p. 291, n. 9.

definition of being (p. 94); finally it is not intuition that the philosopher rejects—"On the contrary everything comes to pass as though he wished to put into words a certain silence he hearkens to within himself" (p. 125); beyond the naïve notion of intuition as the fulfillment of an empty intention by the plenary positivity of being, "we should have to return to this idea . . . of intuition as auscultation or palpation in depth . . ." (p. 128).

What being becomes visible about these paths of hyper-reflection, hyper-dialectic, intuition-palpation?

In his first work Merleau-Ponty had brought forward the notion of structure, of *Gestalt*, as a third notion between facticity and ideality, to name the manner of being proper to the sensible thing. But what, positively, is the *Gestalt*? To say that it is a whole that is not reducible to the sum of its constituent elements, a configuration that is more than the spatio-temporal juxtaposition of its parts, is to supply a negative, exterior designation (p. 204). And it is not yet to understand what makes of the *Gestalt* a sensible being: what makes the unity in it of sensuousness and sense.

"For me it is . . . transcendence that explains . . ." (p. 237). The sensible thing is transcendent: hitherto this has been taken to state the position of its being, but not the manner of its being: it would mean that the sensible thing is exterior to the being of the subject. Thus the account remains within a subject-object epistemology, and the sensible is assimilated to the objective. Merleau-Ponty, defining the thing as a "field being" and as a dimensional fact, unified with the unity of a style, seeks to exhibit transcendence as the manner of being of what becomes visible.[10]

The sensible thing is not *in* the here and *in* the now, but it is not intemporal and aspatial either, an ideality. It presides over a region, it is a field being.

> When through the water's thickness I see the tiling at the bottom of a pool, I do not see it *despite* the water and the reflections there; I see it through them and because of them. If there were no distortions, no ripples of sunlight, if it were without this flesh that I saw the geometry of the tiles, then I would cease to see it *as* it is

10. "We have to pass from the thing (spatial or temporal) as identity, to the thing (spatial or temporal) as difference, i.e., as transcendence, i.e., as always 'behind,' beyond, far-off . . ." (p. 195)

and where it is—which is to say, beyond any identical, specific place. I cannot say that the water itself—the aqueous power, the sirupy and shimmering element—is *in* space; all this is not somewhere else either, but it is not in the pool. It inhabits it, it materializes itself there, yet it is not contained there; and if I raise my eyes toward the screen of cypresses where the web of reflections is playing, I cannot gainsay the fact that the water visits it, too, or at least sends into it, upon it, its active and living essence.[11]

The sensible thing is not in space, but, like a direction, is at work across space, presides over a system of oppositional relationships. It is not inserted in a pre-existing locus of space; it organizes a space of planes and fields about itself. Likewise its presence presents a certain contracted trajectory of time. It is for this that it occupies our vision, that it is not transparent like a sign that effaces before the signified. The sensible thing "stops up my view, that is, time and space extend beyond the visible present, and at the same time they are *behind* it, in depth, in hiding" (p. 113).

The unity of the thing is not that of a contingent cluster of particles, nor that of the ideal foreign to spatial and temporal dispersion; its unity is that of "a certain style, a certain manner of managing the domain of space and time over which it has competency, of pronouncing, of articulating that domain, of radiating about a wholly virtual center—in short a certain manner of being, in the active sense, a certain *Wesen*, in the sense that, says Heidegger, this word has when it is used as a verb" (p. 115).

The moving body gives us the primary analogon of what a style or scheme is. Walking is not a "repeatedly-compensated-for falling"; from the first step already a style of walking, a gait, is initiated, a rhythm of movement that propagates itself. The gesture of the hand is not a simple succession of spasms; from its inaugural phase it is a movement commanded by its final phase. And each gesture which thus accomplishes an ordered system of changes of position across a determined trajectory of time launches itself into a new trajectory of time; every gesture is by essence repeatable, tends to prolong itself into a motor habit. This generation of schemes of unity across time and space, this "instability instituted by the organism itself," this *"fluctuation organized by it,* and consequently dominated" (p.

11. *L'Oeil et l'esprit,* pp. 70–71. [Eng. trans., p. 182.]

230), this auto-schematizing is the very essence of the living body.

And the things too come into presence, come to command a field of presence, by their style. They hold together like the body holds together. Their unity is neither the unity of pure assemblage nor the unity of a law; it is produced and reproduced as the "bringing of a style of being wherever there is a fragment of being" (p. 139). The style is that interior animation of the color,[12] that interior rhythm that assembles the forms and shadows of the rose (p. 174), that organized fluctuation that makes the thing arise as a relief upon a depth of being.[13] The thing is borne into presence by a scheme of contrasts that commands a constellation, that modulates a trajectory of time, and that makes it leave its place to come reverberate in the receptive sensitive flesh that perceives it. Its way of being is verbal, it is transcendence, its style is "nothing else than a brief, peremptory manner of giving in one sole something, in one sole tone of being, visions past, visions to come, by whole clusters." The presence of the sensible thing is a presence by allusion (pp. 191–92, 200, 214, 229), and all perception is tele-perception (pp. 258, 273).[14]

Thus the "wild being," the uncultivated and unconstituted being of the sensible, is not opacity, but dimensionality (p. 257). "What we call a visible is, we said, a quality pregnant with a texture, the surface of a depth, a cross-section upon a massive being, a grain or corpuscle borne by a wave of Being" (p. 136). Serial music, Merleau-Ponty points out (p. 218), discovers the ability of any tone in a series to function as an individual

12. ". . . a naked color, and in general a visible, is not a chunk of absolutely hard, indivisible being, offered all naked to a vision which would be only total or null, but it is rather a sort of straits between exterior horizons and interior horizons ever gaping open, something that comes to touch lightly and make resound at the distances diverse regions of the colored or visible world, a certain differentiation, an ephemeral modulation of this world—less a color or a thing, therefore, than a difference between things and colors, a momentary crystallization of colored being or of visibility" (p. 132).

13. ". . . this piece of wood is neither a collection of colors and tactile data, nor even their total *Gestalt*, but there emanates from it a sort of ligneous essence, these 'sense-data' modulate a certain theme or illustrate a certain style which is the wood itself." *Phénoménologie de la perception*, p. 514. [Eng. trans., p. 450.]

14. Cf. *Signes* (Paris, 1960), p. 24. [English translation by Richard C. McLeary, *Signs* (Evanston, Ill., 1964), p. 16.]

sounded in a field and as the dominant, the field tone, the level at which the melody plays. In the very measure that a color occupies a here and a now it comes to command a field, begins to exist as dominant or color level. "With one sole movement it imposes itself as particular and ceases to be visible as particular" (pp. 217–18). "This becoming-neutral is not a change of the red into 'another color,' it is a modification of the red by its own duration (as the impact of a figure or a line on my vision tends to become dimensional, and to give it the value of an index of the curvature of space)" (p. 247). In the register of visibility every sensible thing is a universal-particular, every point is a pivot, every line a vector,[15] every color a level, every plane a horizon by transparency, every fact a category (p. 218).

"Perception is not first perception of *things*, but perception of *elements* . . . , of *rays of the world*, things which are dimensions, which are worlds . . ." (p. 218). Once we have understood that the thing is a *dimensional this*, we have already understood that the vision of the rose is already an introduction into roseness, into the *species* rose, into a family of like beings (p. 174)— not by an intellectual operation of generalization, but because to be introduced into a style of visible being is already to be introduced to the pregnancy of that style. And pregnancy, Merleau-Ponty tells us, means not only typicality, but also productivity, or generativity (p. 208)—not only the establishing of a type by "a certain manner of managing the domain of space over which it has competency" (p. 115), but generative power, "the equivalent of the cause of itself" (p. 208).

THE INVISIBLE

IN RECOGNIZING TRANSCENDENCE, being-at-a-distance, being "always further on" (p. 217), as the very manner of being of the visible, we come to recognize that the visible is not a multitude of spatio-temporal individuals that would have to be connected and combined by a mind constitutive of relations; it is a field, a relief, a topography unfolding by differentiation, by segregation, which holds together not by laws, but "through the reflections, shadows, levels, and horizons between things (which

15. Cf. *L'Oeil et l'esprit*, pp. 72–77. [Eng. trans., pp. 182–84.]

are not things and are not nothing, but on the contrary mark out by themselves the fields of possible variation in the same thing and in the same world)." [16] And once we conceive the "verbal essence" of the visible, the style it promotes across time and space and across all registers of sensoriality, then we understand that the visible holds together of itself, coheres into things. And we no longer need an ideal unity, intuited by and finally constituted by the mind, in order to account for the unity of sense that the sensible thing embodies.

Has Merleau-Ponty not then banished the ideal from the sensible? Is the ideal perhaps to be relegated to the cultural, the linguistic order only?

Certainly we cannot confine the ideal to the order of language and culture without destroying the very possibility of speaking *of* the visible, of brute being. If we speak about *the things*, it is because the ideal order expressed in language is already prefigured in the things themselves; but if we *speak* about the things it is because what we express is prefigured but not yet accomplished in their silence (pp. 4, 102–3, 125–27, 152–55). But surely it is true that the new morphology of the visible we acquire from Merleau-Ponty's work does implicate a new conception of the ideal, which cannot be defined by opposition to the sensible, nor taken as a second order of positive entities composed in the things (the "positivist bric-a-brac" of concepts, relations, essences . . . [p. 235]).

In the *Phenomenology of Perception* Merleau-Ponty often invoked the immanent logic at work in the sensible field, which governs the relief of the things in sizes and shapes and their staggering out in depth, which commands the distribution of tone and texture and grain in the things and holds all things together in a system. This wild *Logos* was shown to be not a set of principles or laws, but rather a system of levels posited in the sensible field by our body in its primal assuming of position before the tasks of the world. Thus to understand the distribution of things in proximity and in distance, or the differentiation of color in the visible field, it was necessary to discern the spatial levels and the level of illumination. Like the light, these levels and dimensions, this system of lines of force, are not *what* we see; they are that *with which, according to which,* we see.

16. *Signes,* p. 202. [Eng. trans., p. 160.]

This invisible piling upon which the visible is set is therefore not a set of representations or bonds constituted by a priori operations of a mind, nor even a set of positive configurations which would be apprehended, possessed by a mind, converted into "objects of thought." On the contrary to see is to see with, according to the invisible axes and pivots, levels and lines of force of the visible; we are guided by them, *possessed* by them (p. 151). Their authority, their fascinating, indestructible power (p. 150), is precisely due to the fact that here "to comprehend is not to constitute in intellectual immanence, that to comprehend is to apprehend by coexistence, laterally, *by the style*, and thereby to attain at once the far-off reaches of this style . . ." (p. 188).

For the discernment of this invisible filigree everywhere operative in the visible, for the description of this "carnal ideality" of light, of a melody, of relief, of physical voluptuosity, Merleau-Ponty sends us to Proust; but we could also turn to "Eye and Mind," where the "operative essence" of depth, of the line, of the contour, the movement, and the color are analyzed with incomparable virtuosity by Merleau-Ponty himself.

"To see is as a matter of principle to see further than one sees, to reach a being in latency." [17] There is a prejudicative *Logos* that does not emerge into view before eidetic insight or abstraction—that does not emerge into view at all, that remains latent, even in language.

> With the first vision, the first contact, the first pleasure, there is initiation, that is, not the positing of a content, but the opening of a dimension that can never again be closed, the establishment of a level in terms of which every other experience will henceforth be situated. The idea is this level, this dimension. It is therefore not a *de facto* invisible, like an object hidden behind another, and not an absolute invisible, that would have nothing to do with the visible. Rather it is the invisible *of* this world, that which inhabits this world, sustains it, and renders it visible, its own and interior possibility, the Being of this being (p. 151).

This *Logos*, which we do not constitute, which utters itself in us, is also what is at work in our language. Like the visible, language too is a system of differences, which, when cast into

17. *Signes*, p. 29. [Eng. trans., p. 20.]

operation, when it is operative speech, can capture in its own lines of force and movement something invisible, which is not positive thought content, but is rather an *unthought* (pp. 118–19). Merleau-Ponty was preparing a separate text, to be entitled *Introduction to the Prose of the World*,[18] to explore the divergencies, the disequilibriums, the reverberations back over itself that initiate and animate speech. It would explore not the cultivated language that employs a system of explicit relations between signs and meanings, but the operative language, that of literature, of poetry, of conversation, and of philosophy, which possesses meaning less than it is possessed by it, does not speak of it, but speaks *it*, or speaks *according to it*, or lets it speak and be spoken within us, breaks through our present (p. 118). This language "is open upon the things, called forth by the voices of silence, and continues an effort of articulation which is the Being of every being" (pp. 126–27).

Merleau-Ponty believed that the study of this wild *Logos*, not constituted by a mind and not consisting of positive idealities, was destined to renew our understanding of the imaginary, which is not simply the production of mental images, but the "baroque" proliferation of generating axes for visibility in the duplicity of the real. ". . . [T]he 'great unpenetrated and discouraging night of our soul' is not empty, is not 'nothingness'; but these entities, these domains, these worlds that line it, people it, and whose presence it feels like the presence of someone in the dark, have been acquired only through its commerce with the visible, to which they remain attached" (p. 150). In "Eye and Mind" Merleau-Ponty showed how these axes and schemes for visibility, captured in our flesh, were at the origin of that productive and motor imagination that moves the hand of the painter;[19] in the present text we find several working notes (pp. 180, 189–90, 232, 255, 262–63, 269–70) that claim that the invisible substructure of the visible is the key to the unconscious structure of consciousness.[20] "To see is as a matter of principle to see further than one sees, to reach a being in latency."

18. A fragment from this text was published in the *Revue de métaphysique et de morale*, LXXII, No. 2 (April-June, 1967), 139–53.
19. Cf. particularly pp. 22 ff. [Eng. trans., pp. 164 ff.]
20. For Merleau-Ponty's quite critical attitude with regard to his own earlier understanding of the unconscious in *The Structure of*

THE FLESH

THE CONCEPT OF FLESH emerges as the ultimate notion of Merleau-Ponty's thought; it is, he says, an uncomposed notion thinkable by itself (p. 140), and a prototype for Being universally.

The flesh, a concept of "what has no name in any philosophy" (pp. 139, 147), is not just a new term for what the *Phenomenology of Perception* (but already Sartre's *Being and Nothingness*) brought to light as the set of non-objective phenomena by which the subject's own corporeity is given to him as his "lived body" or "I-body," distinguished from his objective body, appearing publicly as a thing among things of the world. The flesh is the body inasmuch as it is the visible seer, the audible hearer, the tangible touch—the sensitive sensible: inasmuch as in it is accomplished an equivalence of sensibility and sensible thing.

The flesh is for itself the *exemplar sensible*. It is so because its manner of being is elemental: [21] "to designate it we should need the old term 'element' . . . in the sense of a *general thing*, midway between the spatio-temporal individual and the idea, a sort of incarnate principle that brings a style of being wherever there is a fragment of being" (p. 139). This teaching was prepared in the *Phenomenology of Perception* especially in the analysis of the corporeal schema, or postural model. The body is able to move itself because it has an awareness of itself and of its situation in the world; this awareness is the postural schema. But the postural schema is not a particular image; it rather gives the body to itself as an "I can," as a system of powers organized according to transposable schemes for movement. The continual auto-production of schemes in the body's mobilizing of itself "gives our life the form of generality and prolongs our personal acts into stable dispositions." [22] Thus "my body is to the

---

Behavior and *Phenomenology of Perception*, see his Preface to A. Hesnard, *L'Oeuvre de Freud* (Paris, 1960).

21. "The flesh is not matter, in the sense of corpuscles of being that would add up or continue on one another to form beings" (p. 139).

22. *Phénoménologie de la perception*, p. 171. [Eng. trans., p. 146.]

greatest extent what every thing is: a *dimensional this . . . a* sensible that is dimensional *of itself"* (p. 260).

It is in this elemental being of the flesh that the secret of sensibility is to be sought. The positivist conception of being, which preconceives being as objectivity posited before a subject, requires that the subject free a clearing in the density of being, about which the visible can be spread. Consequently the positivist conception of the visible implicates a negativist conception of the seer, which must be an incorporeal and nonsensorial knowing agency, an immaterial spirit, finally a pure clearing, a nothingness. In destroying the positivist conception of being we no longer think being posited against the ground of nothingness, and come to think the visible exhibited along the invisible dimensions, the levels, the pilings of the world; we discover a world in degrees, in distance, in depth, and in difference. "The perceived world . . . is the ensemble of my body's routes and not a multitude of spatio-temporal individuals" (p. 247). What makes then of the flesh a seer and of being a visibility is not the production of a clearing by nihilation but an elemental event by which the flesh captures the lines of force of the world, brings itself up to the levels about which visibility is modulated, rises upright before vertical being. This inaugural advent of sensibility in one sensible thing was already discerned, in the *Phenomenology of Perception,* in the study of the light that is not something seen but is that with which, or according to which, one sees: what inaugurates vision of things is the elemental alliance with the invisible light. In like manner what inaugurates touch in a tangible thing is not the production of the absolute untouchable void (for we cannot conceive of a being itself intangible that could touch, just as, after all, the only seer known to us is visible), but rather the capture in a hand of that movement and tempo that "effect the forming of tactile phenomena, as light delineates the configuration of a visible surface.[23]

The things can solicit the flesh without leaving their places because they are transcendencies, rays of the world, each promoting a singular style of being across time and space; and the flesh can capture in itself the allusive, schematic presence of the things because it is itself elemental being, self-positing posture, self-moving motion adjusting itself to the routes and levels and

23. *Phénoménologie de la perception,* p. 364. [Eng. trans., p. 315.]

axes of the visible. This intertwining, this chiasm effected across the substance of the flesh is the inaugural event of visibility.

It is then no incomprehensible conjuncture that the only seer known to us is itself visible (p. 137), and no mystery that the body has two sides, one "phenomenal," the other "objective." For "he who sees cannot possess the visible unless he is possessed by it, unless he *is of it* . . ." (pp. 134–35); "a mind could not be captured by its representations, it would rebel against this insertion into the visible which is essential to the seer" (p. 139). The seer is not a gap, a clearing, in the fabric of the visible; there is no hole in the weave of the visible where I am; the visible is one continuous fabric, since inside of me there are only " 'shadows stuffed with organs'—more of the visible" (p. 138). The manifest visibility of the world closes in over itself across the zone of latent visibility of my flesh. "There really is inspiration and expiration of Being, respiration in Being . . ." [24]

As translator of this book, I am indebted to Editions Gallimard for their permission to undertake this work. It is a pleasure to express my gratitude to Madame Merleau-Ponty for her kind encouragement and to M. Claude Lefort for his patient and generous help in the interpretation of the French manuscript.

ALPHONSO LINGIS

24. *L'Oeil et l'esprit*, pp. 31–32. [Eng. trans., p. 167. The translation has been slightly altered.]

The Visible and Nature:
Philosophical Interrogation

1 / Reflection and Interrogation

I^te (Kant)

THE PERCEPTUAL FAITH AND ITS OBSCURITY[1]

cf. 192

[WE SEE THE THINGS THEMSELVES,] the world is what
we see: formulae of this kind express a faith common to the
natural man and the philosopher—the moment he opens his
eyes; they refer to a deep-seated set of mute "opinions" implicated in our lives. But what is strange about this faith is that if
we seek to articulate it into theses or statements, if we ask
ourselves what is this *we*, what *seeing* is, and what *thing* or
world is, we enter into a labyrinth of difficulties and contradictions.

What Saint Augustine said of time—that it is perfectly familiar to each, but that none of us can explain it to the others—
must be said of the world. [Ceaselessly the philosopher finds
himself][2] obliged to reinspect and redefine the most well-
grounded notions, to create new ones, with new words to designate them, to undertake a true reform of the understanding—at
whose term the evidence of the world, which seemed indeed to be
the clearest of truths, is supported by the seemingly most sophisticated thoughts, before which the natural man now no longer
recognizes where he stood. Whence the age-old ill-humor against

1. EDITOR: Opposite the title of the section, the author notes:
"Notion of faith to be specified. It is not faith in the sense of decision
but in the sense of what is before any position, animal and [?] faith."
2. EDITOR: "Ceaselessly the philosopher finds himself . . .":
these words, which we introduce to give sense to the following
sentences, were the first words of a sentence-body entirely erased by
the author.

[3]

philosophy is reanimated, the grievance always brought against it that it reverses the roles of the clear and the obscure. The fact that the philosopher claims to speak in the very name of the naïve evidence of the world, that he refrains from adding anything to it, that he limits himself to drawing out all its consequences, does not excuse him; on the contrary he dispossesses [humanity] [3] only the more completely, inviting it to think of itself as an enigma.

epoché

This is the way things are and nobody can do anything about it. It is at the same time true that the world is *what we see* and that, nonetheless, we must learn to see it—first in the sense that we must match this vision with knowledge, take possession of it, *say* what *we* and what *seeing* are, act therefore as if we knew nothing about it, as if here we still had everything to learn. But philosophy is not a lexicon, it is not concerned with "word-meanings," it does not seek a verbal substitute for the world we see, it does not transform it into something said, it does not install itself in the order of the said or of the written as does the logician in the proposition, the poet in the word, or the musician in the music. It is the things themselves, from the depths of their

ontological

silence, that it wishes to bring to expression. If the philosopher questions, and hence feigns ignorance of the world and of the vision of the world which are operative and take form continually within him, he does so precisely in order to make them speak, because he believes in them and expects from them all his future science. The questioning here is not a beginning of negation, a perhaps put in the place of being. It is for philosophy the only way to conform itself with the vision we have in fact, to correspond with what, in that vision, provides for thought, with the paradoxes of which that vision is made, the only way to adjust itself to those figured enigmas, the thing and the world, whose massive being and truth teem with incompossible details.

For after all, sure as it is that I see my table, that my vision

3. EDITOR: "Dispossesses humanity" is doubtless to be understood. These words belong to the last part of the preceding sentence, erased by the author, and which we reproduce here between brackets: ". . . the grievance always brought against it that it reverses the roles of the clear and the obscure [and that it arrogates to itself the role of making humanity live in a state of alienation, in the most complete alienation, the philosopher claiming to understand humanity better than it understands itself]."

terminates in it, that it holds and stops my gaze with its insur-
mountable density, as sure even as it is that when, seated before
my table, I think of the Pont de la Concorde, I am not then in my
thoughts but am at the Pont de la Concorde, and finally sure as it
is that at the horizon of all these visions or quasi-visions it is the
world itself I inhabit, the natural world and the historical world,
with all the human traces of which it is made—still as soon as I
attend to it this conviction is just as strongly contested, by the
very fact that this vision is *mine*. We are not so much thinking
here of the age-old argument from dreams, delirium, or illusions,
inviting us to consider whether what we see is not "false." For to
do so the argument makes use of that faith in the world it seems
to be unsettling: we would not know even what the false is, if
there were not times when we had distinguished it from the true.
The argument therefore postulates the world in general, the true
in itself; this is secretly invoked in order to disqualify our perceptions and cast them pell-mell back into our "interior life" along
with our dreams, in spite of all observable differences, for the
sole reason that our dreams were, at the time, as convincing as
they—forgetting that the "falsity" of dreams cannot be extended
to perceptions since it appears only relative to perceptions and
that if we are to be able to speak of falsity, we do have to have
experiences of truth. Valid against naïveté, against the idea of a
perception that would plunge forth to surprise the things beyond
all experience, as the light draws them from the night wherein
they pre-existed, the argument does not [elucidate?]; it is marked
with this same naïveté itself, since it equalizes the perception
and the dream only by setting opposite them a Being that would
be in itself only. If, however, as the argument, in the measure
that it has validity, shows, we must completely reject this phantasm, then the intrinsic, descriptive differences between the
dream and the perceived take on ontological value. And we
answer Pyrrhonism sufficiently by showing that there is a difference of structure and, as it were, of grain between the perception
or true vision, which gives rise to an open series of concordant
explorations, and the dream, which is not *observable* and, upon
examination, is almost nothing but blanks. To be sure, this does
not terminate the problem of our access to the world; on the
contrary it is only beginning. For there remains the problem of
how we can be under the illusion of seeing what we do not see,
how the rags of the dream can, before the dreamer, be worth the

In the
world—
yet it is
mine

close-woven fabric of the true world, how the unconsciousness of not having observed can, in the fascinated man, take the place of the consciousness of having observed. If one says that the void of the imaginary remains forever what it is, is never equivalent to the plenum of the perceived and never gives rise to the *same* certitude, that it is *not taken to be worth* the perceived, that the sleeping man has lost every reference mark, every model, every canon of the clear and the articulate, and that one sole particle of the perceived world introduced in it would instantaneously dissipate the enchantment, the fact remains that if we can lose our reference marks *unbeknown to ourselves* we are never sure of *having* them when we think we have them; if we can withdraw from the world of perception without knowing it, nothing proves to us that we are ever in it, nor that the observable is ever entirely observable, nor that it is made of another fabric than the dream. Then, the difference between perception and dream not being absolute, one is justified in counting them both among "our experiences," and it is above perception itself that we must seek the guarantee and the sense of its ontological function. We will stake out that route, which is that of the philosophy of reflection (*la philosophie réflexive*), when it opens. But it begins well beyond the Pyrrhonian arguments; by themselves they would deter us from any elucidation, since they refer vaguely to the idea of a Being wholly in itself and by contrast count the perceived and the imaginary indiscriminately among our "states of consciousness." At bottom, Pyrrhonism shares the illusions of the naïve man. It is the naïveté that rends itself asunder in the night. Between Being in itself and the "interior life" it does not even catch sight of the *problem of the world*. Whereas it is toward that problem that we are making our way. What interests us is not the reasons one can have to consider the existence of the world "uncertain"—as if one already knew what to exist is and as if the whole question were to apply this concept appropriately. For us the essential is to know precisely what the being of the world means. Here we must presuppose nothing—neither the naïve idea of being in itself, therefore, nor the correlative idea of a being of representation, of a being for the consciousness, of a being for man: these, along with the being of the world, are all notions that we have to rethink with regard to our experience of the world. We have to reformulate the sceptical arguments outside of every ontological preconception and reformulate them precisely so as to know what world-being, thing-being, imaginary being, and conscious being are.

Now that I have in perception the thing itself, and not a representation, I will only add that the thing is at the end of my gaze and, in general, at the end of my exploration. Without assuming anything from what the science of the body of the other can teach me, I must acknowledge that the table before me sustains a singular relation with my eyes and my body: I see it only if it is within their radius of action; above it there is the dark mass of my forehead, beneath it the more indecisive contour of my cheeks—both of these visible at the limit and capable of hiding the table, as if my vision of the world itself were formed from a certain point of the world. What is more, my movements and the movements of my eyes make the world vibrate—as one rocks a dolmen with one's finger without disturbing its fundamental solidity. With each flutter of my eyelashes a curtain lowers and rises, though I do not think for an instant of imputing this eclipse to the things themselves; with each movement of my eyes that sweep the space before me the things suffer a brief torsion, which I also ascribe to myself; and when I walk in the street with eyes fixed on the horizon of the houses, the whole of the setting near at hand quivers with each footfall on the asphalt, then settles down in its place. I would express what takes place badly indeed in saying that here a "subjective component" or a "corporeal constituent" comes to cover over the things themselves: it is not a matter of another layer or a veil that would have come to pose itself between them and me. The stirring of the "appearance" does not disrupt the evidence of the thing—any more than monocular images interfere when my two eyes operate in synergy. The binocular perception is not made up of two monocular perceptions surmounted; it is of another order. The monocular images *are* not in the same sense that the thing perceived with both eyes *is*. They are phantoms and it is the real; they are pre-things and it is the thing: they vanish when we pass to normal vision and re-enter into the thing as into their daylight truth. They are too far from having its density to enter into competition with it: they are only a certain divergence [4] from the imminent true vision, absolutely

4. TRANSLATOR: *Ecart.* This recurrent term will have to be rendered variously by "divergence," "spread," "deviation," "separation."

bereft of its [prestiges?] and therefore drafts for or residues of the true vision, which accomplishes them by reabsorbing them. The monocular images cannot be *compared* with the synergic perception: one cannot put them side by side; it is necessary to choose between the thing and the floating pre-things. We can effect the passage by *looking,* by awakening to the world; we cannot witness it as spectators. It is not a *synthesis;* it is a metamorphosis by which the appearances are instantaneously stripped of a value they owed merely to the absence of a true perception. Thus in perception we witness the miracle of a total-ity that surpasses what one thinks to be its conditions or its parts, that from afar holds them under its power, as if they existed only on its threshold and were destined to lose them-selves in it. But if it is to displace them as it does, it is necessary that the perception maintain in its depth all their corporeal ties: it is by *looking,* it is still with my eyes that I arrive at the true thing, with these same eyes that a moment ago gave me monocu-lar images—now they simply function *together* and as though *for good.* Thus the relation between the things and my body is decidedly singular: it is what makes me sometimes remain in appearances, and it is also what sometimes brings me to the things themselves; it is what produces the buzzing of appear-ances, it is also what silences them and casts me fully into the world. Everything comes to pass as though my power to reach the world and my power to entrench myself in phantasms only came one with the other; even more: as though the access to the world were but the other face of a withdrawal and this retreat to the margin of the world a servitude and another expression of my natural power to enter into it. The world is what I perceive, but as soon as we examine and express its absolute proximity, it also becomes, inexplicably, irremediable distance. The "natural" man holds on to both ends of the chain, thinks *at the same time* that his perception enters into the things and that it is formed this side of his body. Yet coexist as the two convictions do without difficulty in the exercise of life, once reduced to theses and to propositions they destroy one another and leave us in confusion.

What if I took not only my own views of myself into account but also the other's views of himself and of me? Already my body as stage director of my perception has shattered the illusion of a coinciding of my perception with the things themselves. Between them and me there are henceforth hidden powers, that whole vegetation of possible phantasms which it holds in check only in the fragile act of the look. No doubt, it is not entirely my body that perceives: I know only that it can prevent me from perceiving, that I cannot perceive without its permission; the moment perception comes my body effaces itself before it and never does the perception grasp the body in the act of perceiving.* If my left hand is touching my right hand, and if I should suddenly wish to apprehend with my right hand the work of my left hand as it touches, this reflection of the body upon itself always miscarries at the last moment: the moment I feel my left hand with my right hand, I correspondingly cease touching my right hand with my left hand. But this last-minute failure does not drain all truth from that presentiment I had of being able to touch myself touching: my body does not perceive, but it is as if it were built around the perception that dawns through it; through its whole internal arrangement, its sensory-motor circuits, the return ways that control and release movements, it is, as it were, prepared for a self-perception, even though it is never itself that is perceived nor itself that perceives.[5] Before the science of the body (which involves the relation with the other) the experience of my flesh as gangue of my perception has taught me that perception does not come to birth just anywhere, that it emerges in the recess of a body. The other men who see "as we do," whom we see seeing and who see us seeing, present us with but an amplification of the same paradox. If it is already difficult to say that my perception, such as I live it, goes unto the things themselves, it is indeed impossible to grant access to the world to the others' perception; and, by a sort of backlash, they also refuse me this access which I deny to them. For where the others (or myself seen by them) are concerned, one must not only say that the thing is caught up by the vortex of exploratory movements and perceptual behaviors and drawn inward. If perhaps there is for me no sense in saying that my perception and the thing it aims at are "in my head" (it is certain only that they are *"not else-where"*), I cannot help putting the other, and the perception he has, *behind his body.* More exactly, the thing perceived by the

---

* The ἴδιος κόσμος like the monocular image: it is not interposed, isolated, but it is not nothing.

5. TRANSLATOR: . . . *même si ce n'est jamais lui qu'il perçoit ou lui qui le perçoit.*

other is doubled: there is *the one he perceives*, God knows where, and there is the one I see, outside of his body, and which I call the true thing—as he calls true thing the table *he sees* and consigns to the category of appearances the one I see. The true things and the perceiving bodies are this time no longer in the ambiguous relation which a moment ago we found between *my* things and *my* body. Now the true things and the perceiving bodies, whether close-up or distant, are in any case juxtaposed in the world, and perception, which perhaps is not "in my head," is nowhere else than in my body as a thing of the world. From now on it seems impossible to remain in the inner certitude of him who perceives: seen from without perception glides over the things and does not touch them. At most one will say, if one wishes to admit the perception's own perspective upon itself, that each of us has a private world: these private worlds are "worlds" only for their titulars; they are not the world. The sole world, that is, the unique world, would be a κοῖνος κόσμος, and our perceptions do not open upon it.

But upon what then do they open? How are we to name, to describe, such as I see it from my place, that *lived by another* which yet for me is not nothing, since I believe in the other—and that which furthermore concerns me myself, since it is there as another's view upon me?* Here is this well-known countenance, this smile, these modulations of voice, whose style is as familiar to me as myself. Perhaps in many moments of my life the other is for me reduced to this spectacle, which can be a charm. But

* Take up again: Yet, just as above the monocular phantasms could not compete with the thing, so also now one could describe the private worlds as divergence with respect to the *world itself*. How I represent the lived by another to myself: as a sort of duplication of my own lived experience. The marvel of this experience: I can count on what I see, which is in close correspondence with what the other sees (everything attests to this, in fact: we really do see the same thing and the thing itself)—and yet at the same time I never rejoin the other's lived experience. It is in the world that we rejoin one another. Every attempt to reinstate the illusion of the "thing itself" is in fact an attempt to return to my imperialism and to the value of *my* thing. Therefore it does not bring us out of solipsism: it is a new proof of solipsism.

    c) Consequences: underlying obscurity of the natural idea of truth or "intelligible world."

Science will only prolong this attitude: objectivist ontology which undermines itself and collapses under analysis.

should the voice alter, should the unwonted appear in the score of the dialogue, or, on the contrary, should a response respond too well to what I thought without having really said it—and suddenly there breaks forth the evidence that yonder also, minute by minute, life is being lived: somewhere behind those eyes, behind those gestures, or rather before them, or again about them, coming from I know not what double ground of space, another private world shows through, through the fabric of my own, and for a moment I live in it; I am no more than the respondent for the interpellation that is made to me. To be sure, the least recovery of attention persuades me that this other who invades me is made only of my own substance: how could I conceive, precisely as *his, his* colors, *his* pain, *his* world, except as in accordance with the colors I see, the pains I have had, the world wherein I live? But at least my private world has ceased to be mine only; it is now the instrument which another plays, the dimension of a generalized life which is grafted onto my own.

But at the very moment that I think I share the life of another, I am rejoining it only in its ends, its exterior poles. It is in the world that we communicate, through what, in our life, is articulate. It is from this lawn before me that I think I catch sight of the impact of the green on the vision of another, it is through the music that I enter into his musical emotion, it is the thing itself that opens unto me the access to the private world of another. But the thing itself, we have seen, is always for me the thing that *I* see. The intervention of the other does not resolve the internal paradox of my perception: it adds to it this other enigma: of the propagation of my own most secret life in another—another enigma, but yet the same one, since, from all the evidence, it is only through the world that I can leave myself. It is therefore indeed true that the "private worlds" communicate, that each of them is given to its incumbent as a variant of one common world. The communication makes us the witnesses of one sole world, as the synergy of our eyes suspends them on one unique thing. But in both cases, the certitude, entirely irresistible as it may be, remains absolutely obscure; we can live it, we can neither think it nor formulate it nor set it up in theses. Every attempt at elucidation brings us back to the dilemmas.

And it is this unjustifiable certitude of a sensible world common to us that is the seat of truth within us. That a child perceives before he thinks, that he begins by putting his dreams in the things, his thoughts in the others, forming with them, as it were, one block of common life wherein the perspectives of each are not yet distinguished—these genetic facts cannot be simply ignored by philosophy in the name of the exigencies of the intrinsic analysis. Thought cannot ignore its apparent history, if it is not to install itself beneath the whole of our experience, in a pre-empirical order where it would no longer merit its name; it must put to itself the problem of the genesis of its own meaning. It is in terms of its intrinsic meaning and structure that the sensible world is "older" than the universe of thought, because the sensible world is visible and relatively continuous, and because the universe of thought, which is invisible and contains gaps, constitutes at first sight a whole and has its truth only on condition that it be supported on the canonical structures of the sensible world. If we reconstitute the way in which our experiences, according to their ownmost meaning, depend on one another, and if, in order to better lay bare the essential relations of dependency, we try to break them apart in our thought, we come to realize that all that for us is called thought requires that distance from oneself, that initial openness which a field of vision and a field of future and of past are for us. . . . In any case, since we are here only trying to take a first look at our natural certitudes, there is no doubt that, in what concerns the mind and truth, they rest on the primary stratum of the sensible world and that our assurance of being in the truth is one with our assurance of being in the world. We speak and we understand speech long before learning from Descartes (or rediscovering for ourselves) that thought is our reality. We learn to meaningfully handle language (*language*), in which we install ourselves, long before learning from linguistics the intelligible principles upon which our tongue (*langue*) and every tongue are "based" (supposing that it does teach them). Our experience of the true, when it is not immediately reducible to that of the thing we see, is at first not distinct from the tensions that arise between the others and ourselves, and from their resolution. As the thing, as the other, the true dawns through an emotional and almost carnal experience, where the "ideas"—the other's and our own—are rather traits of his physiognomy and of our own, are less understood than welcomed or spurned in love or hatred. To be sure, there are motifs, quite abstract categories, that function very precociously in this wild [6] thought, as the extraordinary anticipations of adult life in childhood show sufficiently; and one can say that the whole of man is already there in his infancy. The child understands well beyond what he knows how to say, responds well beyond what he could define, and this after all is as true of the adult. A genuine conversation gives me access to thoughts that I did not know myself capable of, that I *was* not capable of, and sometimes I feel myself *followed* in a route unknown to myself which my words, cast back by the other, are in the process of tracing out for me. To suppose here that an *intelligible world* sustains the exchange would be to take a name for a solution—and furthermore it would be to grant us what we are maintaining: that it is by borrowing from the world structure that the universe of truth and of thought is constructed for us. When we want to express strongly the consciousness we have of a truth, we find nothing better than to invoke a τόπος νοητός that would be common to minds or to men, as the sensible world is common to the sensible bodies. And this is not only an analogy: it is the same world that contains our bodies and our minds, provided that we understand by world not only the sum of things that fall or could fall under our eyes, but also the locus of their compossibility, the invariable style they observe, which connects our perspectives, permits transition from one to the other, and —whether in describing a detail of the landscape or in coming to agreement about an invisible truth—makes us feel we are two witnesses capable of hovering over [7] the same true object, or at least of exchanging our situations relative to it, as we can exchange our standpoints in the visible world in the strict sense. But here again, more than ever, the naïve certitude of the world, the anticipation of an intelligible world, is as weak when it wishes to convert itself into theses as it is strong in practice. As long as we are dealing with the visible, a mass of facts comes to support it: beyond the divergence of the witnesses it is often easy

6. TRANSLATOR: *Sauvage:* wild in the sense of uncultivated, uncultured. There is doubtless an allusion to Claude Lévi-Strauss's *The Savage Mind* (*La Pensée sauvage*) in the term.

7. TRANSLATOR: *Survoler.* Merleau-Ponty likes to call the unsituated point of view of objectivist thought a *pensée de survol*—a "high-altitude thinking" (as Benita Eisler translates in John-Paul Sartre's *Situations* [New York, 1965], p. 229).

to re-establish the unity and concordance of the world. But as soon as one goes beyond the circle of *instituted* opinions, which are undivided among us as are the Madeleine or the Palais de Justice, much less thoughts than monuments of our historical landscape, as soon as one reaches the true, that is, the invisible, it seems rather that each man inhabits his own islet, without there being transition from one to the other, and we should rather be astonished that sometimes men come to agreement about anything whatever. For after all each of them has begun by being a fragile mass of living jelly, and it is already a great deal that they would have taken the same route of ontogenesis; it is still more of a wonder that all, from the bottom of their retreats, would have let themselves be caught up by the same social functioning and the same language; but, when it comes to using these according to their own wills and to saying what no one sees, neither the type of the species nor that of the society guarantees that they should come to compatible propositions. When one thinks of the mass of contingencies that can alter both, nothing is more improbable than the extrapolation that treats the universe of the truth as one world also, without fissures and without incompossibles.

SCIENCE PRESUPPOSES THE PERCEPTUAL FAITH AND DOES NOT ELUCIDATE IT

ONE MIGHT BE TEMPTED to say that these insoluble antinomies belong to the confused universe of the immediate, lived experience, or the vital man, which by definition is without truth, that hence we must forget them until the sole rigorous knowledge, science, comes to explain these phantasms with which we are troubling ourselves by their conditions and from without. The true is neither the thing that I see, nor the other man whom I also see with my eyes, nor finally that total unity of the sensible world and, at the limit, of the intelligible world which we were presently trying to describe. The true is the *objective*, is what I have succeeded in determining by measurement, or more generally by the *operations* that are authorized by the variables or by the entities I have defined relative to an order of facts. Such determinations owe nothing to our *contact* with the things: they express an effort of approximation that would have no meaning with regard to the lived experience, since the lived is to be taken as such and cannot also be considered "in itself." Thus science began by excluding all the predicates that come to the things from our encounter with them. The exclusion is however only provisional: when it will have learned to invest it, science will little by little reintroduce what it first put aside as subjective; but it will integrate it as a particular case of the relations and objects that define the world for science. Then the world will close in over itself, and, except for what within us thinks and builds science, that impartial spectator that inhabits us, we will have become parts or moments of the Great Object.

We will too often have to return to the multiple variants of this illusion to deal with them now. Here we have to state only what is necessary to rule out the objection of principle that would stop our research at the start: that is, summarily, that the κοσμοθεωρός capable of constructing or of reconstructing the existing world with an indefinite series of its own operations, far from dissipating the obscurities of our naïve faith in the world, is on the contrary its most dogmatic expression, presupposes it, maintains itself only by virtue of that faith. During the two centuries that it pursued its task of objectification without diffi- culty, physics was able to believe that it was simply following out the articulations of the world and that the physical object in itself pre-existed science. But today, when the very rigor of its description obliges physics to recognize as ultimate physical beings in full right relations between the observer and the ob- served, determinations that have meaning only for a certain situation of the observer, it is the ontology of the κοσμοθεωρός and of the Great Object correlative to it that figures as a prescien- tific preconception. Yet it is so natural that the physicist contin- ues to think of himself as an Absolute Mind before the pure object and to count also as truths in themselves the very state- ments that express the interdependence of the whole of the observable with a situated and incarnate physicist. The formula that permits one to pass from one real perspective on astronomi- cal spaces to another and which, being true of all of them, goes beyond the *de facto* situation of the physicist who speaks, does not, however, surpass it unto an absolute knowledge: for it has meaning in physics only when tallied with observations and inserted into a life of cognitions which, for their part, are always situated. What permits the joining together of views which are all perspective is not a view of the universe; it is only the methodic usage. If we give to that formula the value of an absolute Knowledge, if, for example, we seek in it the ultimate and exhaustive meaning of time and space, we do so because the pure operation of science here takes up for its own profit our certitude, which is much older than it and much less clear, of having access "to the things themselves" or of having an absolute power to survey the world from above.

When it gained access to domains that are not naturally given to man—to astronomical spaces or microphysical realities —the more inventiveness in the wielding of algorithm science has exhibited, the more conservative it has shown itself to be in what concerns theory of knowledge. Truths that should not have left its idea of Being unchanged are—at the cost of great difficulties of expression and thought—retranslated into the language of the traditional ontology—as if science needed to except itself from the relativities it establishes, to put itself out of play, as if blindness for Being were the price it has to pay for its success in the determination of beings. The considerations regarding scale, for example, if they are really taken seriously, should not relegate all the truths of physics to the side of the "subjective"—a move that would maintain the rights of the idea of an inaccessible "objectivity"—but they should contest the very principle of this cleavage and make the contact between the observer and the observed enter into the definition of the "real." Yet we have seen many physicists seek in the compact structure and the density of macroscopic appearances, or on the contrary in the loose and lacunate structure of certain microphysical domains, arguments in favor of a determinism, or, contrariwise, of a "mental" or "acausal" reality. These alternatives show enough to what point science, where it is a question of an ultimate understanding of itself, is rooted in pre-science and foreign to the question of the *meaning of being*. When the physicists speak of particles that exist for but a milliard of a second, their first movement is always to suppose that they exist in the same sense as directly observable particles, except for much shorter a time. The microphysical field is considered as a macroscopic field of very small dimensions, where the horizon phenomena, the properties without carriers, the collective beings or beings without absolute localization, are by right only "subjective appearances" which the vision of some giant [would reduce to] [8] the interaction of absolute physical individuals. Yet this is to postulate that the considerations of scale are not ultimate; it is again to think them in the perspective of the in itself, at the very moment when there is a suggestion to renounce that perspective. Thus the "strange" notions of the new physics are strange for it only in the sense that a paradoxical opinion surprises common sense, that is, without instructing it in depth and without changing anything of its categories. We are not implying here that the properties of the new physical beings *prove* a new logic or a new ontology. If one takes "proof" in the mathematical sense, the scientists, who are alone in a position to furnish one, are also alone in a position to evaluate it. That some of them refuse such proof as a case of begging the question [9] suffices for the philosopher not to have the right—nor the obligation either—to admit it. What the philosopher can note—what provokes his thought —is that precisely those physicists who maintain a Cartesian representation of the world [10] admit their "preferences," just as a musician or a painter would speak of his preferences for a style. This permits us to advance the notion that no ontology is exactly *required* by the thought proper to physics at work (whatever be the subsequent fate of the microphysical theory), that in particular the classical ontology of the object cannot claim to be enjoined by it, nor can it claim a privilege *by principle*, when, for those who maintain it, it is only a preference. Either by physics and by science we understand a certain way of operating on the facts with algorithm, a certain procedure of cognition of which those who possess the instrument are the sole judges—in which case they are the sole judges also of the sense in which they take their variables, but have neither the obligation nor even the right to give an imaginative translation of them, to decide in their name the question of *what there is,* or to impugn an eventual *contact* with the world. Or, on the contrary, physics means to say *what is*—but then it is today no longer justified in defining Being

8. EDITOR: "Would reduce to" is crossed out and "would find again" is written over it. We restore the first expression, since the correction is manifestly incomplete.

9. For example, Louis de Broglie, *Nouvelles perspectives sur la microphysique* (Paris, 1956).

10. *Ibid.*

by the Being-object, nor in confining lived experience within the order of our "representations" and the sector of "psychological" curiosities; it must recognize as legitimate an analysis of the procedures through which the universe of measures and operations is constituted starting from the life world (*monde vécu*) considered as the source, eventually as the universal source. Without this analysis, in which the relative rights and the limits of the classical objectification would be recognized, a physics that would maintain as is the philosophical equipment of classical science and project its own results into the order of absolute knowledge would, like the perceptual faith from which it proceeds, live in a state of permanent crisis. It is striking to see Einstein disqualify as "psychology" the experience that we have of the simultaneous through the perception of another and the intersection of our perceptual horizons and those of the others: for him there could be no question of giving ontological value to this experience because it is purely a knowledge by anticipation or by principle and is formed without operations, without effective measurings. This is to postulate that what is is not *that upon which we have an openness,* but only *that upon which we can operate;* and Einstein does not dissemble the fact that this certitude of an adequation between the operation of science and Being is with him prior to his physics. He even emphasizes with humor the contrast between his "wildly speculative" science and his claim for it of a truth in itself. We will have to show how the physical idealization goes beyond, and forgets, the perceptual faith. For the moment it was enough to note that it proceeds from that faith, that it does not lift its contradictions, does not dissipate its obscurity, and nowise dispenses us—far from it— from envisaging it in itself.

We would arrive at the same conclusion if, instead of underscoring the inconsistencies of the "objective" order, we would address ourselves to the "subjective" order which, in the ideology of science, is its counterpart and necessary complement—and perhaps our conclusion would be more easily accepted through this way. For here the disorder and the incoherence are manifest, and one can say without exaggeration that our fundamental concepts—that of the psychism and of psychology—are as mythical as the classifications of the societies called archaic. It was believed that we were returning to clarity by exorcising "introspection." And to do so was indeed necessary: for where, when, and how has there ever been a vision of the inside? There is—and this is something quite different, which retains its value —a life present to itself (*près de soi*), an openness upon oneself, which does not look out upon any world other than the common world—and which is not necessarily a closedness to the others. The critique of introspection too often turns away from that irreplaceable way of access to the other as he is involved in ourselves. And on the other hand, the recourse to the "outside" is by itself nowise a guarantee against the illusions of introspection; it gives only a new form to our confused idea of a psychological "vision"; it only transfers it from the inside to the outside. It would be instructive to make explicit what the psychologists mean by "psychism" and other analogous notions. It is like a deep-lying geological stratum, an *invisible "thing,"* which is found somewhere behind certain living bodies, and with regard to which one supposes that the only problem is to find the correct angle for observation. It is also what, in me, troubles itself with the desire to know the psychism; but there is as it were a continually abortive vocation in it: for how could a thing know itself? The "psychism" is opaque to itself and rejoins itself only in its exterior counterparts. And, in the last analysis, it assures itself that those exterior counterparts resemble itself in the way the anatomist assures himself that he finds in the organ he dissects the very structure of his own eyes: because there is a "species man" . . . If we were to render completely explicit the psychological attitude and the concepts which the psychologist uses as if they were self-evident, we would find a mass of consequences without premises, a very long-standing constitutive labor which is not brought out into the open and whose results are accepted as they are without one even suspecting to what extent they are confused. What is operative here is as always the perceptual faith in the things and in the world. We apply to man as to things the conviction it gives us that we can arrive at what is by an absolute overview, and in this way we come to think of the invisible of man as a thing. The psychologist in his turn establishes himself in the position of the absolute spectator. The investigation of the "psychic," like that of the exterior object, first progresses only by putting itself outside of the play of the relativities it discovers, by tacitly supposing an absolute subject before which is deployed the psychism in general, my own or that of another. The cleavage between the "subjective" and the "objective" according to which physics defines its domain as it commences, and correlatively psychology also establishes its domain, does not prevent these from being conceived according to the same fundamental structure; on the contrary it requires that: they are finally two orders of objects, to be known in their intrinsic properties by a pure thought which determines what they are in themselves. But, as in physics also, a moment comes when the very development of knowledge calls into question the absolute spectator always presupposed. After all, this physicist of whom I speak and to whom I attribute a system of reference is also the physicist who speaks. After all, this psychism of which the psychologist speaks is also his own. This physics of the physicist and this psychology of the psychologist evince that henceforth, for science itself, the being-object can no longer be being-itself: "objective" and "subjective" are recognized as two orders hastily constructed within a total experience, whose context must be restored in all clarity.

This intellectual overture, whose diagram we have now drawn, has determined the history of psychology for the last fifty years, and particularly of Gestalt psychology. It had wished to constitute for itself its own domain of objectivity; it believed it had discovered it in the structures of behavior. Was there not here an original conditioning which would form the object of an original science, as other less complex structures formed the object of the sciences of nature? As a distinct domain, juxtaposed to that of physics, behavior or the psychism, taken objectively, was in principle accessible through the same methods and had the same ontological structure: in both domains, the object was defined by the functional relations it universally observes. There was indeed, in psychology, a *descriptive* way of access to the object, but by principle it could lead only to the same functional determinations, And, indeed, it was possible to specify the conditions on which in fact such and such a perceptual realization, a perception of an ambiguous figure, a spatial or color level depend. Psychology believed it had finally found its firm foundation and expected henceforth an accumulation of discoveries that would confirm it in its status as a science. And yet, today, forty years after the beginnings of *Gestaltpsychologie,* we have again the sentiment of being at a standstill. To be sure, on many points the initial works of the school have been brought to precision; a number of functional determinations have been and are being established. But the enthusiasm is no longer with it; nowhere have we the sentiment of approaching a science of man. It is—the authors of the school very quickly realized—that the relationships they establish operate imperatively and are explicative only in the artificial conditions of the laboratory. They do not represent a *first stratum* of behavior, from which one could proceed little by little unto its total determination; rather they are a first form of integration, privileged cases of simple structuration, relative to which the "more complex" structurations are in reality qualitatively different. The functional relation they state has meaning only at their level; it has no explicative force with regard to higher levels, and finally the being of the psychism is to be defined not as an intersection of elementary "causalities," but by the heterogeneous and discontinuous structurations that are realized in it. In the measure that we have to do with more integrated structures, we come to realize that the conditions account for the conditioned less than they are the occasion of its release. Thus the parallelism postulated between the descriptive and the functional was belied. Easy as it is to explain according to its conditions, for example, such and such an apparent movement of a spot of light in a field that has been artificially simplified and reduced by the experimental apparatus, a total determination of the concrete perceptual field of a given living individual at a given moment appears not provisionally unattainable but definitively meaningless, *because it presents structures that do not even have a name in the* objective *universe of separated and separable "conditions."* When I look at a road that retreats from me toward the horizon, I can relate what I call the "apparent width" of the road at a given distance (i.e., the width I measure, by peering at it with one eye only and gauging it on a pencil I hold before me) with other elements of the field also specified by some procedure of *measurement,* and thus establish that the "constancy" of the apparent size depends on such and such variables, according to the schema of functional dependence that defines the object of classical science. But when I consider the field such as I have it when I look freely with both eyes, outside of every isolating attitude, it is impossible for me to *explain* it by conditionings. Not that these conditionings *escape* me or remain *hidden* from me, but because the *"conditioned" itself ceases to be of an order such as could be described objectively.* For the natural gaze that gives me the landscape, the

[margin note: Conditions in natural experience can't be described objectively]

road in the distance has no "width" one could even ideally calculate; it is as wide as the road close-up, since it is the same road—and it is not as wide, since I cannot deny that there is a sort of shrinking in perspective. Between the road far-off and close-up there is identity and yet μετάβασις εἰς ἄλλο γένος, passage from the apparent to the real, and they are incommensurable. Yet I must not understand the appearance even here as a veil cast between me and the real—the perspective contraction is not a deformation, the road close-up is not "more true": the close, the far-off, the horizon in their indescribable contrast form a system, and it is their relationship within the total field that is the perceptual truth. We have entered into the ambiguous order of perceived being, upon which functional dependence has no "grip." The psychology of vision can be only artificially and verbally maintained in this ontological framework: the "conditions" for depth —the disappearance of the retinal images, for example—are not really conditions, since the images are defined as disparate only by relation to a perceptual apparatus that seeks its equilibrium in the fusion of analogous images, and hence here the "conditioned" conditions the condition. To be sure, a perceived world would not appear to a man if these conditions were not given in his body; but it is not they that *explain* that world. A perceived world is in terms of its field laws and laws of intrinsic organization, and not—like the *object*—according to the exigencies of a "side to side" causality. The "psychism" is not an object; but— we emphasize—there is here no question of showing, in terms of the "spiritualist" tradition, that certain realities "escape" scientific determination. Such a demonstration results only in circumscribing a domain of anti-science which ordinarily remains conceived —in the terms of the ontology which precisely is in question—as another "order of realities." Our purpose is not to oppose to the facts objective science coordinates a group of facts that "escape" it—whether one calls them "psychism" or "subjective facts" or "interior facts"—but to show that the being-object and the being-subject conceived by opposition to it and relative to it do not form the alternative, that the perceived world is beneath or beyond this antinomy, that the failure of "objective" psychology is—conjointly with the failure of the "objectivist" physics—to be understood not as a victory of the "interior" over the "exterior" and of the "mental" over the "material," but as a call for the revision of our ontology, for the re-examination of the notions of "subject" and "object." The same reasons that keep us from treating perception as an object also keep us from treating it as the operation of a "subject," in whatever sense one takes the term. If the "world" upon which it opens, the ambiguous field of horizons and distances, is not a region of the objective world, it resists as much being ranked on the side of "facts of consciousness" or "spiritual acts": psychological or transcendental immanence cannot account for what a horizon or a "remoteness" is any better than can "objective" thought. For whether it be given to itself in "introspection," or whether it be the consciousness constitutive of the perceived, perception would have to be, as it were by position and by principle, knowledge and possession of itself —it could not open upon horizons and distances, that is, upon a world which is there for it from the first, and from which alone it knows itself, as the anonymous incumbent toward which the perspectives of the landscape travel. The idea of the subject, and that of the object as well, transforms into a cognitive adequation the relationship with the world and with ourselves that we have in the perceptual faith. They do not clarify it; they utilize it tacitly, they draw out its consequences. And since the development of knowledge shows that these consequences are contradictory, it is to that relationship that we must necessarily return, in order to elucidate it.

We have addressed ourselves to the psychology of perception in general in order to better show that the crises of psychology result from reasons of principle and not from some delay of the research in this or that particular domain. But once we have seen it in its generality, we find again the same difficulty of principle in the specialized branches of research.

For example, one does not see how a social psychology would be possible within the regime of objectivist ontology. If one really thinks that perception is a *function* of exterior *variables*, this schema is (and approximatively indeed) applicable only to the corporeal and physical conditioning, and psychology is condemned to that exorbitant abstraction that consists in considering man as only a set of nervous terminations upon which physico-chemical agents play. The "other men," a social and historical constellation, can intervene as stimuli only if we also recognize the efficacity of ensembles that have no physical existence and that operate on man not according to their immediately sensible properties but by reason of their social configuration, within a social space and time, according to a social code, and finally as symbols rather than as causes. From the sole fact that social psychology is practiced, one is outside the objectivist ontology, and one can remain within it only by restricting the "object" one gives oneself in a way that compromises the research. Here the objectivist ideology is directly contrary to the development of knowledge. It was, for example, evident to the man brought up in the objective cognition of the West that magic or myth has no intrinsic truth, that magical effects and the mythical and ritual life are to be explained by "objective" causes and what is left over ascribed to the illusions of Subjectivity. Yet if social psychology wishes truly to *see* our society such as it *is*, it cannot start with this postulate, which itself is part of Western psychology; in adopting it we would be presupposing our conclusions. As the ethnologist in the face of societies called archaic cannot presuppose that, for example, those societies have a lived experience of time like ours—according to the dimensions of a past that is no longer, a future that is not yet, and a present that alone fully is—and must describe a mythical time where certain events "in the beginning" maintain a continued efficacity; so also social psychology, precisely if it wishes to really know our own societies, cannot exclude a priori the hypothesis of mythical time as a component of our personal and public history. To be sure, we have repressed the magical into the subjectivity, but there is no guarantee that the relationship between men does not inevitably involve magical and oneiric components. Since here it is precisely the society of men that is the "object," the rules of "objectivist" thought cannot determine it a priori; on the contrary they must themselves be seen as the particularities of certain socio-historical wholes, to which they do not necessarily give the key. Of course there are also no grounds for postulating at the start that objective thought is only an effect or a product of certain social structures, and has no rights over the others: that would be to posit that the human world rests on an incomprehensible foundation, and this irrationalism also would be arbitrary. The sole attitude proper to a social psychology is to take "objective" thought for what it is, that is, as a method that has founded science and is to be employed without restriction, unto the limit of the possible, but which, where nature, and a fortiori history are concerned, represents a first phase of elimination [11] rather than a means of total explanation. Social psychology, qua psychology, necessarily encounters the questions of the philosopher—what is another man, what is a historical event, where is the historical event or the State?—and cannot in advance class the other men and history among "objects" or "stimuli." It does not deal with these questions head-on: that is the business of philosophy. It deals with them laterally, by the very manner in which it invests its "object" and progresses toward it. And it does not render useless, it on the contrary requires an ontological elucidation of them.

When it fails to accept resolutely the rules for true "objectivity" in the domain of man and to admit that the laws of functional dependence are here rather a manner of circumscribing the irrational than of eliminating it, psychology will give only an abstract and superficial view of the societies it studies by comparison with what history can offer, and this in fact is what often happens. We said above that the physicist frames with an objectivist ontology a physics that is no longer objectivist. We have to add that it is no different with the psychologist and that it is even from psychology that the objectivist preconceptions return to haunt the general and philosophical conceptions of the physicists. One is struck in this regard when one sees a physicist [12] who has liberated his own science from the classical canons of mechanism and objectivism take up again without hesitation the Cartesian distinction between primary and secondary qualities as soon as he turns to the philosophical problem of the ultimate reality of the physical world, as if the critique of the mechanist postulates within the physical world should in no way affect our manner of conceiving its action upon our body, as if that critique ceased to be valid at the frontier of our body and did not call for a revision of our psycho-physiology. It is, paradoxically enough, more difficult to abandon the schemata of the mechanist explanation in the investigation of the action of the world on man—where they nonetheless have continuously aroused obvious difficulties—than in the investigation of physical actions within the world, where for centuries they could with

11. EDITOR: We should no doubt understand: elimination of the irrational.

12. For example, Eddington. [EDITOR: Arthur Eddington. Cf. in particular *New Pathways in Science* (Cambridge, 1934).]

good reason pass for justified. This is because in physics itself this revolution of thought can apparently be accomplished within the traditional ontological frameworks, whereas in the physiology of the senses it immediately implicates our most inveterate notion of the relations between being and man and the truth. As soon as we cease thinking of perception as the action of the pure physical object on the human body, and the perceived as the "interior" result of this action, it seems that every distinction between the true and the false, between methodic knowledge and phantasms, between science and the imagination, is ruined. Thus it is that physiology is participating less actively than physics in the methodological renewal of today; the scientific spirit sometimes persists there in archaic forms; and the biologists remain more materialist than the physicists. But they too are materialist only when they function as philosophers, and are much less so in the practice of their biology. One day it will indeed be necessary for them to liberate their practice entirely, to pose also the question whether the human body is an object, and hence the question whether its relation with exterior nature is that of function to variable. What is important for us is the fact that this relation has already ceased to be consubstantial with psycho-physiology, as have all the notions that are bound up with it—that of sensation as the proper and constant effect of a physically defined stimulus, and then the notions of attention and judgment as complementary abstractions, charged with explaining what does not follow the laws of sensation. . . . At the same time that it "idealized" the physical world by defining it by wholly intrinsic properties, by what it is in its pure being as an object before a thought itself purified, Cartesianism, whether it intended to do so or not, did inspire a science of the human body that decomposes that body also into a network of objective processes and, with the notion of sensation, prolongs this analysis unto the "psychism." These two idealizations are bound up with one another and must be undone together. It is only by returning to the perceptual faith to rectify the Cartesian analysis that we will put an end to the crisis situation in which our knowledge finds itself when it thinks it is founded upon a philosophy that its own advances undermine.

Because perception gives us faith in a world, in a system of natural facts rigorously bound together and continuous, we have believed that this system could incorporate all things into itself, even the perception that has initiated us into it. Today we no longer believe nature to be a continuous system of this kind; a fortiori we are far removed from thinking that the islets of "psychism" that here and there float over it are secretly connected to one another through the continuous ground of nature. We have then imposed upon us the task of understanding whether, and in what sense, what is not nature forms a "world," and first what a "world" is, and finally, if world there is, what can be the relations between the visible world and the invisible world. Difficult as it may be, this labor is indispensable if we are to get out of the confusion in which the philosophy of the scientists leaves us. It cannot be accomplished entirely by them because scientific thought moves within and presupposes the world, rather than taking it for its theme. But this labor is not foreign to science; it does not install us outside the world. When along with other philosophers we said that the stimuli of perception are not the causes of the perceived world, that they are rather its developers [13] or its releasers, we do not mean that one could perceive without a body; on the contrary we mean that it is necessary to re-examine the definition of the body as pure object in order to understand how it can be our living bond with nature; we do not establish ourselves in a universe of essences—on the contrary we ask that the distinction between the *that* and the *what*,[14] between the essence and the conditions of existence, be reconsidered by referring to the experience of the world that precedes that distinction. Philosophy is not science, because science believes it can soar over its object and holds the correlation of knowledge with being as established, whereas philosophy is the set of questions wherein he who questions is himself implicated by the question. But a physics that has learned to situate the physicist physically, a psychology that has learned to situate the psychologist in the socio-historical world, have lost the illusion of the absolute view from above: they do not only tolerate, they enjoin a radical examination of our belongingness to the world before all science.

13. TRANSLATOR: *Révélateur*—in the sense of a photographic developer fluid.

14. TRANSLATOR: "That," "what": in English in the text.

The natural attitude

THE PERCEPTUAL FAITH AND REFLECTION

THE METHODS of *proof* and of *cognition* invented by a thought already established in the world, the concepts of *object* and *subject* it introduces, do not enable us to understand what the perceptual faith is, precisely because it is a faith, that is, an adherence that knows itself to be beyond proofs, not necessary, interwoven with incredulity, at each instant menaced by non-faith. Belief and incredulity are here so closely bound up that we always find the one in the other, and in particular a germ of non-truth in the truth: the certitude I have of being connected up with the world by my look already promises me a pseudo-world of phantasms if I let it wander. It is said that to cover one's eyes so as to not see a danger is to not believe in the things, to believe only in the private world; but this is rather to believe that what is for us is absolutely, that a world we have succeeded in seeing as without danger is without danger. It is therefore the greatest degree of belief that our vision goes to the things themselves. Perhaps this experience teaches us better than any other what the perceptual presence of the world is: [not affirmation and negation of the same thing in the same respect, positive and negative judgment, or, as we said a moment ago, belief and incredulity—which would be impossible; beneath affirmation and negation, beneath judgment (those critical opinions, ulterior operations), it is our experience, prior to every opinion, of inhabiting the world by our body, of inhabiting the truth by our whole selves, without there being need to choose nor even to distinguish between the assurance of seeing and the assurance of seeing the true, because in principle they are one and the same thing—faith, therefore, and not knowledge, since the world is here not separated from our hold on it, since, rather than affirmed, it is taken for granted, rather than disclosed, it is non-dissimulated, non-refuted.]

The faith of world:

openness

description not enough — must explain how...

If philosophy is to appropriate to itself and to understand this initial openness upon the world which does not exclude a possible occultation, it cannot be content with describing it; it must tell us how there is openness without the occultation of the world being excluded, how the occultation remains at each instant possible even though we be naturally endowed with light. The philosopher must understand how it is that these two possibilities, which the perceptual faith keeps side by side within itself, do not nullify one another. He will not succeed if he remains at their level, oscillating from the one to the other, saying in turn that my vision is at the thing itself and that my vision is my own or "in me." He must abandon these two views, he must eschew the one as well as the other; since taken literally they are incompossible, he must appeal beyond them to himself who is their titular and therefore must know what motivates them from within; he must lose them as a state of fact in order to reconstruct them as his own possibilities, in order to learn from himself what they mean in truth, what delivers him over to both perception and to phantasms—in a word, he must *reflect*. But as soon as he does so, beyond the world itself and beyond what is only "in us," beyond being in itself and being for us, a third dimension seems to open up, wherein their discordance is effaced. With the conversion to reflection, perceiving and imagining are now only two modes of *thinking*.* From vision and feeling (*sentir*) will be retained only what animates them and sustains them indubitably, the pure thought of seeing or of feeling. It is possible to describe that thought, to show that it is made of a strict correlation between my exploration of the world and the sensorial responses it arouses. The imaginary will be submitted to a parallel analysis, and we will come to realize that the thought of which it is made is not in this precise sense a thought of seeing or of feeling, that it is rather the intent to not apply and even forget the criteria of verification and to take as "good" what is not and could not be seen. Thus the antinomies of the perceptual faith seem to be lifted; it is true indeed that we perceive the thing itself, since the thing is nothing but what we see— but not by the occult power of our eyes. For our eyes are no longer the subjects of vision; they have joined the number of things seen. And what we call vision rises from the power of thought that certifies that the appearance here has responded to the movements of our eyes according to a rule. When perception is full or effective, it is the thought of perceiving. If therefore it reaches the thing itself, it is necessary to say, without this being a contradiction, that it is entirely our work, and our own through and through, like all our thoughts. Open upon the thing itself, the perception is no less our own work, because the thing is

* Ideality (idea and immanence of truth).

henceforth exactly what we think we see—*cogitatum* or noema. It no more leaves the circle of our thoughts than does the imagination, which is also a thought of seeing, but a thought that does not seek the exercise, the proof, the plenitude, that therefore presumes on itself and is only half-thought. Thus the real becomes the correlative of thought, and the imaginary is, within the same sphere, the narrow circle of objects of thought that are only half-thought, half-objects or phantoms that have no consistency, no place of their own, disappearing before the sun of thought like the mists of dawn, and that are, between the thought and what it thinks, only a thin layer of the unthought. The reflection retains everything contained in the perceptual faith: the conviction that there is something, that there is the world, the idea of truth, the true idea given. It simply reduces that crude (*barbare*) conviction of going to the things themselves—which is incompatible with the fact of illusion—to what it means or signifies. It converts it into its truth; it discovers in it the adequation and assent of the thought with thought, the transparency of what I think for myself who thinks it. The brute and prior existence of the world I thought I found already there by opening my eyes is only the symbol of a being that is for itself as soon as it is because appearing, and therefore appearing to itself, is its whole being—that is the being we call mind.* Through the conversion to reflection, which leaves nothing but ideates, *cogitata*, or noemata subsisting before the pure subject, we finally leave the equivocations of the perceptual faith, which paradoxically assured us that we have access to the things themselves and that we gain access to them through the intermediary of the body, which therefore opened us to the world only by sealing us up in the succession of our private events. From now on everything seems clear; the blend of dogmatism and scepticism, the confused convictions of the perceptual faith, are called into question. I no longer think I see with my eyes things exterior to myself who sees them: they are exterior only to my body, not to my thought, which soars over it as well as them. Nor do I any longer allow myself to be impressed by that evidence that the other perceiving subjects do not go to the things themselves, that their perception takes place within them—an evidence that ends

* Passage to ideality as a solution of the antinomies. The world is numerically one with my *cogitatum* and with that of the others insofar as it is ideal (ideal identity, beneath the several and the one).

by rebounding upon my own perception, since after all I am "an other" in their eyes, and my dogmatism, communicated to the others, returns to me as scepticism. For if it is true that, seen from the outside, the perception of each seems to be shut up in some retreat "behind" his body, reflection precisely relegates this exterior view to the number of phantasms without consistency and confused thoughts: one does not think a thought from the outside, by definition thought is thought only inwardly. If then the others are thoughts, as such they are not behind their body which I see—they are, like myself, nowhere; they are, like myself, coextensive with being, and there is no problem of incarnation. At the same time that the reflection liberates us from the false problems posed by bastard and unthinkable experiences, it also accounts for them through the simple transposition of the incarnate subject into a transcendental subject and of the reality of the world into an ideality: we all reach the world, and the same world, and it belongs wholly to each of us, without division or loss, because it is *that which* we think we perceive, the undivided object of all our thoughts. Its unity, if it is not the numerical unity, is not the specific unity either: it is that ideal unity or unity of signification that makes the triangle of the geometer be the same in Tokyo and in Paris, the same in the fifth century before Christ and now. This unity suffices and it untangles every problem, because the divisions that can be opposed to it, the plurality of the fields of perception and of lives, are as nothing before it, do not belong to the universe of ideality and of meaning, and cannot even be formulated or articulated into distinct thoughts, and finally, because we have through reflection recognized at the heart of all the situated, bogged-down, and incarnated thoughts the pure appearing of thought to itself, the universe of internal adequation, where everything *true* that we have is integrated without difficulty. . . .

This movement of reflection will always at first sight be convincing: in a sense it is imperative, it is truth itself, and one does not see how philosophy could dispense with it. The question is whether it has brought philosophy to the harbor, whether the universe of thought to which it leads is really an order that suffices to itself and puts an end to every question. Since the perceptual faith is a paradox, how could I remain with it? And if I do not remain with it, what else can I do except re-enter into myself and seek there the abode of truth? Is it not evident that, precisely if my perception is a perception of the world, I must find in my commerce with the world the reasons that induce me to see it, and in my vision the meaning of my vision? From whom would I, who am in the world (*suis au monde*), learn what it is to be in the world if not from myself, and how could I say that I am in the world if I did not know it? Without even presuming that I know everything of myself, it is certain at least that, among other things, I am a knowing; this attribute assuredly belongs to me, even if I have others. I cannot imagine that the world irrupts into me or I into it: the world can present itself to this knowing which I am only by offering it a meaning, only in the form of a thought of the world. The secret of the world we are seeking must necessarily be contained in my contact with it. Inasmuch as I live it, I possess the meaning of everything I live, otherwise I would not live it; and I can seek no light concerning the world except by consulting, by making explicit, my frequenting of the world, by comprehending it from within. What will always make of the philosophy of reflection not only a temptation but a route that must be followed is that it is true in what it denies, that is, the exterior relation between a world in itself and myself, conceived as a process of the same type as those that unfold within the world—whether one imagines an intrusion of the world in myself, or, on the contrary, some excursion of my look among the things. But does it conceive properly the natal bond between me who perceives and what I perceive? And because we assuredly must reject the idea of an exterior relation between the perceiving and the perceived, must we pass to the antithesis of immanence, be it wholly ideal and spiritual, and say that I who perceives am the thought of perceiving, and the perceived world a thing thought? Because perception is not an entering of the world into myself and is not centripetal, must it be centrifugal, as is a thought I form or the signification I give by judgment to an indecisive appearance? The philosophy of reflection practices the philosophical interrogation and the resultant effort toward explicitness in a style that is not the sole possible one; it mixes in presuppositions which we have to examine and which in the end reveal themselves to be contrary to what inspires the reflection. It thinks it can comprehend our natal bond with the world only by *undoing* it in order to *remake* it, only by constituting it, by fabricating it. It thinks it finds clarity through analysis, that is, if not in the most simple elements, at least in the most fundamental conditions implicated in the brute product, in the premises from which it results as a consequence, in a *source of meaning* from which it is derived.* It is therefore essential to the philosophy of reflection that it bring us back, this side of our *de facto* situation, to a center of things from which we proceeded, but from which we were decentered, that it retravel this time starting from us a route already traced out from that center to us. The very effort toward internal adequation, the enterprise to reconquer explicitly all that we are and do implicitly, signifies that what we are finally as *naturata* we first are actively as *naturans*, that the world is our birthplace only because first we as minds are the cradle of the world. But, in this, if the reflection confines itself to this first movement, if it installs us by regression in the immanent universe of our thoughts and strips whatever may be left over of any probative power with respect to itself, dismissing it as confused, mutilated, or naïve thought, the reflection then falls short of its task and of the radicalism that is its law. For the movement of recovery, of recuperation, of return to self, the progression toward internal adequation, the very effort to coincide with a *naturans* which is already ourselves and which is supposed to unfold the things and the world before itself—precisely inasmuch as they are a return or a reconquest, these operations of reconstitution or of re-establishment which come second cannot by principle be the mirror image of its internal constitution and its establishment, as the route from the Etoile to the Notre-Dame is the inverse of the route from the Notre-Dame to the Etoile: the reflection recuperates everything except itself as an effort of recuperation, it clarifies everything except its own role. The mind's eye too has its blind spot, but, because it is of the mind, cannot be unaware of it, nor treat as a simple state of non-vision, which requires no particular mention, the very act of reflection which is *quoad nos* its act of birth. If it is not unaware of itself—which would be

reflective constitution clarifies everything but itself —

---

* Idea of return—of the latent: idea of the reflection coming back over the traces of a constitution. Idea of intrinsic possibility of which the constituted is its unfolding. Idea of a *naturans* of which it is the *naturata*. Idea of the originating as intrinsic. Hence the reflective thought is an anticipation of the whole; it performs all its operations under the guarantee of the totality that it claims to engender. Cf. Kant: if a world is to be possible. . . . This reflection does not find the originating.

contrary to its definition—the reflection cannot feign to unravel the same thread that the mind would first have woven, to be the mind returning to itself within me, when by definition it is I who reflect. The reflection must appear to itself as a progression toward a subject X, an appeal to a subject X. As the reflection's very assurance that it rejoin a universal *naturans* cannot come from some prior contact with it (since precisely it is still ignorance), reflection evokes it and does not coincide with it. That assurance can come only from the world—or from my thoughts insofar as they form a world, insofar as their cohesion, their vanishing lines, designate beneath reflection a virtual focus with which I do not yet coincide. As an effort to found the existing world upon a *thought* of the world, the reflection at each instant draws its inspiration from the prior presence of the world, of which it is tributary, from which it derives all its energy. When Kant justifies each step of his Analytic with the famous refrain "if a world is to be possible," he emphasizes the fact that his guideline is furnished him by the unreflected image of the world, that the necessity of the steps taken by the reflection is suspended upon the hypothesis "world," and that the thought of the world which the Analytic is charged with disclosing is not so much the foundation as the second expression of the fact that for me there has been an experience of a world—in other words, that the intrinsic possibility of the world as a thought rests upon the fact that I can see the world, that is, upon a possibility of a wholly different type, which we have seen borders on the impossible. It is by a secret and constant appeal to this impossible-possible that reflection can maintain the illusion of being a return to oneself and of establishing itself in immanence, and our power to re-enter into ourselves is exactly measured by a power to leave ourselves, which is neither older nor more recent than it, which is exactly synonymous with it. The whole reflective analysis is not false, but still naïve, as long as it dissimulates from itself its own mainspring and as long as, in order to constitute the world, it is necessary to have a notion of the world as preconstituted—as long as the procedure is in principle delayed behind itself. The reply will perhaps be that the great philosophies of reflection know this very well, as the reference to the true idea given in Spinoza or the very conscious reference to a pre-critical experience of the world in Kant shows, but that the circle of the unreflected and the reflection is deliberate in these philosophies—that one begins with the unreflected, because one does have to begin, but that the universe of thought that is opened up by reflection contains everything necessary to account for the mutilated thought of the beginning, which is only the ladder one pulls up after oneself after having climbed it. . . . But if this is so, there is no longer any philosophy of reflection, for there is no longer the originating and the derived; there is a thought traveling a circle where the condition and the conditioned, the reflection and the unreflected, are in a reciprocal, if not symmetrical, relationship, and where the end is in the beginning as much as the beginning is in the end. We are not saying anything different. The remarks we made concerning reflection were nowise intended to disqualify it for the profit of the unreflected or the immediate (which we know only through reflection). It is a question not of putting the perceptual faith in place of reflection, but on the contrary of taking into account the total situation, which involves reference from the one to the other. What is given is not a massive and opaque world, or a universe of adequate thought; it is a reflection which turns back over the density of the world in order to clarify it, but which, coming second, reflects back to it only its own light.

It is indeed true that, in order to disentangle myself from the perplexities in which the perceptual faith casts me, I can address myself only to my experience of the world, to that blending with the world that recommences for me each morning as soon as I open my eyes, to that flux of perceptual life between it and myself which beats unceasingly from morning to night, and which makes my own secret thoughts change the aspect of faces and landscapes for me, as, conversely, the faces and landscapes bring me the help sometimes and the menace sometimes of a manner of being a man which they infuse into my life. But it is just as sure that the relation between a thought and its object, between the *cogito* and the *cogitatum*, contains neither the whole nor even the essential of our commerce with the world and that we have to situate that relation back within a more muted relationship with the world, within an initiation into the world upon which it rests and which is always already accomplished when the reflective return intervenes. We will miss that relationship—which we shall here call the openness upon the world (*ouverture au monde*)—the moment that the reflective effort tries to capture it, and we will then be able to catch sight of the reasons that prevent it from succeeding, and of the way through which we would reach it. I see, I feel (*sens*), and it is certain that for me to account for what seeing and feeling are I must cease accompanying the seeing and the feeling into the visible and the sensible into which they throw themselves, and I must contrive, on this side of them, a sphere they do not occupy and whence they would become comprehensible according to their sense and their essence. To understand them is to suspend them, since the naïve vision occupies me completely, and since the attention to vision that is added on subtracts something from this total gift, and especially since to understand is to translate into disposable significations a meaning first held captive in the thing and in the world itself. But this translation aims to convey the text; or rather the visible and the philosophical explicitation of the visible are not side by side as two sets of signs, as a text and its version in another tongue. If it were a text, it would be a strange text, which is directly given to us all, so that we are not restricted to the philosopher's translation and can compare the two. And philosophy for its part is more and less than a translation: more, since it alone tells us what the text means; less, since it is useless if one does not have the text at one's disposal. The philosopher therefore suspends the brute vision only in order to make it pass into the order of the expressed: that vision remains his model or measure, and it is upon that vision that the network of significations which philosophy organizes in order to reconquer it must open. Hence the philosopher does not have to *consider as inexistent* what was seen or felt, and the vision or the feeling themselves, to replace them, according to the words of Descartes, with the "thought of seeing and of feeling," which for its part is considered unshakable only because it presumes nothing about what effectively is, only because it entrenches itself in the apparition to the thought of what is thought—from which it is indeed inexpugnable. To reduce perception to the thought of perceiving, under the pretext that immanence alone is sure, is to take out an insurance against doubt whose premiums are more onerous than the loss for which it is to indemnify us: for it is to forego comprehending the effective world and move to a type of certitude that will never restore to us the "there is" of the world. Either the doubt is only a state of rending and obscurity, in which case it teaches me nothing—or if it teaches me something, it is because it is deliberate, militant, systematic, and then it is an act, and then, even if subsequently its own existence imposes itself upon me as a limit to the doubt, as a something that is not nothing, this something is of the order of acts, within which I am henceforth confined. The illusion of illusions is to think now that to tell the truth we have never been certain of anything but our own acts, that from the beginning perception has been an inspection of the mind, and that reflection is only the perception returning to itself, the conversion from the knowing of the thing to a knowing of oneself of which the thing was made, the emergence of a "binding" that was the bond itself. We think we prove this Cartesian "spirituality," this *identity* of space with the mind, by saying that it is obvious that the "far-off" object is far-off only by virtue of its relation with other objects "further off" or "less distant"—which relation belongs properly to neither of them and *is* the immediate presence of the mind to all; the doctrine finally replaces our belongingness to the world with a view of the world from above. But it gets its apparent evidence only from a very naïve postulate (and one suggested to us precisely by the world) according to which it is always *the same* thing I think when the gaze of attention is displaced and looks back from itself to what conditions it. This is a massive conviction drawn from external experience, where I have indeed the assurance that the things under my eyes remain *the same* while I approach them to better inspect them, but this is because the functioning of my body as a possibility for changing point of view, a "seeing apparatus," or a sedimented science of the "point of view," assures me that I am approaching the same thing I saw a moment ago from further off. It is the perceptual life of my body that here sustains and guarantees the perceptual explicitation, and far from it itself being a cognition of intra-mundane or inter-objective relations between my body and the exterior things, it is presupposed in every notion of an object, and it is this life that accomplishes the primary openness to the world. My conviction that I see the thing itself does not *result* from the perceptual exploration, it is not a word to designate the proximal vision; on the contrary it is what gives me the notion of the "proximal," of the "best" point of observation, and of the "thing itself." Having therefore learned through perceptual experience what it is to "see well" the thing, that to do so one must and one can approach it, and that the new data thus acquired are deter-

[right margin handwritten note:] rejecting the claim that reflection doesn't affect the object -

[right margin handwritten note:] the body affects change

minations of the *same* thing, we transfer this certitude to the interior, we resort to the fiction of a "little man in the man," and in this way we come to think that to reflect on perception is, *the perceived thing and the perception remaining what they were,* to disclose the true subject that inhabits and has always inhabited them. But in fact I should say that there was there a thing perceived and an openness upon this thing which the reflection has neutralized and transformed into perception-reflected-on and thing-perceived-within-a-perception-reflected-on. And that the functioning of reflection, like the functioning of the exploring body, makes use of powers obscure to me, spans the cycle of duration that separates the brute perception from the reflective examination, and during this time maintains the permanence of the perceived and the permanence of the perception under the gaze of the mind only because my mental inspection and my attitudes of mind prolong the "I can" of my sensorial and corporeal exploration. To found the latter on the former, and the *de facto* perception on the essence of perception such as it appears to reflection, is to forget the reflection itself as a distinct act of recovery. In other words, we are catching sight of the necessity of another operation besides the conversion to reflection, more fundamental than it, of a sort of *hyper-reflection* (*sur-réflexion*) that would also take itself and the changes it introduces into the spectacle into account. It accordingly would not lose sight of the brute thing and the brute perception and would not finally efface them, would not cut the organic bonds between the perception and the thing perceived with a hypothesis of inexistence. On the contrary, it would set itself the task of thinking about them, of reflecting on the transcendence of the world as transcendence, speaking of it not according to the law of the word-meanings inherent in the given language, but with a perhaps difficult effort that uses the significations of words to express, beyond themselves, our mute contact with the things, when they are not yet things said. If therefore the reflection is not to presume upon what it finds and condemn itself to putting into the things what it will then pretend to find in them, it must suspend the faith in the world only so as to *see it,* only so as to read in it the route it has followed in becoming a world for us; it must seek in the world itself the secret of our perceptual bond with it. It must use words not according to their pre-established signification, but *in order to state* this prelogical bond. It must plunge into the world

instead of surveying it, it must descend toward it such as it is
instead of working its way back up toward a prior possibility of
thinking it—which would impose upon the world in advance the
conditions for our control over it. It must question the world, it
must enter into the forest of references that our interrogation
arouses in it, it must make it say, finally, what in its silence *it
means to say. . . .* We know neither what exactly is this order
and this concordance of the world to which we thus entrust
ourselves, nor therefore what the enterprise will result in, nor
even if it is really possible. But the choice is between it and a
dogmatism of reflection concerning which we know only too well
where it goes, since with it philosophy concludes the moment it
begins and, for this very reason, does not make us comprehend
our own obscurity.

A philosophy of reflection, as methodic doubt and as a reduction of the openness upon the world to "spiritual acts," to intrinsic relations between the idea and *its* ideate, is thrice untrue to
what it means to elucidate: untrue to the visible world, to him
who sees it, and to his relations with the other "visionaries." To
say that perception is and has always been an "inspection of the
mind" is to define it not by what it gives us, but by what in it
withstands the hypothesis of *non-existence;* it is to identify from
the first the positive with a negation of negation; it is to require
of the innocent the proof of his non-culpability, and to reduce in
advance our contact with Being to the discursive operations with
which we defend ourselves against illusion, to reduce the true to
the credible, the real to the probable. It has often been pointed
out [15] that even the most credible imagination, the most conformable to the context of experience, does not bring us one step
closer to "reality" and is immediately ascribed by us to the imaginary—and that conversely an even absolutely unexpected and
unforeseeable noise is from the first perceived as real, however
weak be its links with the context. This simple fact imposes upon
us the idea that with the "real" and the "imaginary" we are
dealing with two "orders," two "stages," or two "theaters"—that
of space and that of phantasms—which are set up within us
before the acts of discrimination (which intervene only in the
equivocal cases), and in which what we live comes to settle of

15. EDITOR: In particular by Sartre, *L'Imagination.* [English
translation by Forrest Williams, *Imagination: A Psychological Critique*
(Ann Arbor, 1962).]

itself, outside of all criteriological control. The fact that sometimes the controls become necessary and result in judgments of
reality which rectify the naïve experience does not prove that
judgments of this sort are at the origin of this distinction, or
constitute it, and therefore does not dispense us from understanding it for itself. If we do so, we then will have to not define
the real by its coherence and the imaginary by its incoherence or
its lacunae: the real is coherent and probable because it is real,
and not real because it is coherent; the imaginary is incoherent
or improbable because it is imaginary, and not imaginary because it is incoherent. The least particle of the perceived incorporates it from the first into the "perceived," the most credible
phantasm glances off at the surface of the world; it is this
presence of the whole world in one reflection, its irremediable
absence in the richest and most systematic deliriums, that we
have to understand, and this difference is not a difference of the
more and the less. It is true that it gives rise to mistakes or to
illusions, whence the conclusion is sometimes drawn that it
therefore cannot be a difference of nature, and that the real,
after all, is only the less improbable or the more probable. This is
to think the true by the false, the positive by the negative—and it
is to ill-describe indeed the experience of dis-illusion, wherein
precisely we learn to know the fragility of the "real." For when an
illusion dissipates, when an appearance suddenly breaks up, it is
always for the profit of a new appearance which takes up again
for its own account the ontological function of the first. I
thought I saw on the sands a piece of wood polished by the sea,
and *it was* a clayey rock. The breakup and the destruction of the
first appearance do not authorize me to define henceforth the
"real" as a simple probable, since *they are only another name for
the new apparition,* which must therefore figure in our analysis
of the *dis-illusion.* The dis-illusion is the loss of one evidence
only because it is the acquisition of *another evidence.* If, out of
prudence, I decide to say that this new evidence is "in itself"
doubtful or only probable (in itself—that is: for me, in a moment, when I will have gotten a little closer to it or looked more
closely), the fact remains that at the moment I speak it incon-
testably gives itself as "real" and not as "very possible" or probable; and if subsequently it breaks up in its turn, it will do so only
under the pressure of a new "reality." What I can conclude from
these disillusions or deceptions, therefore, is that perhaps "real-

ity" does not belong definitively to any particular perception, that in this sense it lies *always further on;* but this does not authorize me to break or to ignore the bond that joins them one after the other to the real, a bond that cannot be broken with the one without first having been established with the following, so that there is no *Schein* without an *Erscheinung,* that every *Schein* is the counterpart of an *Erscheinung,* and that the meaning of the "real" is not reduced to that of the "probable," but on the contrary the "probable" evokes a definitive experience of the "real" whose accomplishment is only deferred. When faced with a perceptual appearance we not only know that it can subsequently "break up," we also know that it will do so only for having been so well replaced by another that there remains no trace of it, and that we seek in vain in this chalky rock what a moment ago *was* a piece of wood polished by the sea. Each perception is mutable and only probable—it is, if one likes, only an *opinion;* but what is not opinion, what each perception, even if false, verifies, is the belongingness of each experience to the same world, their equal power to manifest it, as *possibilities of the same world.* If the one takes the place of the other so well—to the point that one no longer finds any trace of it a moment after the illusion—it is precisely because they are not successive hypotheses about an unknowable Being, but perspectives upon the same familiar Being, which we know cannot exclude the one without including the other and which we know in any case to be itself beyond contestation. And this is why the very fragility of a perception, attested by its breakup and by the substitution of another perception, far from authorizing us to efface the index of "reality" from them all, obliges us to concede it to all of them, to recognize all of them to be variants of the same world, and finally to consider them not as all false but as "all true," not as repeated failures in the determination of the world but as progressive approximations. Each perception envelops the possibility of its own replacement by another, and thus of a sort of disavowal from the things. But this also means that each perception is the term of an approach, of a series of "illusions" that were not merely simple "thoughts" in the restrictive sense of Being-for-itself and the "merely thought of," but possibilities that could have been, radiations of this unique world that "there is" . . . —and which, as such, never revert to nothingness or to subjectivity as if they had never appeared, but are rather, as Husserl puts it well, "crossed out" or "cancelled" by the "new" reality. The philosophy of reflection is not wrong in considering the false as a mutilated or partial truth: its error is rather to act as if the partial were only a *de facto* absence of the totality, which does not need to be accounted for. This finally destroys any consistency proper to the appearance, integrates it in advance into Being, deprives it of its tenor of truth because it is partial, makes it disappear into an internal adequation where Being and the reasons for being are one. The movement toward adequation, to which the facts of dis-illusion bear witness, is not the returning to itself of an adequate Thought that would have inexplicably lost sight of itself—nor is it a blind progress of probability, founded on the number of signs and concordances. It is the prepossession of a totality which is there before one knows how and why, whose realizations are never what we would have imagined them to be, and which nonetheless fulfills a secret expectation within us, since we believe in it tirelessly.

The reply will no doubt be that if, in order to save what is original in the "world" as a preobjective theme, we refuse to make of it the immanent correlative of a spiritual act, then the natural light, the openness of my perception upon the world, can result only from a preordination whose effects I record, a finality to whose law I am subjected, as I undergo the law of finality of all my organs. And that moreover once this passivity is introduced in me, it will vitiate everything when I proceed, as one must, to the order of thought and will have to explain how I think about my perceptions. Either I reinstate at this level the autonomy I renounced at the level of the perceived—but then one does not see how this active thinker could recover possession of the reasons of a perception that is given to him ready-made— or (as in Malebranche) the passivity overtakes the order of thought also, which, like the perception, loses every efficacity of its own and has to await its light from a causality that functions in it without it, as the perception obtains its light only through the play of the laws of the union of the soul and the body—and consequently the thought's grasp upon itself and the light of the intelligible become an incomprehensible mystery, in a being for whom the true is at the term of a natural inclination, conformable to the pre-established system according to which his mind functions, and is not *truth*, conformity of self with self, light. . . . And it is indeed certain that every attempt to fit a passivity upon an activity ends up either in extending the passivity to the whole—which amounts to detaching us from Being, since, for lack of a contact of myself with myself, I am in every operation of knowledge delivered over to an organization of my thoughts whose premises are masked from me, to a mental constitution which is given to me as a fact—or ends up by restoring the activity to the whole. This is in particular the flaw in the philosophies of reflection that do not follow themselves through; after having defined the requirements for thought, they add that these do not impose any law upon the things and evoke an order of the things themselves which, in contradistinction to the order of our thoughts, could receive only exterior rules. But we are not opposing to an interior light an order of the things in themselves into which it could not penetrate. There can be no question of fitting together passivity before a transcendent with an activity of immanent thought. It is a question of reconsidering the interdependent notions of the active and the passive in such a way that they no longer place us before the antinomy of a philosophy that accounts for being and the truth, but does not take the world into account, and a philosophy that takes the world into account, but uproots us from being and the truth. The philosophy of reflection replaces the "world" with the "being-thought." One cannot, while recognizing this deficiency, justify it in spite of everything because of the untenable consequences of an exterior regulation of our thoughts, for only from the point of view of a philosophy of reflection is this the alternative, and it is the reflective analysis that we find questionable. What we propose is not to stop the philosophy of reflection after having started as it does—this is indeed impossible, and, all things considered, a philosophy of total reflection seems to us to go further, be it only in circumscribing what in our experience resists it; what we propose is to take another point of departure.

To remove all equivocation on this point, let us repeat that we reproach the philosophy of reflection not only for transforming the world into a noema, but also for distorting the being of the reflecting "subject" by conceiving it as "thought"—and finally for rendering unthinkable its relations with other "subjects" in the world that is common to them. The philosophy of reflection starts with the principle that if a perception is to be able to be my own it must from the start be one of my "representations"—in other words, that I, qua "thought," must be what effects the connection between the aspects under which the object presents itself and their synthesis into an object. The reflection, the return to the interior, would not modify the perception, since it would limit itself to bringing out what from the first made up its framework or its joints, and since the thing perceived, if it is not nothing, is the set of connecting operations which the reflection enumerates and makes explicit. One is barely permitted to say that the reflective gaze turns back from the object toward me, since I qua thought am what makes there be a distance and in general any relation whatever from one point of the object to another. With one stroke the philosophy of reflection metamorphoses the effective world into a transcendental field; in doing so it only puts me back at the origin of a spectacle that I could never have had unless, unbeknown to myself, I organized it. It only makes me be consciously what I have always been distractedly; it only makes me give its name to a dimension behind myself, a depth whence, in fact, already my vision was formed. Through the reflection, the *I* lost in its perceptions rediscovers itself by rediscovering them as thoughts. It thought it had quit itself for them, spread itself out in them; it comes to realize that if it had quit itself they would not be and that the very outspread of the distances and the things was only the "outside" of its own inward intimacy with itself, that the unfolding of the world was the coiling up upon itself of a thought which thinks anything whatever only because it thinks itself first.

Once one is settled in it, reflection is an inexpugnable philosophical position, every obstacle, every resistance to its exercise being from the first treated not as an adversity of the things but as a simple state of non-thought, a gap in the continuous fabric of the acts of thought, which is inexplicable, but about which there is nothing to say since it is literally *nothing*. But are we to enter into reflection? In its inaugural act is concealed a decision to play a double game which, once unmasked, divests it of its apparent evidence; in one move the philosophical lie is perpetrated with which one first pays for this henceforth invulnerable method. It is essential to the reflective analysis that it start from a *de facto* situation. If it did not from the first take as given the true idea, the internal adequation of my thought with what I think, or the thought in act of the world, it should have to suspend every "I think" upon an "I think that I think," and this upon an "I think that I think that I think," and so on. . . . The search for the conditions of possibility is in principle posterior to an actual experience, and from this it follows that even if subsequently one determines rigorously the *sine qua non* of that experience, it can never be washed of the original stain of having been discovered *post festum* nor ever become what positively founds that experience. This is why we must say not that it precedes the experience (even in the transcendental sense) but that it must be able to accompany it, that is, that it translates or expresses its essential character but does not indicate a prior possibility whence it would have issued. Never therefore will the philosophy of reflection be able to install itself in the mind it discloses, whence to see the world as its correlative. Precisely because it is reflection, re-turn, re-conquest, or re-covery, it cannot flatter itself that it would simply coincide with a constitutive principle already at work in the spectacle of the world, that, starting with this spectacle, it would travel the very route that the constitutive principle had followed in the opposite direction. But this is what it would have to do if it is really a *return*, that is, if its point of arrival were also the starting point—and this exigency is no optional clause, since if it were not fulfilled the regressive analysis, declining to make any progressive synthesis, would be abandoning the pretension to disclose the sources to us and would be nothing more than the technique of a philosophical quietism. The reflection finds itself therefore in the strange situation of simultaneously requiring and excluding an inverse movement of constitution. It requires it in that, without this centrifugal movement, it should have to acknowledge itself to be a retrospective construction; it excludes it in that, coming in principle after an experience of the world or of the true which it seeks to render explicit, it thereby establishes itself in an order of idealization and of the "after-the-fact" which is not that wherein the world is formed. This is what Husserl brought frankly into the open when he said that every transcendental reduction is also an eidetic reduction, that is: every effort to comprehend the spectacle of the world from within and from the sources demands that we detach ourselves from the effective unfolding of our perceptions and from our perception of the world, that we cease being one with the concrete flux of our life in order to retrace the total bearing and principal articulations of the world upon which it opens. To reflect is not to coincide with the flux from its source unto its last ramifications; it is to disengage from the things, perceptions, world, and perception of the world, by submitting them to a systematic variation, the intelligible nuclei that resist, and to proceed from one intelligible nucleus to the next in a way that is not belied by experience but gives us only its universal contours.] It therefore by principle leaves untouched the twofold problem of the genesis of the existent world and of the genesis of the idealization performed by reflection and finally evokes and requires as its foundation a *hyper-reflection* where the ultimate problems would be taken seriously. To tell the truth, it is not even certain that the reflection that proceeds by way of the essences can accomplish its propaedeutic task and fulfill its role of being a discipline of the understanding. For there is no guarantee that the whole of experience can be expressed in essential invariants, that certain beings—for example, the being of time—do not in principle elude this fixation and do not require from the start, if they are to be able to be thought by us, the consideration of the fact, the dimension of facticity and the hyper-reflection, which would then become, at least in regard to them, not a superior degree at the ultimate level of philosophy, but philosophy itself. But if time should elude the reflection, space too would be involved in this secession, since time is bound to the present through all its fibers, and, through the present, to the simultaneous; one would also have to describe in terms of facticity, and not in terms of essences, a subjectivity situated in space and in time. Little by little it is the whole of experience—the essence itself, and the subject of the essences, and the reflection itself as eidetic—that would require reconsideration. The legitimate function of the fixing of the eidetic invariants would be no longer to confine us within the consideration of the *what*,[16] but to make evident the divergence between the eidetic invariants and the effective functioning and to invite us to bring the experience itself forth from its obstinate silence. . . . In recognizing that every reflection is eidetic and, as such, leaves untouched the problem of our unreflected being and that of the world, Husserl simply agrees to take up the problem which the reflective attitude ordinarily avoids—the discordance between its initial situation and its ends.

Confronting the mind, focus of all clarity, with the world reduced to its intelligible schema, a consistent reflection dissi-

16. TRANSLATOR: In English in the text.

pates every question concerning the relationship between them. Henceforth their relationship will be one of pure correlation: the mind is what thinks, the world what is thought; one could conceive neither of encroachment of the one upon the other, nor of confusion of one with the other, nor of passage from one to the other, nor even of contact between them. Since they are related to one another as the bound to the binding or the *naturata* to the *naturans,* they are too perfectly coextensive for the one to ever be able to be preceded by the other, too irremediably distinct for the one ever to be able to envelop the other. Philosophy therefore impugns as meaningless every encroachment of the world upon the mind, or of the mind upon the world. That the world could pre-exist my consciousness of the world is out of the question: is it not obvious that every world without me that I could think of becomes, by the very fact that I think of it, a world for me; that the private world I divine at the origin of another's gaze is not so private as to prevent me from becoming at that very moment its quasi-spectator? What we express by saying that the world is in itself, or that it is beyond the perception I and the others have of it, is simply the signification "world," which is the same for all and independent of our phantasms, just as the properties of the triangle are the same in all places and at all times and do not begin to be true the day they are recognized. There is a pre-existence of the world with regard to our perception, of the aspects of the world which the other perceives to the perception I will have of them later, of my world to that of men yet to be born, and all these "worlds" make one unique world, but do so only in that the things and the world are objects of thought with their intrinsic properties, are of the order of the true, of the valid, of the signification, and are not of the order of events. The question whether the world be unique for all the subjects loses all meaning once one has admitted the ideality of the world; it no longer makes any sense to ask if my world and that of the other are numerically or specifically the same, since, as an intelligible structure, the world lies always beyond my thoughts as events, but also beyond those of the others, so that it is not divided by the knowledge we acquire of it, nor unique in the sense that each of us is unique. In all that they signify, my perception and the perception another man has of the world are the same, even though our lives be incommensurable, because the *signification,* the meaning—being an internal adequation, a relation of self with self, pure interiority and total openness all at once—never descend into us as subjected to a perspective (for as such we are never our own light to ourselves), and because thus all our truths as truths rejoin of themselves and form by right one sole system. Thus, with the correlation between thought and the object of thought set up as a principle, there is established a philosophy that knows neither difficulties nor problems nor paradoxes nor reversals: once and for all, I have grasped within myself, with the pure correlation between him who thinks and what he thinks, the truth of my life, which is also the truth of the world and of the other lives. Once and for all, the being-object is placed before me as alone meaningful for me, and every inherence of the others in their bodies, and of myself in my own, is impugned as a confusion—once and for all, the being-self is given to me in the adequation of my thought with itself, and, from this side also, there is no question of taking seriously the compound of the mind with the body. I am forever subjected to the centrifugal movement that makes an object of thought be for a thought, and there is no question of my quitting this position and examining what Being can indeed be before it be thought by me or (what amounts to the same thing) by another, what indeed can be the intermundane space (*l'intermonde*) where our gazes cross and our perceptions overlap: there is no brute world, there is only an elaborated world; there is no intermundane space, there is only a signification "world". . . . And here too the reflective attitude would be inexpugnable if it did not belie in the hypothesis and as reflection what it affirms in the thesis about what is reflected on. For before the reflection I thought myself situated in an actual world by my body, in the midst of other men situated in it by their bodies; I thought I saw them perceive the same world I perceive, and thought I was one of them occupied in seeing their world—and where else have I found, if not in this naïve initiation and in these confused perceptions, the meaning first sighted that I wanted to approach by the reflection? * How was I able to appeal to myself as to the universal source of meaning—which is to reflect—if not because the spectacle had meaning for me before I discovered that I am he who gives it meaning, that is—since a philosophy of reflection identifies my being with what I think of it—before being this?

* Show that the reflection suppresses the intersubjectivity.

My access to a universal mind via reflection, far from finally discovering what I always was, is motivated by the intertwining of my life with the other lives, of my body with the visible things, by the intersection of my perceptual field with that of the others, by the blending in of my duration with the other durations. If I pretend to find, through reflection, in the universal mind the premise that had always backed up my experience, I can do so only by forgetting this non-knowing of the beginning which is not nothing, and which is not the reflective truth either, and which also must be accounted for. I was able to appeal from the world and the others to myself and take the route of reflection, only because first I was outside of myself, in the world, among the others, and constantly this experience feeds my reflection. Such is the total situation that a philosophy must account for. It will do so only by admitting the double polarity of reflection and by admitting that, as Hegel said, to retire into oneself is also to leave oneself.*

* Perhaps write a separate paragraph (at the end) on reflection as Husserl understands it. It is a reflection that finally is not installed in an active constituting agent (*Auffassungsinhalt-Auffassung*), but finds at the origin of every reflection a massive presence to self, the Retention's *Noch im Griff*, and, through it, the *Urimpression*, and the absolute flux which animates them. It presupposes the reduction of Nature to immanent unities. Yet the *Tönen* is not immanence—unless one understands immanence in the sense of ecstasy!—it utilizes the very structure of the flux.

Distinguish perhaps: 1) reflection, contact with self (Kantian, the Binding)—conditions of possibility. 2) Specular reflection, gaze (Husserl). Thematization of the psychological immanence, of the internal time. 3) Reflection of the absolute flux.

2 / Interrogation and Dialectic

[Kant, Hs, Sartre]

Perceptual Faith and Negativity

PHILOSOPHY BELIEVED it could overcome the contradictions of the perceptual faith by suspending it in order to disclose the motives that support it. The operation seems to be inevitable, and absolutely legitimate too, since in sum it consists in stating what our life takes as understood. Yet it reveals itself to be fallacious in that it transforms the perceptual faith, which is to be understood; it makes of it a belief among others, founded like any other on reasons—the reasons we have to *think that there is* a world. But it is clear that in the case of perception the conclusion comes before the reasons, which are there only to take its place or to back it up when it is shaken. If we search after the reasons, it is because we no longer succeed in seeing, or because other facts, like that of illusion, incite us to impugn the perceptual evidence itself. But to identify it with the reasons which we have to restore to it some value once it has been shaken is to postulate that the perceptual faith has always been a resistance to doubt, and the positive a negation of negation. The procedure of reflection, as an appeal to "the interior," retreats back from the world, consigns the faith in the world to the rank of things said or *statements*.[1] But then we have the feeling that this "explicitation" is a transformation without reconversion, that it rests upon itself, on the perceptual faith whose tenor it claims to give us and whose measure it claims to be: it is because first I believe in the world and in the things that I believe in the

1. TRANSLATOR: In English in the text.

[50]

order and the connection of my thoughts. We are therefore led to seek, beneath the reflection itself, and as it were *in front of* the philosopher who reflects, the reasons for belief which he seeks within himself, in his thoughts, on the hither side of the world.

This critique of reflection does not only apply to its rudimentary forms, to a psychological reflection which turns away from the things in order to look back upon the "states of consciousness" through which the things are given to us, upon our "thoughts" taken in their formal reality as events situated in a stream of consciousness. Even a reiterated reflection, more self-conscious, which treats the states of consciousness in their turn as unities constituted before an absolute subject, liberates that absolute subject from all inherence in psychological events and defines our thoughts as pure relations to their "objective reality," their ideate, or their signification—even this purified reflection is not free from the reflective vice of transforming the openness upon the world into an assent of self with self, the institution of the world into an ideality of the world, the perceptual faith into acts or attitudes of a subject that does not participate in the world. If we wish to avoid this first, irretrievable, lie, it is therefore, with and through the reflection, the Being-subject and Being itself that we have to conceive anew, by concentrating our attention on [the horizon of the world,] at the confines of the universe of reflection. For it is the horizon of the world that secretly guides us in our constructions and harbors the truth of the procedures of reflection by which we pretend to reconstitute it—a first positivity of which no negation of our doubts could be the equivalent.

One will say, then, that before the reflection, and in order to make it possible, a naïve frequenting of the world is necessary, and that the *Self* to which one returns is preceded by an alienated Self or a Self in ec-stasy in Being. The world, the things, what is, is (one will say) of itself, without common measure with our "thoughts." If we try to find out what "the thing" means for us, we find that it is what rests in itself, that it is exactly what it is, wholly in act, without any virtuality or potency, that it is by definition "transcendent," outside, absolutely foreign to all interiority. If it is perceived by someone, and in particular by me, this is not constitutive of its meaning as a thing, which on the contrary is to be there in indifference, in the night of identity, as

[Marginal notes in handwriting:]
Even pure Rf. based on Tr. Ego transforms wld into ideal –

Fix attention on the horizon of the world –

naïve frequenting of the wld is ∪ for Rf.

pure in-itself. Such would be the description of Being to which we would be led if we really wished to rediscover the prereflective zone of the openness upon Being. And in order that this openness take place, in order that decidedly we get out of our thoughts, in order that nothing stand between us and it, it would be correlatively necessary to empty the Being-subject of all the phantoms with which philosophy has encumbered it. If I am to be in ec-stasy in the world and in the things, it is necessary that nothing detain me within myself far from them—no "representation," no "thought," no "image," and not even that epithet "subject," "mind," or "Ego," with which the philosopher wishes to distinguish me absolutely from the things, but which becomes misleading in its turn, since, like every designation, in the end it devolves into the positive, reintroduces a phantom of reality within me, and makes me think that I am a *res cogitans*—a very particular, elusive, invisible thing, but a thing all the same. The only way to ensure my access to the things themselves would be to purify my notion of the subjectivity completely: there is not even any "subjectivity" or "Ego"; the consciousness is without "inhabitant," I must extricate it completely from the secondary apperceptions that make of it the reverse of a body, the property of a "psychism," and I must discover it as the "nothing," the "void," which has the capacity for receiving the plenitude of the world, or rather which needs it to bear its own emptiness.

It is with this intuition of Being as absolute plenitude and absolute positivity, and with a view of nothingness purified of all the being we mix into it, that Sartre expects to account for our primordial access to the things, always tacitly understood in the philosophies of reflection, and always taken in realism as an action of the things upon us—which is unthinkable. From the moment that I conceive of myself as negativity and the world as positivity, there is no longer any interaction. I go with my whole self to meet a massive world; between it and myself there is neither any point of encounter nor point of reflection, since it is Being and I am nothing. We are and remain strictly opposed and strictly commingled precisely because we are not of the same order. Through the center of myself I remain absolutely foreign to the being of the things—and, precisely as such, destined for them, made for them. Here what one says of being and what one says of nothingness *are* but one and the same thing—they are the obverse and the reverse of the same thought; the clear vision of being such as it is under our eyes—as the being of the thing that is peaceably, obstinately itself, seated in itself, absolute non-me—is complementary or even synonymous with a conception of oneself as absence and elusion. The intuition of being is solidary with a sort of negintuition of nothingness (in the sense that we speak of negentropy), with the impossibility of our reducing ourselves to anything whatever—a state of consciousness, thought, an *ego,* or even a "subject." [2] Here everything depends on the strictness with which we will be able to think through the negative. We are not thinking it as negative if we treat it as an "object of thought" or try to say *what it is:* that is to make of it a more subtle or more rarefied species of being, it is to reintegrate it into being. [3] The only way to think of the negative is to think that it *is not,* and the only way to preserve its negative purity is (instead of juxtaposing it to being as a distinct substance, which is to immediately contaminate it with positivity) to see it out of the corner of one's eye as the sole *frontier* of being, implicated in being as what being would lack, if absolute fullness could lack anything—more precisely, as calling for being in order to not be nothing, and, as such, called forth by being as the sole supplement to being that would be conceivable, a lack of being, but at the same time a lack that constitutes itself into a lack, hence a fissure that deepens in the exact measure that it is filled. Take the *this* which is under my eyes and which seems to choke the void I am with its mass. In reality, this glass, this table, this room can be sensibly present to me only if nothing separates me from them, only if I am in them and not in myself, in my representations or my thoughts, only if I am nothing. Yet (one will say) inasmuch as I have *this* before myself I am not an absolute nothing, I am a determined nothing: not this glass, nor this table, nor this room; my emptiness is not indefinite, and to this extent at least my nothingness is filled or nullified. In reality, this pseudo-positivity of my present is only a more profound or re-

2. I am absolutely foreign to being and this is what makes me be open to being qua "absolute plenitude and entire positivity" (Sartre, *L'Etre et le néant* [Paris, 1943], p. 50). [English translation by Hazel E. Barnes, *Being and Nothingness* (New York, 1956), p. 15. The translations from this book have been slightly altered. A.L.]

3. Sartre accepts all the arguments against the idea of nothingness one could offer: they prove that nothingness is not, which is precisely its sole manner of being.

doubled negation. It has its weight as an effective present; it occupies in full force the field of my life only because it is new, because it [breaks forth?] on the ground of the total world, but this also means that it is about to be reabsorbed into it: in another instant it will have disappeared, while I was speaking of it, and given place to another *this;* it will have fused into the rest of the world. It determines my emptiness only because it is ephemeral, constitutionally menaced by another *this.* What I call its force and its presence is the infinitesimal suspension of this menace, is the momentary retreat of the whole. Its "pressure" on me is only the unsure absence of the rest, the negation of those other negations which the past *thises* "have been" (*ont été*), which the future *thises* "will be," a negation that will soon rejoin them in the inactual and will have to be recommenced. Thus to fill up the fissure is in reality to deepen it, since the present one throws into it does not negate the negations that have been or will be in their own time, and displaces them only by exposing itself to the same imminent fate. The very plenitude of the present reveals itself upon examination to be our constitutive void carried to the second power. An effective or primordial negation must bear within itself what it negates, must be actively a negation of itself:

> In the measure . . . that the being that lacks— *is not* what it lacks, we apprehend a negation it it. But if this negation is not to vanish into pure exteriority—and along with it all possibility of negation in general—its foundation lies in the necessity for the being that lacks— *to be* what it lacks. Thus the foundation of the negation is a negation of negation. But this negation-foundation is no more a *given* than is the lack of which it is an essential moment: it is as having to be. . . . It is only as a lack *to be suppressed* that the lack can be an internal lack for the for-itself.[4]

Finally it is with the same movement that nothingness hollows itself out and fills itself. A philosophy that really thinks the negation, that is, that thinks it as what is not through and through, is also a philosophy of Being.* We are beyond monism and dualism, because dualism has been pushed so far that the opposites, no longer in competition, are at rest the one against

4. *L'Etre et le néant,* pp. 248–49. [Eng. trans., p. 198.]
* The destiny of nothingness and that of being are the same if one thinks nothingness properly.

the other, coextensive with one another. Since nothingness is what is not,

> . . . knowledge is reabsorbed into being: it is neither an attribute nor a function nor an accident of being; but *there is* only being. . . . At the end of this book we shall even be able to consider this articulation of the For-itself with respect to the In-itself as the perpetually moving outline of a quasi-totality which we can call *Being*. From the point of view of this totality, the upsurge of the For-itself is not only the absolute event of the For-itself, it is also *something that happens to the In-itself*, the sole adventure of the In-itself possible: for everything comes to pass as if the For-itself, by its very nihilation, constituted itself as "consciousness of—" that is, by its very transcendence escapes that law of the In-itself by which affirmation is choked up by the affirmed. The For-itself, through its self-negation, becomes affirmation *of* the In-itself. The intentional affirmation is like the reverse of the internal negation. . . . But then within the quasi-totality of Being, affirmation *happens* to the In-itself; it is the adventure of the In-itself *to be affirmed*. It happens to the In-itself that this affirmation, which could not be effected as the affirmation *of* self by the In-itself without destroying its being-in-itself, is realized by the For-itself; it is as a passive ec-stasy of the In-itself, which leaves it unaltered and which nonetheless is effected in it and on the basis of it. Everything comes to pass as if the For-itself had a Passion to lose itself in order that the affirmation "world" happen to the In-itself.[5]

From the point of view of a philosophy of the absolute negativity —which is at the same time a philosophy of the absolute positivity—all the problems of the classical philosophy volatilize, for they were problems about "compound" or "union," and compound and union are impossible between what is and what is not, but, for the same reason that makes the compound impossible, the one could not be thought without the other. Thus disappears the antinomy of idealism and realism: it is true that "knowledge" as nihilation is sustained only by the things themselves in which it is founded, that it could not affect being, that it "adds nothing" to it and "takes nothing" from it,[6] that it is a "shimmering of nothingness" at its surface [7]—and at the same time it is true that, again as nihilation, and inasmuch as nothing-

5. *Ibid.*, pp. 268–69. [Eng. trans., pp. 216–17.]
6. *Ibid.*, p. 232. [Eng. trans., p. 183.]
7. *Ibid.*, p. 268. [Eng. trans., p. 216.]

ness is absolutely unknown to being, "knowledge" gives it this negative but original determination of being "Being *such as it is,*" the being recognized or acknowledged, the sole being that *would have a meaning:*

> . . . this being which "invests me" from all sides and from which *nothing* separates me, it is precisely *nothing* that separates me from it, and this nothing, because it is nothingness, is untraversable . . . ; the For-itself is immediate presence to being and, at the same time, there slips in as an infinite distance between itself and being.[8]

Likewise it is true that the things are forever distinct from every "object of thought" or every "state of consciousness," transcendent, and at the same time that the consciousness that knows them is defined by its presence to itself, its immanence, the strict identity of appearing and being in it. The consciousness is immanence because it is nihilation, void, transparency; and it is open upon transcendent things because by itself this void would be *nothing,* because the existent consciousness is always gorged full of qualities, engulfed in the being it nihilates and over which it has, so to speak, no motor power, being of another order than it. My apprehension of myself is coextensive with my life, as its own possibility by principle—or, more exactly, it is this possibility that is me; I am this possibility, and, through it, all the others. But it is a possibility of nihilation, it leaves untouched the absolute actuality of my incarnate being as it does that of every being, it leaves intact the opacity of my life as long as I do not apply myself to it by reflection; and the *cogito* as an experience of my own being is a prereflective *cogito,* it does not pose my own being as an object before me. By position, and before all reflection, I touch myself through my situation; it is from it that I am referred back to myself; I am unaware of myself as nothingness, I believe only in the things. Precisely because, in what is most proper to me, I am nothing, nothing ever separates me from myself, but also nothing draws my attention to myself, and I am in ec-stasy in the things. If the negative is recognized for what it is,[9] if we practice negintuition in its regard, there is no longer a choice to be made between the unreflected and the reflection, between the perceptual faith and the immanence of my thoughts

8. *Ibid.,* pp. 269–70. [Eng. trans., pp. 217–18.]
9. One should say: for what it is.

to myself who thinks: it is the same thing to be nothing and to inhabit the world; between the knowledge of self and the knowledge of the world there is no longer any debate over even ideal priority. In particular the world is no longer *founded on* the "I think," as the bound on the binding. What I "am" I am only at a distance, yonder, in this body, this personage, these thoughts, which I push before myself and which are only my least remote distances (*mes lointains les moins éloignés*); and conversely I adhere to this world which is not me as closely as to myself, in a sense it is only the prolongation of my body [10]—I am justified in saying that I am in the world. Idealism and the reflective cramp disappear because the relation of knowledge is based on a "relation of being," because for me to be is not to remain in identity, it is to bear before myself the identifiable, *what there is*, to which I add nothing but the tiny doublet "such as it is." And even this passage from the brute being to the acknowledged being or to its truth is required from the depths of the exterior being by its very quality of being exterior, while self-negation is required by the radical negation that I am.

If now we consider that other certitude of the perceptual faith, that of having access to the very world the others perceive, here is how it is translated in a truly negativist philosophy. *What I see is not mine* in the sense of being a private world. Henceforth the table is the table; even the perspective views which I have of it and which are bound to the position of my body are part of being and not of myself; even the aspects of the table that are bound to my psychophysical constitution—its singular color, if I am color-blind and the table is painted red—are still part of the system of the world. What is mine in my perception are its lacunae, and they would not be lacunae if the thing itself, behind them, did not betoken them to be such. Thus finally there remains, to constitute the "subjective" face of perception, only the secondary redoubling of the thing which is expressed in saying that we see it *such as it is.* Suppose now that there is another

10. As Bergson said in *Les Deux Sources:* my body extends unto the stars. (EDITOR: *Les Deux Sources de la morale et de la religion* [Paris, 1932], p. 277: "For if our body is the matter upon which our consciousness applies itself, it is coextensive with our consciousness. It includes everything that we perceive, it extends unto the stars.") [English translation by R. Ashley Audra and Cloudesley Brereton, *The Two Sources of Morality and Religion* (New York, 1935), p. 246.]

man before me who "looks at" what I call "the table." Between the table of my field (which is not one of my thoughts, but the table itself) and this body, this gaze, a relation is established which is neither of the two relations that a solipsist analysis furnishes: the gaze of the other man on the thing is neither a negation swept away by itself and opening upon the thing itself, nor is it the thing in the night of identity now installing itself in full light through the space I supply for it, or its plenitude now decompressing due to the void I provide about it. For the other's gaze on it is not a nothing for me, its exterior witness; whatever it may be in the last analysis, it is not nothing as I am nothing for myself, it does not have the power I have to push the things unto their truth or their meaning and to grasp them "such as they are." The perception others have of the world always leaves me with the impression that it is a blind palpation, and we are quite surprised when they say something about it that rejoins our perception, as we marvel when an infant begins to "understand." . . . And correlatively, the things, at the end of another's look, do not call for that look as a confirmation of their being, as that which makes them true or acknowledged things. It is always *my* things that the others look at, and the contact they have with those things does not incorporate them into a world that would be theirs. The perception of the world by the others cannot enter into competition with my own perception of it, for my position is not comparable to theirs; I live my perception from within, and, from within, it has an incomparable power of ontogenesis. This very power I have to reach the thing and hence to go beyond my private states of consciousness, because it is proper to the perception lived from within, that is, to my own perception, reduces me to a solipsism (this time transcendental) the very moment I thought myself delivered from it. This power of ontogenesis becomes my speciality and my difference. But for this very reason the intervention of the foreign spectator does not leave my relationship with the things untouched. Insinuating into the world "such as it is" the sub-universe of a behavior or of a private life, his intervention puts my devotion to being to the test; it calls into question the right I arrogated to myself to think it for all, it takes my generosity at its word, it summons me to keep the promises I made when I admitted that I was *nothing* and that I was surpassed by being. The gaze of the other men on the things is being which claims its due and which enjoins me to admit that my relationship with it passes through them. I remain the sole witness of the ontogenesis, the others can add nothing to the evidence of being for me. Before they intervene I already knew that being owes nothing to my states of consciousness; but the nothing I am and the being I see all the same formed a closed sphere. The other's gaze on the things is a second openness. Within this openness which I am, it is a question mark opposite the *solipsist* sphere, it is the possibility of a divergence between the nothing that I am and being. I remain the sole *ipse;* the other, as long as he does not speak, remains an inhabitant of my world, but he reminds me very imperiously that the *ipse* is a nothing, that this anonymity does not form the spectacle for itself, that it forms it for X, for all those presumptively who might wish to take part in it. One sole condition is laid down for their coming on the scene: that they could present themselves to me as other focuses of negativity. It is true that one does not see how they could fulfill that condition, since they are in front of me, on the side of being. But if one does not very well see how they could appear in the world, and if the privilege of my perspective seems to be absolute and my perception indeclinable, I have only provisionally acquired this privilege: it is not the privilege of a "subjective" series reserved for me; I as it were do everything that depends on me in order that the world lived by me be open to participation by others, since I am distinguishable only as a nothing which takes nothing from it, since I put into the arena of the world my body, my representations, my very thoughts qua mine, and since everything that one calls me is in principle open to a foreign gaze, should it but be willing to appear.

Will it appear? It cannot appear in the things. Whatever be the common opinion, it is not in their bodies, nor *anywhere,* that I see the others. It is not from a point of space that the other's gaze emanates. The other is born *from my side,* by a sort of propagation by cuttings or by subdivision, as the first other, says Genesis, was made from a part of Adam's body. But how is it conceivable that what is nothing be doubled? How would one discern one "nothing" from another? The question only shows that we have forgotten our principle on the way, that we have come to forget that nothingness is not, that we grasp it by negintuition and as the reverse of being. If there can be several beings, there will be as many nothingnesses. The question is not how one would discern one nothingness from another, for to say that I am nothing (in the sense of identity) is to say that I am (in the active sense) my body and my situation, and, reduced to its true terms, the question is whether there can be more than one body and more than one situation. But as soon as it is put in these terms, it is solved: to be sure, I will never find in *my* situation the proof that there actually are other situations (with their titular incumbents who also make being be—the same being as I do), but if my situation were to prove that, it would prove much more than it should, since then the existence of the other would result from my own existence. All one can ask is that my situation—that region of being that is the least distant from my constitutive nothingness—not be for me just one object among all those over which my look soars, that, as Descartes said, there be a certain particular right by which I call it my own, that it be a region of being which I assume first and foremost, through which I assume all the rest, that I have a certain particular bond with it, that it restrict the universality of my gaze in such a way that my view of being not be coextensive with being, and that beyond what I see the place be marked out for what the others see, if they come to be. But this is included in the very notion of situation and in the negintuition of nothingness: if I am nothing and if in order to come to the world I support myself particularly on one part of being, then, since that part does not thereby cease to be *outside* and to be subject to the actions that traverse the world, and since I am not informed about all those actions, there are some whose consequences I will have to assume as brute facts; my situation is opaque to my own eyes, it presents aspects that escape me and upon which an exterior look, if such were possible, would have more light. What I am all told overflows what I am for myself, my universality as nothingness is only presumption on my part, and since it is operative only through my situation, an exterior look that would encompass that situation would encompass my nothingness also. If I succeed in thinking the non-being of my non-being completely, I would agree that in order to be truly non-being, it renounces itself in favor of what I am as a whole or in fact. From then on everything is ready, not for an experience of the other (which we have seen is not positively possible), not for a proof of the other (which would proceed against its objective by rendering the other necessary on the basis of myself), but for an experience of my passivity within being—not that being could by itself alone close in over my nothingness, but because it includes at least all the attributes which my nothingness is decked out with in fact. Since I inevitably identify myself with these attributes from the sole fact that they are my situation, since being is and nothingness is not, in this measure I am exposed, menaced. That this possibility is realized is in fact attested by the experience of shame, or my being reduced to what is visible in my situation. There is no positive experience of another, but there is an experience of my total being as compromised in the visible part of myself. For reflection, we—the others and myself—could not have in common a world that would be numerically the same, we could only rejoin one another in the common signification of our thoughts and in the indivision of ideality. If, on the contrary, we follow out the consequences of the negintuition all the way, we understand how our transcendental being and our empirical being are the obverse and the reverse of one another; we understand, through this expedient, that we are visible, we are not the adequate cause of all that we are, that the world is not only the term of our private ontogenesis but is what already sustains us while we traverse it with a look that, in its own way, is a part of it. I do not *know* the others, in the strong sense that I *know* myself; I therefore cannot flatter myself in supposing that I participate with them in a thought of the world which would be ideally the same thought. But my perception of the world feels it has an exterior; I feel at the surface of my visible being that my volubility dies away, that I become flesh, and that at the extremity of this inertia that was me there is something else, or rather an other who is not a thing. He then is seated nowhere, he is everywhere around me with the ubiquity of oneiric or mythical beings: for he is not entirely *ipse*—I alone am—but he is not caught up in the fabric of what I call being either. He encompasses it, he is a look come from nowhere and which therefore envelops me, me and my power for ontogenesis, from all sides. I knew very well that I was *nothing* and that this nothing swept itself away in favor of being. There remained for me to learn from the other that even this sacrifice does not suffice to equal the plenitude of being, that my fundamental negation is not complete as long as it has not itself been negated from without, and, by a foreign gaze, counted in with the beings. . . . But at the same time, since there are no degrees in nothingness, the other's intervention can teach me nothing about my nothingness of which I would have been absolutely ignorant. The solipsist being is already in himself the absolute other which he becomes for himself with the apparition of the other. I already have in the night of the In-itself all that is necessary in order to fabricate the other's private world, as the beyond inaccessible to me. The experience of the other's gaze upon me only prolongs my inward conviction of being nothing, of living only as a parasite on the world, of inhabiting a body and a situation. All told, therefore, a rigorous philosophy of negintuition accounts for the private worlds without shutting us up in them: strictly speaking there is no intermundane space; each one inhabits only his own, sees only according to his own point of view, enters into being only through his situation. But because he is nothing and because his relationship with his situation and with his body is a relation of being, his situation, his body, his thoughts do not form a screen between him and the world; on the contrary they are the vehicle of a relation to Being in which third parties, witnesses, can intervene. Their place is marked out in advance in the lacunae of my private world, which I know very well to be lacunae, since the "nothing" which I am would need the totality of being in order to be completely realized, and since it is evident that my situation, my body, my thoughts are only a part of it. While a philosophy of consciousness or of reflection can justify the perceptual faith in the unicity of the world only by reducing it to a consciousness of the identity of the world, and by making of illusion a simple privation, a philosophy of negativity entirely ratifies the pretension of the perceptual faith to open to us a world numerically one, common to all, through perspectives that are our own, because the *solus ipse*, as fundamental negation, is in advance open upon a background-world that exceeds all its perspectives, because the "incomparable monster" is in its heart convinced that its views are unequal to the whole, is all ready, if it encounters someone, to found a family, and because it has the momentum to go beyond itself. For the philosophy of reflection it is an inextricable difficulty to comprehend how a constitutive consciousness can pose another that would be its equal, and hence also constitutive—since the first must forthwith pass on to the rank of the constituted. The difficulty results from the fact that both are conceived as centrifugal acts, spiritual syntheses, in which case one does not see how they could ebb back toward their source. On the contrary it is for a philosophy of the negative the very definition of the *ipse* to adhere to a *de facto* situation or to sustain it as its bond with Being. This exterior at the same time confirms it in its particularity, renders it visible as a partial being to the others' look, and connects it back to the whole of Being. What was a stumbling block for the philosophy of reflection becomes, from the point of view of negativity, the principle of a solution. Everything really does come down to a matter of thinking the negative rigorously.

Finally the thought of the negative (*pensée du négatif*) satisfies the third exigency of the perceptual faith we spoke of at the start. We said that before all philosophy, perception is convinced that it has to do with a confused totality where all things, the bodies and the minds, are together, and which it calls the *world*. Here again the reflection attains its rigor only by destroying what we experience: it replaces the pell-mell of the world with a set of parallel consciousnesses, each observing its own law if it had been regulated by the same clockmaker as the others, or each observing the laws of a universal thought that is immanent in all. From the point of view of a negativist philosophy, the synchronism of the consciousnesses is given by their common belongingness to a Being to which no one has the key and whose law they all observe—or rather, let us no longer say that there is synchronization: each experiences himself as involved with the others; there is a meeting ground which is Being itself inasmuch as each of us inheres in it through his situation. "There is only Being": each experiences himself given over to a body, to a situation, through them to being, and what he knows of himself passes entirely over to the other the very instant he experiences the other's medusan power. Hence each one knows that he himself and the others are *inscribed* in the world; what he feels, what he lives, what the others feel and live, even his dreams or their dreams, his illusions and theirs, are not islets, isolated fragments of being: all this, by reason of the fundamental exigency of our constitutive nothingnesses, is *of being,* has consistence, order, meaning, and there is a way to comprehend it. Even if what I live at present should reveal itself to be illusory, the critique of my illusion will not simply cast it out of the world, but on the contrary will show me its place, its relative legitimacy, its *truth.* If nothingness is destined for Being, my presence as a nothingness is an exigency for totality, for cohesion; it postulates that everywhere it is a matter of the same being. . . . All that is partial is to be reintegrated, every negation is in reality a determination, the being-self and the being-other and the being in itself are fragments of one sole being. The negativism, if it is rigorous, absolute, is a sort of positivism. The very movement by which a *this* is pronounced in my life, or this life in the world, is but the climax of negation, the negation that destroys itself. If a nothingness that is truly conceived as nothingness as such eludes all contamination with being and refuses to form a whole by juxtaposition with it, at the same time it demands to be all, it backs up being in its integral exigency, and, through a reversal of the pro and the con, is incorporated into being. When we have gone beyond the first steps, the radical distinction between being and nothingness, the analysis—which are abstract and superficial—we find at the center of things that the opposites are exclusionary to such an extent that the one without the other would be only an abstraction, that the force of being is supported by the frailty of the nothingness which is its accomplice, that the obscurity of the In Itself is for the clarity of the For Itself in general, if not for that of "my consciousness." The famous ontological problem, the "why is there something rather than nothing" disappears along with the alternative: there is not something *rather than nothing,* the nothing could not *take the place* of something or of being: nothingness inexists (in the negative sense) and being is, and the exact adjusting of the one upon the other no longer leaves room for a question. Everything is obscure when one has not thought out the negative; everything is clear when one has thought it as negative. For then what is called negation and what is called position appear as accomplices and even in a sort of equivalence. They confront one another "in a tumult like unto silence"; the world is like that band of foam on the ocean which appears immobile when seen from an airplane, but which suddenly, because it has extended itself by a line, is understood to be shimmering and living from close up. But one also understands that, seen from high enough, the amplitude of being will never exceed that of nothingness, nor the noise of the world its silence.

In a sense the thought of the negative provides us with what we were searching for, terminates our research, brings philoso-

phy to a standstill. We said that philosophy needs a contact with
being prior to reflection, a contact which makes reflection itself
possible. The "negintuition" of nothingness *is* the philosophical
attitude that puts reflection and spontaneity in a sort of equivalence. If I really understand that nothingness is not, and that this
is its own way of being, I understand that there can be no question of incorporating it into being, that it will always be this side
of it, that I qua negativity am always behind all the things, cut off
from them by virtue of my status as witness, always capable of
suspending my adhesion to the world in order to make of it a
thought of the world. And yet at the same time I understand that
this thought of the world is *nothing*, that in this return to myself
I do not discover a set of premises of which the world would be
the consequence, that on the contrary it is the premise and my
consciousness of it the consequence, that my intentions in themselves are empty, that they are only the flight of my emptiness
after being, and that this flight owes its direction and its meaning to being, that our reconstructions or reconstitutions are
suspended upon a primary evidence of the world which itself indicates its articulations to me. What I find "in myself," is always
the reference to this originating presence, and to retire into
oneself is identical to leaving oneself. For him who thinks the
negative in its purity, there are not two movements—the aban-
donment to the world and the recovery by reflection; there are
not two attitudes—the one, natural, of attention to the things,
and the other, philosophical, of attention to the signification of
the things, each retaining, as in reserve, the possibility of transforming itself into the other; there is a perception of being and
an imperception of nothingness which are coextensive with one
another, which are but one. An absolute negativism—that is, one
that thinks the negative in its originality—and an absolute positivism—that is, one that thinks being in its plenitude and its
self-sufficiency—are exactly synonymous; there is not the least
divergence between them. To say that nothingness is not is the
same as to say that there is only being—in other words, that one
could not find nothingness among the things that are, as one of
them, that *therefore* it must be backed up against them, that it
must be no more than what makes them not be each for its own
account, what makes them be together, what makes them be one
sole Being. . . . The perspective in which Being and Nothingness
are absolutely opposed, and the perspective in which Being itself,

by definition given as identical with itself, eminently contains a contact—established, broken and re-established—with Nothingness, its being recognized, its negation negated—these two perspectives are but one; as absolutely opposed, Being and Nothingness are indiscernible. It is the absolute inexistence of Nothingness that makes it need Being and makes it hence be not visible except in the guise of "lakes of non-being," relative and localized non-beings, reliefs or lacunae in the world. It is precisely because Being and Nothingness, the yes and the no, cannot be blended together like two ingredients that, when we see being, nothingness is immediately there, and not in the margin like the zone of non-vision around our field of vision, but over the whole expanse of what we see, as what installs it and disposes it before us as a spectacle. The strict thought of the negative is invulnerable, since it is also a thought of the absolute positivity and hence already contains everything one could oppose to it. It cannot be shown wanting nor be found shorthanded.

But is this not because it is ungraspable? It begins by opposing being and nothingness absolutely, and it ends by showing that the nothingness is in a way within being, which is the unique universe. When are we to believe it? At the beginning or at the end? The answer will be: it amounts to the same thing and there is no difference. Yet there is a difference between Being in the restricted sense with which one begins—which over its whole extension is absolutely exclusive of nothingness, and which nothingness needs if it is to be able to be named—and Being in the broad sense which one ends up with—which in a way contains nothingness, invokes it in order to become fully being, in order to become Being "such as it is." The two movements—that by which nothingness invokes being and that by which being invokes nothingness—do not merge into one: they cross. According to the first, being is negation of negation, it has an infrastructure of nothingness, it is an attribute of knowledge; according to the second, nothingness finally is reiterated position, position of position, it has an infrastructure of being, and knowledge is an attribute of being. In the first approach, being is considered from the point of view of nothingness. In the second, nothingness is considered from the point of view of being. Even if, in both cases, one ends up at an identification, it takes place in the first case for the profit of nothingness, in the second for the profit of being, and the two relationships are not identical. Let us examine each in turn.

One can first think starting from the pure negative. One shows that I, who question myself about being, am nothing. With this statement, one circumscribes an anti-nature which is me: I am what has no nature, I am a nothing. This conceptual or verbal fixation is only a first moment of analysis, but it is indispensable to introduce what follows, it commands it. It motivates the conclusions themselves, quite opposed to it, at which the thought of the negative will arrive; it co-determines their meaning by establishing them in advance in an order of univocal truth where the opposites can drive out one another but not pass into one another. In positing that nothingness is not, that non-being is its manner of being, that it is non-being through and through, the thought of the negative condemns itself to define being as absolute plenitude and proximity, it posits that being is. Because he who questions about being is a nothing, it is necessary that everything be absolutely outside of him, at a distance, and one could not conceive of a more or a less in this remoteness which is by principle. He who questions, having been once and for all defined as *nothing,* is installed at infinity; from there he apperceives all things in an absolute equidistance: before what is not, they are all, without any degree, of being, of the absolutely full and positive. Because the negative is the founding, the founded being is absolute positivity. One cannot even say that there is any *inference* here: the negintuition of nothingness is already the immediate presence to being. The power conceded to the philosopher to name this nothingness which he is, to coincide with this fissure in being, is already a variant of the principle of identity which defines being. In thinking on the basis of the pure negative we already decide to think according to identity; we are already in identity, since this negative which nothing can limit in its own order, having to go on to the limit of itself, will be also, and fundamentally, a negation of itself, and therefore will be pronounced in the form of an advent of pure being. There is a trap inherent in the thought of the negative: if we say that it is, we destroy its negativity; but if we maintain strictly that it is not, we still elevate it to a sort of positivity, we confer upon it a sort of being, since through and through and absolutely it is *nothing.* The negative becomes a sort of quality precisely because one fixes it in its power of refusal and evasion. A negativist thought is identical to a positivist thought, and in this reversal remains the same in that, whether considering the void of nothingness or the absolute fullness of being, it in every case ignores density, depth, the plurality of planes, the background worlds. When, starting from nothingness, it comes to pose being as absolute plenitude and positivity—more: to declare that there is only being and that being in a sense invokes and includes nothingness—it is not reintroducing elements that it would first methodically have excluded, it is not approaching the concrete, it is not following out the articulations of the whole: it is compensating for one abstraction with a counter-abstraction. One must grant to it that the pure negative calls for pure being, but far from one having thus found for philosophy a position where self-consciousness would not be prejudicial to the transcendence of the thing, one compromises both of these, one accumulates the difficulties. For it is quite obvious that there is pure negation only in principle and that the existent For Itself is encumbered with a body, which is not outside if it is not inside, which intervenes between the For Itself and itself. Likewise pure being is nowhere to be found, for every alleged thing soon reveals itself to be an appearance, and these alternating and antagonistic images are not comprehensible as images of one sole being, for lack of degrees of being, for lack of organization in depth, and because this being, in order to be positive and full, must be flat, and hence remains *what it is* beyond the ambivalence to which we are confined. It is in appearance only that the immanent consciousness and the transcendence of being are reconciled by an analytic of Being and Nothingness: it is not being that is transcendent, it is I who hold it at arm's length by a sort of abnegation; it is not the world that is thick, it is I who am agile enough to make it be yonder. When here one moves from nothingness to being, and then to the ec-stasy of being in the nothingness that recognizes that being "such as it is," in fact there is neither progress nor synthesis, there is no transformation of the initial antithesis: one pushes unto its limits the initial analysis which remains valid to the letter, and which always animates the integral view of Being. Being's invoking of nothingness is *in truth* an invoking of Being by nothingness, an autonegation. Nothingness and being are always absolutely other than one another, it is precisely their isolation that unites them; they are not really united, they only more quickly succeed one another before thought.* Since the void of the For Itself fills up, since man is not immediately present to everything, but more especially to a body, to a situation, and only through them to the world, one admits the denseness of an unreflected being in the For Itself, and one admits that the reflective operation is second: one speaks of a *prereflective cogito*. But the ambivalence of the word conveys the ambivalence of a thought that can either remain itself, or negate itself in the night of the In Itself, but cannot find any inertia in itself: is the prereflective *cogito* something in us that is more ourselves than the *cogito* and the reflection that introduces it, or is it a *cogito* that from the depths of ourselves precedes itself, pronounces itself before we have pronounced it, because thought is what we are? The first hypothesis is precluded if I am a nothing; and the second restores to me my emptiness just when the question is to understand how my life can be opaque for itself. The very progress of the investigation cannot change the idea we form of Being and Nothingness; it can only disclose its unnoticed implications, so long as one thinks on the basis of the signification of being and the non-sense of nothingness. Even if the explanation apparently reverses the perspectives, the reversal is not effective; everything takes place between this entity and this negentity (*négatité*), and being, which is said to undergo a sort of assumption into nothingness, remains pure In Itself, absolute positivity; it is only as such that it knows this adventure—and this pure In Itself was from the beginning destined to be recognized, since it was as an autonegation of the negative that it had appeared. There is no first apprehension of ipseity and being which is transformed or surpassed; the reversal of the pro and the con is another formulation of the initial antithesis, which does not cease in it, which on the contrary is renewed in it. The thought of the pure negative or of the pure positive is therefore a high-altitude thought, which operates on the essence or on the pure negation of the essence, on terms whose signification has been fixed and which it holds in its possession. Sartre does indeed say that *at the end of his book* it will be permissible to move to a broader sense of Being, which

* I said in turn that "nothingness is not" and "being is" are the same thought—and that nothingness and being are not united. Connect the two: they are not united precisely because they are the same thing in two contradictories = ambivalence.

contains Being and nothingness. But this is not because the initial opposition would have been overcome; it remains in all its rigor, it is that initial opposition that justifies its own reversal, that triumphs in this defeat; the passion of the For Itself, which sacrifices itself in order that being be, is still its own negation by itself. It is tacitly understood that from one end of the book to the other we are speaking of the same nothingness and of the same being, that one unique spectator is witness to the progress, that he is not himself caught up in the movement, and that inasmuch as that is so the movement is illusory. A negativist or positivist thought rediscovers that postulate of the philosophy of reflection that no result of the reflection can retroactively compromise him who operates the reflection nor change the idea we form of him for ourselves. And it cannot be otherwise if one starts with the pure negative: for it will never admit anything into itself, and even if one comes to recognize that it has need of Being, it will need Being only as a distant environment that does not adulterate it. It will dispose it about itself, as a pure spectacle or as what it has to be, it will elevate it to truth or to signification; but it will itself remain the nothingness it was, its devotion to Being will confirm it as nothingness.

The negativist (or positivist) thought establishes between nothingness and being a massive cohesion, both rigid and fragile at the same time: rigid since they are finally indiscernible, fragile since they remain unto the end absolute opposites. Their relation is, as the psychologists say, labile. This will be seen each time it is a question of comprehending how nothingness receives being into itself, and hence not only, as we said a moment ago, when it is a question of comprehending my incarnation, but also when it is a question of comprehending how I can assume the view another has of me, or finally our common belongingness to the world. It is as always by means of the negative purity of the For Itself that one seeks to comprehend the fact that it recognizes beings like unto itself: because I am no thing, and because all the same I have to be this emptiness, to make it be in the world, I take up again on my own account my body and my situation and the other's gaze which I see posed on this exterior that is me. For me there is no activity and presence of an other; there is on my part the experience of a passivity and of an alienation which I recognize concern me, because, being nothing, I have to be my situation. In the last analysis, therefore, the relationship remains one between me as nothingness and me as a man, and I do not deal with others, at most I deal with a neutral non-me, with a diffused negation of my nothingness. I am drawn out of myself by the other's gaze, but his power over me is exactly measured by the consent which I have given to my body, to my situation; he has alienating force only because I alienate myself. Philosophically speaking, there is no experience of the other. For the encounter with another to be thought, no transformation of the idea of myself that I form by myself is required. The encounter actualizes what was already possible on the basis of me alone. What the encounter brings is only the force of the fact: this consent to my body and to my situation which I prepared, whose principle I possessed, but only the principle, since a passivity that one poses oneself is not effective —here suddenly it is realized. The relation with another, says Sartre, is [evidently?] a fact, otherwise I should not be myself and he would not be other; the other exists in fact and for me exists only in fact. But just as "being is" *adds* nothing to "nothingness is not" and the recognition of Being as absolute plenitude and positivity changes nothing in the negintuition of nothingness, so also the other's gaze which suddenly congeals me adds to my universe no new dimension—it only confirms for me an inclusion in being which I knew from within; I only learn that there is about my universe an outside in general, as I learn by perception that the things it illuminates lived before it in the night of identity. The other is one of the empirical forms of the engulfment into Being. . . . And, to be sure, this analysis has its truth: to the whole extent that it is true that I am nothing, the other cannot appear to me otherwise than as the ultra-world from which emanates a gaze whose impact I feel on my body alone; to the whole extent that I am a thought, a consciousness, I am compelled to enter into the world only through it, and the other consciousnesses, the other thoughts, will be forever but the doubles or the younger sisters of my own. I will never live any but my own life and the others will never be but other myselves. But is this solipsism, this aspect of the phenomena, this structure of the relationship with another the whole or even the essential? It is but one empirical variant of it [11]—the ambivalent

11. EDITOR: The preceding sentence, to which the beginning of this one is linked, suffers from an apparently incomplete correction. The first version, which was rejected, was: "but the question is

or labile relationship with the other—in which, moreover, analysis would rediscover the normal, canonical form, subjected in the particular case to a distortion that makes of the other an anonymous, faceless obsession, an other in general.

Let us even suppose that the other be the X titular of this look which I feel posed upon me and which congeals me: I do not advance one step into the elucidation of the phenomenon in saying that it is prepared for by me from within, that I, nothingness, have exposed myself to this look by taking up on my own account my body, my situation, my exterior, and that finally the other is the limiting case of my engulfment in Being. For as long as it is I who insert myself into Being, the one who inserts and the inserted keep their distances. Whereas the other's gaze—and it is here that it brings me something new—envelops me wholly, being and nothingness. This is what, in the relationship with another, depends on no interior possibility and what obliges us to say that it is a pure fact. But though this relationship be a part of my facticity, though it be an encounter that cannot be deduced from the For Itself, still it does present a sense for me; it is not a nameless catastrophe that leaves me petrified (*médusé*), it is the entry on the scene of someone else. I do not simply feel myself frozen, I am frozen by a look, and if it were for example an animal that looked at me, I would know only a feeble echo of this experience. Therefore, far from the sense of the other's look being exhausted in the burning it leaves at the point of my body he looks at, it is necessary that there be something in the other's look that designates it to me as a look of an other. It is necessary that something teach me that I am wholly implicated, being and nothingness, in this perception that takes possession of me and that the other perceive me soul and body. Hence, by making of the ambivalent relation the canonical form of the relationship with the other and by bringing to the foreground the objectification I suffer, one does not avoid having to recognize a positive perception of the ipseity by an exterior ipseity: the ambivalent relation refers to it as to its condition. In other words, the thought of the negative can very well found every position on a negation of negation, every centripetal relation on a centrifugal

whether the negativist or positivist thought disclosing this aspect of the phenomena, this structure of the relationship with another, grasps the whole or even the essential. We say that, in principle, it can only grasp one empirical variant of it. . . ."

relation, but, whether in dealing with being in general or the being of the other, a moment comes when the negation of negation crystallizes into the simplicity of a *this:* there is a thing, here is someone. These events are more than the infrastructure of the For Itself—the For Itself's power for negation henceforth derives from their sovereign positivity. My knowledge only sanctions what being already was in itself, only rejoins it "such as it is"—and, likewise, instead of my shame constituting the whole sense of the other's existence, the other's existence is the truth of my shame. Finally, if we consider my relationship no longer with the solipsist Being and with the other, but now with Being inasmuch as it is aimed at by all of us, inasmuch as it is crammed full of others who perceive one another and perceive the same world—and the same one that I also perceive—the negativist thought is once again faced with the alternative: either remain faithful to the definition of myself as nothingness and Being as pure positivity—in which case we do not have before us a world as the whole of nature, humanity, and history, including me; the negations are only a shimmering on the surface of being, and the hard core of being is found only after one has effaced from it every possible, every past, all movement, all the imaginary or illusory attributes which are of me and not of it. Or if one does not mean to drive being back to this limit of pure positivity where there is nothing, and ascribe to the For Itself what makes up the whole content of our experience, then, in accordance with the very movement of the negativity when it goes all the way in its negation of itself, it is necessary to incorporate into being a whole quantity of negative attributes, the transitions, and the becoming, and the possible. As always the same negativist thought oscillates between these two images without being able to sacrifice one of them nor to unite them. It is ambivalence itself, that is, the absolute contradiction and the identity of being and nothingness, it is the "ventriloquial" thought that Plato speaks of, that which always affirms or denies in the hypothesis what it denies or affirms in the thesis, that which as high-altitude thinking belies the inherence of being in nothingness and of nothingness in being.

A philosophy of reflection, if it is not to be ignorant of itself, is led to question itself about what precedes itself, about our contact with being within ourselves and outside of ourselves, before all reflection. Yet by principle it can conceive of that contact with being only as a reflection before the reflection, because it develops under the domination of concepts such as "subject," "consciousness," "self-consciousness," "mind," all of which, even if in a refined form, involve the idea of a *res cogitans,* of a positive being of thought—whence there results the immanence in the unreflected of the results of reflection. We have therefore asked ourselves if a philosophy of the negative would not restore to us the [brute being of the unreflected] without compromising our power of reflection: a subjectivity that is nothing is in the immediate presence of being or in contact with the world, and at the same time as close to itself as one could like, since no opaqueness in it could separate it from itself. And yet, this analytic of being and nothingness leaves us with a difficulty. By principle it opposes them absolutely, it defines them as mutually exclusive—but if they are absolute opposites they are not defined by anything that would be proper to them. As soon as the one is negated the other is there, each of them is only the exclusion of the other, and nothing prevents them, in the end, from exchanging their roles: there subsists only the split between them. Reciprocally alternative as they may be, they together compose one sole universe of thought, since each of them is only its retreat before the other. To think the total being—what is totally, and hence also that to which nothing is lacking, what is the whole of being—it is necessary to be outside of it, a margin of non-being; but this margin excluded from the whole prevents it from being all—the true totality should contain it too, which, since it is a margin of non-being, is quite impossible. Thus, if being and nothingness are absolutely opposed, they are together founded in a sort of [Hyper-being,] which is mythical, since the force that requires it is their absolute repulsion. Such is the circle we have traversed, and which leads from absolute opposition to an identity which is only another figure of the opposition—either one thinks them in their opposition between what is and what is not, or on the contrary one identifies them by making of being either a redoubling of negation, or, inversely, a positivity so perfect that it contains eminently the recognition that the nothingness brings to it. But there is no progress, transformation, irreversible order from one of these relationships to the other; what leads us from the one to the other is not a movement of what is thought, it is the shifting of our attention or the choice we make of the one or other point of departure. But this reproach of ambivalence has no cogency against an analytic of Being and Nothingness that is a description in accordance with the fundamental structures of our contact with being: if this contact really is ambivalent, it is for us to accommodate ourselves to it, and logical difficulties cannot prevail against this description. In reality, the definitions of being as what is in all respects and without restriction, and of nothingness as what is not in any respect—this appropriation of an immediate being and of an immediate nothingness by thought, this intuition and this negintuition—are the abstract portrait of an experience, and it is on the terrain of experience that they must be discussed. Do they express well our contact with being, do they express it in full? They do assuredly express the experience of vision: the vision is a panorama; through the holes of the eyes and from the bottom of my invisible retreat, I survey the world and rejoin it where it is. There is a sort of madness in vision such that with it I go unto the world itself, and yet at the same time the parts of that world evidently do not coexist without me (the table in itself has nothing to do with the bed a yard away); the world is the vision of the world and could not be anything else. Being is bordered along its whole extension with a vision of being that is not a being, that is a non-being. For him who really coincides with the gaze and truly installs himself in the position of the seer, this is incontestable. But is this the whole truth, and can one then formulate it by saying that there is the In Itself as position, and that the For Itself inexists as negation? This formula is evidently abstract: taken literally it would make the experience of vision impossible, for if being is wholly in itself, it is itself only in the night of identity, and my look, which draws it therefrom, destroys it as being; and if the For Itself is pure negation, it is not even For Itself, it is unaware of itself for want of *there being* something in it to be known. I never have being as it is, I have it only as interiorized, reduced to its meaning as a spectacle. And, to top it all, I do not have nothingness either—which is entirely pledged to being, and which, it is true, always misses it: but this repeated failure does not render to non-being its purity. What then do I have? I have a nothingness filled with being, a being emptied by nothingness, and if this is not the destruction of each of the terms by the other, of me by the world and of the world by me, it is necessary that the annihilation of being and the sinking of the nothingness into it not be exterior relations and not be two distinct operations. This is what one tries to achieve by thinking vision as *nihilation*. Understood in this way, it makes the In Itself itself pass to the status of a world seen, and makes the For Itself pass to the status of a For Itself sunken into being, situated, incarnated. As an operative nothingness, my vision is a ubiquitous presence to the world itself, since it is without inertia and without opacity,* and at the same time irremediably distinct from what it sees, from which it is separated by the very emptiness that permits it to be vision.[12] But we find again here, in the analysis of experience, what we have found above in the dialectic of being and nothingness: if one really abides by their opposition —if to see is to not be, and if what is seen is being—one understands that vision would be an immediate presence to the world, but one does not see how the nothingness I am could at the same time separate me from being. If it does so, if being is transcendent to the vision, it is that then one has ceased to think of it as pure non-being, and moreover has ceased to think of being as pure In Itself. Either the analytic of being and nothingness is an idealism and does not give us the brute or prereflective being we seek, or, if it is something else, this is because it goes beyond and transforms the initial definitions. Then I am no longer the pure negative, to see is no longer simply to nihilate, the relation between what I see and I who see is not one of immediate or frontal contradiction; the things attract my look, my gaze caresses the things, it espouses their contours and their reliefs, between it and them we catch sight of a complicity. As for being, I can no longer define it as a hard core of positivity

---

* The layer of the being-for-me of the world reveals: 1) a *depth* of being in itself; 2) an *opacity* of the being for itself.

12. EDITOR: These lines have been inserted here, in the course of the text itself:

"1) To say I am separated from being by a sheath of non-being— is true. But this sheath of non-being is not *me;* vision is not cognition, the I of vision is not nothingness.

2) The hard 'core of being' Sartre speaks of. There is no core with, around the [no ?] that would be me (negations, shimmering at the surface of being). That being is transcendent means precisely: it is appearances crystallizing, it is full and *empty,* it is *Gestalt* with horizon, it is duplicity of planes, it is, itself, *Verborgenheit*—it is it that perceives itself, as it is it that speaks in me."

under the negative properties that would come to it from my vision: if one subtracts them all there no longer remains anything to see; and nothing permits me to attribute them to the For Itself, which moreover is itself sunken into Being. The negations, the perspective deformations, the possibilities, which I have learned to consider as extrinsic denominations, I must now reintegrate into Being—which therefore is staggered out in depth, conceals itself at the same time that it discloses itself, is abyss and not plenitude. The analytic of Being and Nothingness spread over the things themselves an impalpable film: their *being for me,* which let us see them in themselves. Now, while on my side there has appeared the stratum of corporeal being into which my vision sinks, on the side of the things there is a profusion of perspectives which are not as nothing and which oblige me to say that the thing itself is always further on. Vision is not the immediate relationship of the For Itself with the In Itself, and we are invited to redefine the seer as well as the world seen. The analytic of Being and Nothingness is the seer who forgets that he has a body and that what he sees is always beneath what he sees, who tries to force the passage toward pure being and pure nothingness by installing himself in pure vision, who makes himself a visionary, but who is thrown back to his own opacity as a seer and to the depth of being. If we succeed in describing the access to the things themselves, it will only be through this opacity and this depth, which never cease: there is no thing fully observable, no inspection of the thing that would be without gaps and that would be total; we do not wait until we have observed it to say that the thing is there; on the contrary it is the appearance it has of being a thing that convinces us immediately that it would be possible to observe it. In the grain of the sensible we find the assurance for a series of cross-checkings, which do not constitute the ecceity of the thing but are derived from it. Conversely, the imaginary is not an absolute inobservable: it finds in the body analogues of itself that incarnate it. This distinction, like the others, has to be reconsidered and is not reducible to that between the full and the void.

For a philosophy that is installed in pure vision, in the aerial view of the panorama, there can be no encounter with another: for the look dominates; it can dominate only things, and if it falls upon men it transforms them into puppets which move only by springs. From the heights of the towers of Notre-Dame, I cannot, when I like, feel myself to be on equal footing with those who, enclosed within those walls, there minutely pursue incomprehensible tasks. High places attract those who wish to look over the world with an eagle-eye view. Vision ceases to be solipsist only up close, when the other turns back upon me the luminous rays in which I had caught him, renders precise that corporeal adhesion of which I had a presentiment in the agile movements of his eyes, enlarges beyond measure that blind spot I divined at the center of my sovereign vision, and, invading my field through all its frontiers, attracts me into the prison I had prepared for him and, as long as he is there, makes me incapable of solitude. In every case, in the solipsism as in the alienation, how would we ever find a mind, an invisible, at the end of our look? Or, if the other also is pure vision, how would we see his vision? One would have to be him. The other can enter into the universe of the seer only by assault, as a pain and a catastrophe; he will rise up not before the seer, in the spectacle, but laterally, as a radical casting into question of the seer. Since he is only pure vision, the seer cannot encounter an other, who thereby would be a thing seen; if he leaves himself, it will only be by a turning back of the vision upon himself; if he finds an other, it will only be as his own being seen. There is no perception of the other by me; abruptly my ubiquity as a seer is belied, I feel myself seen—and the other is that X yonder which I do indeed have to think in order to account for the visible body that I suddenly feel myself to have. In appearance this manner of introducing the other as the unknown is the sole one that takes into account and accounts for his alterity. If there is an other, by definition I cannot install myself in him, coincide with him, live his very life: I live only my own. If there is an other, he is never in my eyes a For Itself, in the precise and given sense that I am, for myself. Even if our relationship leads me to admit or even to experience that "he too" thinks, that "he too" has a private landscape, I am not that thought as I am my own, I do not have that private landscape as I have my own. What I say of it is always derived from what I know of myself by myself: I concede that *if I inhabited* that body I should have another solitude, comparable to that which I have, and always divergent perspectively from it. But the "if I inhabited" is not a hypothesis; it is a fiction or a myth. The other's life, such as he lives it, is not for me who speaks an eventual experience or a possible: it is a prohibited experience, it is an impossible, and this is as it must be if the other is really the other. If the other is really the other, that is, a For Itself in the strong sense that I am for myself, *he must never be so before my eyes;* it is necessary that this other For Itself never fall under my look, it is necessary that there be no perception of an other, it is necessary that the other be my negation or my destruction. Every other interpretation, under the pretext of placing us, him and myself, in the same universe of thought, ruins the alterity of the other and hence marks the triumph of a disguised solipsism. Conversely, it is in making the other not only inaccessible but invisible for me that I guarantee his alterity and quit solipsism. Yet we are not at the end of our troubles, and the labyrinth is still more difficult than we thought. For if we formulate what we have just said into theses—that is: the other can be for me, and hence can be only my being seen, the other is the unknown incumbent of that zone of the not-mine which I am indeed obliged to mark out with dotted lines in being, since I feel myself seen—this agnosticism in regard to the other's being for himself, which appeared to guarantee his alterity, suddenly appears as the worst of infringements upon it. For he who states it implies that it is applicable to all those who hear him. He does not speak only of himself, of his own perspective, and for himself; he speaks for all. He says: *the For Itself* (in general) is alone . . . , or: *the being for another* is the death of the For Itself, or things of this kind—without specifying whether this concerns the being for itself such as he lives it or the being for itself such as those who hear him live it, the being for another such as he experiences it or the being for another such as the others experience it. This singular that he permits himself—the For Itself, the For the Other—indicates that he means to speak in the name of all, that in his description he implies the power to speak for all, whereas the description contests this power. Hence I only apparently confine myself to my own experience— to my being for myself and to my being for another—and only apparently respect the radical originality of the for itself of another and his being for me. From the sole fact that I open in the wall of my solipsism the breach through which the gaze of another passes, it is no longer a dichotomy that I am dealing with—that of "the" For Itself and of "the" For the Other—it is a

[handwritten margin note: Other is inaccessible & invisible to me —]

four-term system: my being for me, my being for the other, the for itself of another, and his being for me. The void that I wished to provide at the horizon of my universe, in order to lodge in it the author of my shame and the inconceivable image of me he forms, is not, whatever I may think, a void; it is not the simple or immediate negation of myself and of my universe. From the sole fact that I circumscribe it, be it with dotted lines, it is cut out in my universe; there is an intersection of my universe with that of another. We do not have *the* For Itself in general with *the* In Itself in general which it sustains, *the* For the Other in general, that is, the possibility for *every* For Itself to be incorporated into *the* In Itself in general by a foreign look; in other words we do not have my being for me and my being for the other virtually multiplied to *n* samples—we have face to face my being for myself, this same being for me offered as a spectacle to the other, the gaze of another as bearer of a being for itself which is a rejoinder of my own, but capable of petrifying (*méduser*) my own, and finally this same being for itself of the other aimed at and in some way reached, perceived, by my gaze upon him. There is, to be sure, no question of a reciprocal relationship between me and the other, since I am alone to be myself, since I am for myself the sole original of humanity, and the philosophy of vision is right in emphasizing the inevitable dissymmetry of the I-Other relation. But, in spite of appearances, it is the philosophy of vision that installs itself dogmatically in all the situations at the same time, by declaring them impenetrable, by thinking each of them as the absolute negation of the others. I cannot even go the length of this absolute in negation; the negation here is a dogmatism, it secretly contains the absolute affirmation of the opposites. It is necessary that there be transition from the other to me and from me to the other precisely in order that I and the others not be posed dogmatically as universes equivalent by principle, and in order that the privilege of the For Itself for itself be recognized. In founding the experience of the other upon that of my objectification before him, the philosophy of vision believed it established between him and me a relationship that would be at the same time a relation of being—since it is in my very being that I am affected by the view the other gets of me—and a relation of pure negation, since this objectification which I undergo is literally incomprehensible to me. Here once again we find that one must choose: either [13] the relationship is really a relationship of being, in which case it is necessary that the other have in my eyes the status of a For Itself, that the outside of myself on which he has a hold also put me at his mercy as a pure For Itself, that my constitutive nothingness sink into my situation under my own eyes. And finally it is necessary that, instead of the other and me being two parallel For Itselfs each on his own stricken with the same mortal evil—the other's presence, which crushes us each in turn in the midst of our own universe of the In Itself—we be some for the others [14] a system

13. EDITOR: There is no *or* expressed in the continuation of the text. The reflection on the first term of the alternative decides the issue of the second. For, as will immediately become apparent, to say that the other does not crush me into my universe of the in itself is the same as to say that he is not the inexplicable negation of the For Itself I am. The author moreover returns to this latter idea in the note below.

14. Some for the others and not only each for the other (*Les uns pour les autres et non pas seulement l'un pour l'autre*). The problem of the other is always posed by the philosophies of the negative in the form of the problem of *the* other, as though the whole difficulty were to pass from the *one* to the *other*. This is significant: the other is not here *an other;* he is the non-I in general, the judge who condemns me or acquits me, and to whom I do not even think of opposing other judges. But, if one can show, as was done, for example, in Simone de Beauvoir's *She Came to Stay*, that a trio decomposes into three couples, and—in supposing that there are, outside of all abstract reciprocity, successful couples—that there can be no trio that would be successful in the same sense, since it adds to the difficulties of the couple those of the concord between the three possible couples of which it is composed—still the fact remains that the problem of the other is not reducible to that of *the* other, and so much the less so in that the most strict couple always has its witnesses in third parties. Perhaps it even would be necessary to reverse the customary order of the philosophies of the negative, and say that the problem of *the* other is a particular case of the problem of others, since the relation with someone is always mediated by the relationship with third parties, that these have relationships among themselves that command those of *the* one and those of *the* other—and that this is so as far back as one goes toward the beginnings of life, since the Oedipus situation is still a triangular one. Now this is not only a matter of psychology, but also of philosophy —not only of the contents of the relationship with an other, but of its form and its essence as well: if the access to the other is an entry into a constellation of others (where there are of course stars of several magnitudes), it is difficult to maintain that the other be nothing but

of For Itselfs, sensitive to one another, such that the one knows the other not only in what he suffers from him, but more generally as a witness, who can be challenged because he is also himself accused, because he is not a pure gaze upon pure being any more than I am, because his views and my own are in advance inserted into a system of partial perspectives, referred to one same world in which we coexist and where our views intersect. For the other to be truly the other, it does not suffice and it is not necessary that he be a scourge, the continued threat of an absolute reversal of pro and con, a judge himself elevated above all contestation, without place, without relativities, faceless like an obsession, and capable of crushing me with a glance into the dust of my world. It is necessary and it suffices that he have the power to decenter me, to oppose his centering to my own, and he can do so only because we are not two nihilations installed in two universes of the In Itself, incomparable, but two entries to the same Being, each accessible to but one of us, but appearing to the other as *practicable by right*, because they both belong to the same Being. It is necessary and it suffices that the other's body which I see and his word which I hear, which are given to me as immediately present in my field, *do present to me in their own fashion what I will never be present to*, what will always be invisible to me, what I will never directly witness—an absence therefore, but not just any absence, a certain absence and a certain difference in terms of dimensions which are from the first common to us and which predestine the other to be a mirror of me as I am of him, which are responsible for the fact

---

the absolute negation of myself. For when it is a matter of absolute negation there is but one of them; it absorbs into itself every rival negation. Even if we have one *principal other*, from whom are derived many secondary others in our life, the sole fact that he is not the unique other obliges us to comprehend him not as an absolute negation but as a negation-model, that is, in the last analysis, not as what contests my life but as what forms it, not as another universe in which I would be alienated but as the preferred variant of a life that has never been only my own. Even if each of us has his own archetype of the other, the very fact that he is open to participation, that he is a sort of cipher or symbol of the other, obliges us to pose the problem of the other, not as a problem of access to another nihilation, but as a problem of initiation to a symbolics and a typicality of the others of which the *being for itself* and the *being for the other* are reflective variants and not the essential forms.

that we do not have two images side by side of someone and of ourselves, but one sole image in which we are both involved, which is responsible for the fact that my consciousness of myself and my myth of the other are not two contradictories, but rather each the reverse of the other. It is perhaps all that that is meant when it is said that the other is the X responsible for my being-seen. But then it would be necessary to add that he can be this only because I see that he looks at me, and that he can look at me —me, the invisible—only because we belong to the same system of being for itself and being for another; we are moments of the same syntax, we count in the same world, we belong to the same Being. But this has no meaning for man taken as a pure vision: he does indeed have the conviction of going unto the things themselves, but, surprised in the act of seeing, suddenly he becomes one of them, and there is no passage from the one view to the other. Pure seer, he becomes a thing seen through an ontological catastrophe, through a pure event which is for him the impossible. Or, if he can comprehend it, it will be only by backing down on the alleged ubiquity of the vision, by foregoing the idea of being everything, that is, of being nothing, by learn-ing to know, within the vision itself, a sort of palpation of the things, within the overhead survey itself, an inherence. To be sure, our world is principally and essentially visual; one would not make a world out of scents or sounds. But the privilege of vision is not to open *ex nihilo* upon a pure being *ad infinitum:* the vision too has a field, a range. Only at very great distances are the things it gives us pure things, identical to themselves and wholly positive, like the stars, and this horizon of the In Itself is visible only as the background of a zone of nearby things which, for their part, are open and inexhaustible.

Whether we are considering my relations with the things or my relations with the other (the two problems are but one, since the insularity of the For Itselfs is spanned only by their openness to the "same" things), the question is whether in the last analysis our life takes place between an absolutely individual and abso-lutely universal nothingness behind us and an absolutely individ-ual and absolutely universal being before us—in which case we have the incomprehensible and impossible task of restoring to Being, in the form of thoughts and actions, everything we have taken from it, that is, everything that we are—or whether every relation between me and Being, even vision, even speech, is not a carnal relation, with the flesh of the world. In this case "pure" being only shows through at the horizon, at a distance which is not nothing, which is not spread out by me, which is something, which therefore itself belongs to being, which, between the "pure" being and myself, is the thickness of its being for me, of its being for the others—and which finally makes what merits the name of being be not the horizon of "pure" being but the system of perspectives that open into it, makes the integral being be not before me, but at the intersection of my views and at the intersection of my views with those of the others, at the intersection of my acts and at the intersection of my acts with those of the others, makes the sensible world and the historical world be always intermundane spaces, since they are what, beyond our views, renders them interdependent among themselves and interdependent with those of the others; they are the instances to which we address ourselves as soon as we live, the registers in which is inscribed what we see, what we do, to become there thing, world, history. Far from opening upon the blinding light of pure Being or of the Object, our life has, in the astronomical sense of the word, an atmosphere: it is constantly enshrouded by those mists we call the sensible world or history, the one [15] of the corporeal life and the one of the human life, the present and the past, as a pell-mell ensemble of bodies and minds, promiscuity of visages, words, actions, with, between them all, that cohesion which cannot be denied them since they are all differences, extreme divergencies of one same something. Before this inextricable involvement, there are two types of error; one is to deny it—under the pretext that it can be broken up by the accidents of my body, by death, or simply by my freedom. But this does not mean that when it does take place it would be only the sum of the partial processes without which it does not exist. The principle of principles here is that one cannot judge the powers of life by those of death, nor define without arbitrariness life as the sum of the forces that resist death, as if

15. TRANSLATOR: The indefinite pronoun *on* used to name the anonymous, prepersonal subject. "We must conceive of a primordial [One] (*on*) that has its own authenticity and furthermore never ceases but continues to uphold the greatest passions of our adult life and to be experienced anew in each of our perceptions" (*Signes* [Paris, 1960], p. 221). [English translation by Richard C. McCleary, *Signs* (Evanston, Ill., 1960), p. 175.]

it were the necessary and sufficient definition of Being to be the suppression of non-being. The involvement of men in the world and of men in one another, even if it can be brought about only by means of *perceptions* and *acts*, is transversal with respect to the spatial and temporal multiplicity of the actual. But this must not lead us into the inverse error, which would be to treat this order of involvement as a transcendental, intemporal order, as a system of a priori conditions: that would be to postulate once again that life is only death nullified, since one thinks oneself obliged to explain by an outside principle everything in it that exceeds the simple summation of its necessary conditions. The openness upon a natural and historical world is not an illusion and is not an a priori; it is our involvement in Being. Sartre expressed this by saying that the For Itself is necessarily haunted by an imaginary In-Itself-for-itself. We only say that the In-Itself-for-itself is more than imaginary. The imaginary is without consistence, inobservable; it vanishes when one proceeds to vision. Thus the In-Itself-for-itself breaks up before the philosophical consciousness to give place to the Being which is and the Nothingness which is not, to the rigorous thought of a Nothingness which needs Being, which attains it by being a negation of itself, and which thus accomplishes the silent self-affirmation that was immanent in Being. The truth of the Sartrean In-Itself-for-itself is the intuition of pure Being and the negintuition of Nothingness. It seems to us that on the contrary it is necessary to recognize in it the solidity of myth, that is, of an operative imaginary, which is part of our institution, and which is indispensable for the definition of Being itself. With this difference, we are indeed speaking of the same thing; and Sartre has himself pointed out what intervenes between Being and Nothingness.

A philosophy of negativity, which lays down nothing qua nothing (and consequently being qua being) as the principle of its research, thinks these invisibles in their purity, and at the same time admits that the knowing of nothingness is a nothingness of knowing, that nothingness is accessible only in bastard forms, is incorporated into being. The philosophy of negativity is indissolubly logic and experience: in it the dialectic of being and nothingness is only a preparation for experience, and in return experience, such as it has described it, is sustained and elaborated by the pure entity of being, the pure negentity of nothingness. The pure negative, in negating itself, sacrifices itself to the positive; the pure positive, insofar as it affirms itself without restriction, sanctions this sacrifice—this movement of significations, which is only the being of being and the inexistence of nothingness followed into their consequences, the principle of non-contradiction put into application, gives the schema of a pure vision with which the philosopher coincides. If I identify myself with my view of the world, if I consider it in act and without any reflective withdrawal, it is indeed the concentration in a point of nothingness, where being itself, being such as it is in itself, becomes being-seen. What there is common to both the concrete descriptions and the logical analysis—even more: what in a philosophy of the negative identifies the absolute distinction between being and nothingness and the description of nothingness sunken into being—is that they are two forms of immediate thought. On the one hand, one seeks being and nothingness in the pure state, one wishes to approach them as closely as possible, one aims at being itself in its plenitude and nothingness itself in its vacuity, one presses the confused experience until one draws the entity and the negentity out of it, one squeezes it between them as between pincers; beyond the visible one trusts entirely in *what* we think under the terms of being and nothingness, one practices an "essentialist" thought which refers to significations beyond experience, and thus one constructs our relations with the world. And at the same time one installs oneself in our condition of being seers, one coincides with it, one oneself exercises the vision of which one speaks, one says nothing that does not come from the vision itself lived from within. The clarification of the significations is one with the exercise of life because it is tacitly understood that to live or to think is always (as one wants to say) to identify oneself, or to nihilate. If a philosophy of the negative is at the same time a determination of essences and a coinciding with lived experience, this is not due to accident, inconsistency, or eclecticism, but because spontaneity consists in being in the mode of not-being, the reflective critique in not being in the mode of being, and because these two relationships form a circuit which is us. In this universal ambivalence, the philosophy of the negative is, we said, ungraspable: and indeed everything one opposes to it, it accepts. That nothingness is not? That the idea of nothingness is a pseudo-idea? That being is transcendent or that the "human reality" is access to a being? That it is not man that has being, but being that has man? It is the first to agree; these are its own principles. The only thing is that in it they are identified with the opposite principles: precisely because the *nichtiges Nichts* is not, the "there is" is reserved to a being unalloyed, positive, full. Precisely because there is no idea of nothingness, nothingness nihilates freely while being is. Precisely because transcendence is access to a Being and flight from the Self, this centrifugal and impalpable force, which is us, presides over every apparition of Being, and it is in starting from the Self, by ec-stasy or alienation, that the "there is" is produced. Being has man, but because man gives himself to it. Whence comes that sort of sentiment of uneasiness that a philosophy of the negative leaves: it described our factual situation with more penetration than had ever before been done —and yet one retains the impression that this situation is one that is being surveyed from above, and indeed it is: the more one describes experience as a compound of being and nothingness, the more their absolute distinction is confirmed; the more the thought adheres to experience, the more it keeps it at a distance. Such is the sorcery of the thought of the negative. But this also means that it cannot be circumscribed or discerned by what it affirms—it affirms everything—but only by what it leaves aside, precisely in its will to be everything: that is to say, the situation of the philosopher who speaks as distinct from what he speaks of, insofar as that situation affects what he says with a certain latent content which is not its manifest content, insofar as it implies a divergence between the essences he fixes and the lived experience to which they are applied, between the operation of living the world and the entities and negentities in which he expresses it. If one takes this residue into account, there is no longer identity between the lived experience and the principle of non-contradiction; the thought, precisely as thought, can no longer flatter itself that it conveys all the lived experience: it retains everything, save its density and its weight. The lived experience can no longer recognize itself in the idealizations we draw from it. Between the thought or fixation of essences, which is the aerial view, and life, which is inherence in the world or vision, a divergence reappears, which forbids the thought to project itself in advance in the experience and invites it to recommence the description from closer up. For a philosophy conscious of itself as a cognition, as a second fixation of a pre-existing experience, the formula *being is, nothingness is not* is an idealization, an approximation of the total situation, which involves, beyond *what* we say, the mute experience from which we draw what we say. And just as we are invited to rediscover behind the vision, as immediate presence to being, the flesh of being and the flesh of the seer, so also must we rediscover the common milieu where being and nothingness are only λέκτα laboring each against the other. Our point of departure shall not be *being is, nothingness is not* nor even *there is only being*— which are formulas of a totalizing thought, a high-altitude thought—but: there is being, there is a world, there is *something;* in the strong sense in which the Greek speaks of τὸ λέγειν, there is cohesion, there is meaning. One does not arouse being from nothingness, *ex nihilo;* one starts with an ontological relief where one can never say that the ground be nothing. What is primary is not the full and positive being upon a ground of nothingness; it is a field of appearances, each of which, taken separately, will perhaps subsequently break up or be crossed out (this is the part of nothingness), but of which I only know that it will be replaced by another which will be the truth of the first, because there is a world, because there is something—a world, a something, which in order to be do not first have to nullify the nothing. It is still saying too much of nothingness to say that it *is not,* that it is pure negation: that is to fix it in its negativity, to treat it as a sort of essence, to introduce the positivity of words into it, whereas it can count only as what has neither name, nor repose, nor nature. By principle, a philosophy of the negative cannot start from "pure" negation, nor make of it the agent of its own negation. In reversing the positions of the philosophy of reflection, which put all the positive within and treated the outside as a simple negative, by on the contrary defining the mind as the pure negative which lives only from its contact with the exterior being, the philosophy of the negative bypasses the goal: once again, even though now for opposite reasons, it renders impossible that *openness upon being* which is the perceptual faith. The philosophy of reflection did not account for it, for lack of providing a distance between the idea and the idea of the idea, between the reflecting and the unreflected. It is again that distance that is lacking now, since he who thinks, being nothing, cannot be separated by anything from him who perceived naïvely, nor he who perceived naïvely from what he perceived. There is no openness upon being for a philosophy of thought and of our immanent thoughts—but there is none either for a philosophy of nothingness and being, for no more in this case than in the other is being far-off, at a distance, for good. Thought is too much closed in upon itself, but nothingness is too much outside of itself for one to be able to speak of openness upon being, and in this respect immanence and transcendence are indistinguishable. Let it be so, it will perhaps be said; let us start then with the openness upon being. Yet is it not necessary, in order for there really to be openness, that we leave the metaphysical plenum, that *he* who is open to being and who sees be an absolute lacuna in being, and finally that he be purely negative? Otherwise are we not driven from appearance to appearance, like the vulgar relativism, without the absolute appearance or consciousness, nor being in itself, ever coming to pass? Without the absolute negativity, are we not in a universe of physical or psychic images which float about without anyone being conscious of them? The objection postulates what is in question, that is, that one can think only beings (physical, physiological, "psychic") or "consciousnesses" absolutely foreign to existence as a thing. It announces the return to the reflective dichotomies of a thought that has less surmounted them than incorporated them in advance into the spontaneous life.

We do not think then that the dichotomy of Being and Nothingness continues to hold when one arrives at the descriptions of nothingness sunken into being; it seems to us therefore that it is an abstract introduction to those descriptions and that from the introduction to the descriptions there is movement, progress, surpassing. Could we not express this simply by saying that for the intuition of being and the negintuition of nothingness must be substituted a *dialectic*? From the most superficial level to the most profound, dialectical thought is that which admits reciprocal actions or interactions—which admits therefore that the total relation between a term *A* and a term *B* cannot be expressed in one sole proposition, that that relation covers over several others which cannot be superimposed, which are even opposed, which define so many points of view logically incompossible and yet really united within it—even more that each of these relations leads to its opposite or to its own reversal, and does so by its own movement. Thus Being, through the very exigency of each

[margin notes: wants / Nothingness / Sunk into / being -]

[margin notes: dialectical / thought - / that wch / admits / reciprocal / actions & / interaction]

of the perspectives, and from the exclusive point of view that defines it, becomes a system with several entries. Hence it cannot be contemplated from without and in simultaneity, but must be effectively traversed. In this transition, the stages passed through are not simply passed, like the segment of the road I have traveled; they have called for or required the present stages and precisely what is new and disconcerting in them. The past stages continue therefore to be in the present stages—which also means that they are retroactively modified by them. Hence there is a question here not of a thought that follows a pre-established route but of a thought that itself traces its own course, that finds itself by advancing, that makes its own way, and thus proves that the way is practicable. This thought wholly subjugated to its content, from which it receives its incitement, could not express itself as a reflection or copy of an exterior process; it is the engendering of a relation starting from the other. Being neither an outside witness nor a pure agent, it is implicated in the movement and does not view it from above. In particular it does not formulate itself in successive statements which would have to be taken as they stand; each statement, in order to be true, must be referred, throughout the whole movement, to the stage from which it arises and has its full sense only if one takes into account not only what it says expressly but also its place within the whole which constitutes its latent content. Thus, he who speaks (and that which he understands tacitly) always codetermines the meaning of what he says, the philosopher is always implicated in the problems he poses, and there is no truth if one does not take into account, in the appraising of every statement, the presence of the philosopher who makes the statement. Between the manifest content and the latent content, there can be not only differences but also contradiction, and yet this double meaning belongs to the statement—as when we want to consider a thing *in itself,* and in doing so, concentrating ourselves on it, we come to determine it such as it is *for us.* Hence for the dialectical thought, the idea of the In Itself and the idea of the For Us have each its truth outside of itself, do not belong to the total or full thought, which would define itself throughout a limitless explicitation. In sum, therefore, whether in the relations within being or in the relations of being with me, dialectical thought is that which admits that each term is itself only by proceeding toward the opposed term, becomes what it is through the movement, that it is one and the same thing for each to pass into the other or to become itself, to leave itself or to retire into itself, that the centripetal movement and the centrifugal movement are one sole movement, because each term is its own mediation, the exigency for a becoming, and even for an auto-destruction which gives the other. If such is the dialectical thought, is this not what we have tried to apply to the dichotomy of Being and Nothingness? Has not our discussion consisted in showing that the relationship between the two terms (whether one takes them in a relative sense, within the world, or in an absolute sense, as the index of the thinker and of what he thinks) covers a swarm of relations with double meaning, incompatible and yet necessary to one another (complementary, as the physicists say today), and that this complex totality is the truth of the abstract dichotomy from which we started? Is not the dialectic, through its avatars, in every case the reversal of relationships, their solidarity throughout the reversal, the intelligible movement which is not a sum of positions or of statements such as *being is, nothingness is not* but which distributes them over several planes, integrates them into a being in depth? Particularly in what concerns the relations between thought and Being, is not the dialectic the refusal of high-altitude thinking, of the wholly exterior being as well as the reflexivity? Is it not thought at work within Being, in contact with Being, for which it opens a space for manifestation, but in which all its own initiatives are inscribed, recorded, or sedimented, if only as errors surmounted, and take on the form of a history which has its sense, even if it turns in circles or marches in zigzags? In sum, is it not exactly the thought we are seeking, not ambivalent, "ventriloquial," but capable of differentiating and of integrating into one sole universe the double or even multiple meanings, as Heraclitus has already showed us opposite directions coinciding in the circular movement? This thought is capable of effecting this integration because the circular movement is neither the simple sum of the opposed movements nor a third movement added to them, but their *common meaning,* the two component movements visible as one sole movement, *having become* a totality, that is, a spectacle: thus because the dialectic is the thought of the Being-seen, of a Being that is not simple positivity, the In Itself, and not the Being-posed by a thought, but *Self-manifestation,* disclosure, in the process of forming itself. . . .

The dialectic is indeed all this, and it is, in this sense, what we are looking for. If nonetheless we have not hitherto said so, it is because, in the history of philosophy, it has never been all that unadulteratedly; it is because the dialectic is unstable (in the sense that the chemists give to the word), it is even essentially and by definition unstable, so that it has never been able to formulate itself into theses without denaturing itself, and because if one wishes to maintain its spirit it is perhaps necessary to not even name it. The sort of being to which it refers, and which we have been trying to indicate, is in fact not susceptible of being designated positively. It abounds in the sensible world, but on condition that the sensible world has been divested of all that the ontologies have added to it. One of the tasks of the dialectic, as a situational thought, a thought in contact with being, is to shake off the false evidences, to denounce the significations cut off from the experience of being, emptied—and to criticize itself in the measure that it itself becomes one of them. But this is what it is in danger of becoming as soon as it is stated in theses, in univocal significations, as soon as it is detached from its ante-predicative context. It is essential to it that it be autocritical—and it is also essential to it to forget this as soon as it becomes what we call *a philosophy*. The very formulas by which it describes the movement of being are then liable to falsify that movement. Take the profound idea of *self-mediation* (*médiation par soi*), of a movement through which each term ceases to be itself in order to become itself, breaks up, opens up, negates itself, in order to realize itself. It can remain pure only if the mediating term and the mediated term—which are "the same"—are yet not the same in the sense of identity: for then, in the absence of all difference, there would be no mediation, movement, transformation; one would remain in full positivity. But there is no self-mediation either if the mediator is the simple or absolute negation of the mediated: the absolute negation would simply annihilate the mediated and, turning against itself, would annihilate itself also, so that there would still be no mediation, but a pure and simple retreat toward positivity. It is therefore ruled out that the mediation have its origin in the positive term, as though it were one of its *properties*—but it is likewise precluded that the mediation come to the positive term from an abyss of exterior negativity, which would have no hold on it and would leave it intact. Yet it is in this second manner that the

dialectic is translated when it ceases to be a way of deciphering
the being with which we are in contact, the being in the process
of manifesting itself, the situational being, and when it wishes to
formulate itself once and for all, without anything left over, state
itself as a doctrine, sum itself up. Then, to get to the end, the
negation is carried to the absolute, becomes negation of itself; at
the same time being sinks back to the pure positive, the negation
concentrates itself beyond it as absolute subjectivity—and the
dialectical movement becomes pure identity of the opposites,
ambivalence. It is thus that in Hegel, God, defined as abyss or
absolute subjectivity, negates himself in order that the world be,
that is, in order that there be a view upon himself that would not
be his own and to which he would appear as posterior to being;
in other words, God makes himself man—so that the philosophy
of Hegel is an ambivalence of the theological and the anthropo-
logical. It is not otherwise that, for Sartre, the absolute opposition of Being and Nothingness gives place to a return to the
positive, to a sacrifice of the For Itself—except that he rigorously
maintains the consciousness of the negative as a margin about
being, the negation of negation is not for him a speculative
operation, an unfolding of God, and the In-Itself-for-itself consequently remains for him the natural illusion of the For Itself.
But, with these reservations, the same metamorphosis of the
dialectic, the same relapse into ambivalence occurs in both
cases, and for the same reason: because the thought ceases to
accompany or to be the dialectical movement, converts it into
signification, thesis, or thing said, and thereby falls back into the
ambivalent image of the Nothingness that sacrifices itself in
order that Being be and of the Being that, from the depths of its
primacy, tolerates being recognized by the Nothingness. There is
a trap in the dialectic: whereas it is the very movement of the
content, as it is realized by auto-constitution, or the art of retrac-
ing and following the relations between the appeal and the response, the problem and the solution, whereas the *dialectic* is by
principle an epithet, as soon as one takes it as a motto, speaks
of it instead of practicing it, it becomes a power of being, an explicative principle. What was Being's manner of being becomes
an evil genius. Oh, Dialectic! says the philosopher, when he
comes to recognize that perhaps the true philosophy flouts philosophy. Here the dialectic is almost someone; like the irony of
things, it is a spell cast over the world that turns our expectations

into derision, a sly power behind our back that confounds us, and, to top it all, has its own order and its rationality; it is not only a risk of non-sense, therefore, but much worse: the assurance that the things have *another sense* than that which we are in a position to recognize in them. Already we are on the way of the bad dialectic, that which, against its own principles, imposes an external law and framework upon the content and restores for its own uses the pre-dialectical thought. Dialectical thought by principle excludes all *extrapolation,* since it teaches that there can always be a supplement of being in being, that quantitative differences veer into the qualitative, that the consciousness as consciousness of the exterior, being partial, abstract, is always deceived by the event. But this very slipping away of life and of history, which resolves the problems otherwise than the consciousness of the exterior would have done (sometimes better, sometimes not so well), is understood as a vector, a polarity of the dialectical movement, a preponderant force that always works in the same direction, that, in the name of the process, extends over the process, and therefore authorizes the determination of the ineluctable. And this is what happens as soon as the *meaning* of the dialectical movement is defined apart from the concrete constellation. The bad dialectic begins almost with the dialectic, and there is no good dialectic but that which criticizes itself and surpasses itself as a separate statement; the only good dialectic is the hyperdialectic. The bad dialectic is that which does not wish to lose its soul in order to save it, which wishes to be dialectical immediately, becomes autonomous, and ends up at cynicism, at formalism, for having eluded its own double meaning. What we call hyperdialectic is a thought that on the contrary is capable of reaching truth because it envisages without restriction the plurality of the relationships and what has been called ambiguity. The bad dialectic is that which thinks it recomposes being by a thetic thought, by an assemblage of statements, by thesis, antithesis, and synthesis; the good dialectic is that which is conscious of the fact that every *thesis* is an idealization, that Being is not made up of idealizations or of things said, as the old logic believed, but of bound wholes where signification never is except in tendency, where the inertia of the content never permits the defining of one term as positive, another term as negative, and still less a third term as absolute suppression of the negative by itself. The point to be noted is this: that the dialectic without synthesis of which we speak is not therefore scepticism, vulgar relativism, or the reign of the ineffable. What we reject or deny is not the idea of a surpassing that reassembles, it is the idea that it results in a new positive, a new position. In thought and in history as in life the only surpassings we know are concrete, partial, encumbered with survivals, saddled with deficits; there is no surpassing in all regards that would retain everything the preceding phases had acquired, mechanically add something more, and permit the ranking of the dialectical phases in a hierarchical order from the less to the more real, from the less to the more valid. But, on a defined part of the route, there can be progresses; especially there are solutions excluded in the long run. In other words, what we exclude from the dialectic is the idea of the pure negative, what we seek is a dialectical definition of being that can be neither the being for itself nor the being in itself—rapid, fragile, labile definitions, which, as Hegel rightly said, lead us back from the one to the other—nor the In-Itself-for-itself which is the height of ambivalence, [a definition] [16] that must rediscover the being that lies before the cleavage operated by reflection, about it, on its horizon, not outside of us and not in us, but there where the two movements cross, there where "there is" something.

PERCEPTUAL FAITH AND INTERROGATION

THESE REMARKS concerning negativity permit us already to make more precise the meaning of our question before the world, for the most difficult part is to avoid mistaking what it is, what it can be, its exact and proper meaning, what it asks. We already know that it is not a question as to whether the world really is, or whether it is only a well-regulated dream: that question covers over others; it supposes that the dream, the image, be known, and be better known—it interrogates the world only in the name of an alleged positivity of the psychic. It casts over the world the shadow of a possible non-existence—but it does not elucidate the mental existence it substitutes for it, which in fact it conceives as a weakened or degraded real existence. And if the doubt thus understood were lifted through some

16. EDITOR: We reintroduce this term between brackets to eliminate ambiguity.

argument, the "real" existence which would be restored to our dreams would be the very same real existence, obscure and incomprehensible, with which we started, and everything would have to be begun over again. We are not asking ourselves if the world exists; we are asking what it is for it to exist. But even thus transformed, the question is not yet radical. For one can understand it still in a surface sense that hides its true mainspring. When we ask what it is for the things and for the world to exist, one might think that it is only a matter of defining a word. After all, the questions take place in language. Even if it seems to us that an affirmative thought can detach itself from words and rest on its internal adequation, negation and especially interrogation, which do not express any property intrinsic to the things, can be sustained only by the apparatus of language. One can therefore be tempted to count the philosophical question concerning the world among the facts of language, and it would seem that the response can be sought only in the meanings of words, since it is in words that the question will be answered. But our previous reflections have already taught us that this would be to evade it: the question concerning the meaning of the world's being is so little solvable by a definition of words—which would be drawn from the study of language, its powers, and the effective conditions for its functioning—that on the contrary it reappears within the study of language, which is but a particular form of it. One can reduce philosophy to a linguistic analysis only by supposing that language has its evidence within itself, that the signification of the word "world" or "thing" presents in principle no difficulty, that the rules for the legitimate use of the word can be clearly read in a univocal signification. But the linguists teach us that this is precisely not the case, that the univocal signification is but one part of the signification of the word, that beyond it there is always a halo of signification that manifests itself in new and unexpected modes of use, that there is an operation of language upon language which, even without other incitements, would launch language back into a new history, and makes of the word-meaning itself an enigma. Far from harboring the secret of the being of the world, language is itself a world, itself a being—a world and a being to the second power, since it does not speak in a vacuum, since it speaks *of* being and *of* the world and therefore redoubles their enigma instead of dissipating it. The philosophical interrogation concerning the world therefore does not consist in referring from the world itself to what we say of the world, since it is reiterated within language. To philosophize is not to cast the things into doubt in the name of the words, as if the universe of things said were clearer than that of the brute things, as if the effective world were a canton of language, perception a confused and mutilated speech, the signification of words a perfectly reassuring sphere of positivity. But this observation does not only argue against a positivism of language: it affects every attempt to seek the source of meaning in pure significations, even when no mention is made of language. The philosophical interrogation about the world cannot consist, for example, in casting into doubt the world in itself or the things in themselves for the profit of an order of "human phenomena," that is, of the coherent system of appearances such as we men can construct it, in the factual conditions that are ours, according to our psychophysical constitution and the types of connections that make the relation to an "object" possible for us. Whether this construction of the object be understood in terms of the method of the sciences and by the means of algorithm, or whether one confronts the *constructa* with the concrete because science after all wishes to be a *scientia intuitiva*, an understanding of the world itself, or whether finally one envisages more generally rendering explicit the acts and attitudes of all kinds—emotional, practical, axiological—by which a consciousness refers itself to objects or quasi-objects, refers them to one another, and effects the transition from one attitude to another—in all cases the question posed is not yet radical, ultimate. For over against the things and the world, which are obscure, one gives oneself the field of operations of consciousness and of the constructed significations whose terminal product one supposes the world and the things to be—and, before this field as before the field of language (which in fact it presupposes), the philosopher must ask himself if it is closed, if it suffices to itself, if, as an *artefact*,[17] it does not open upon an original perspective of natural being, if, even supposing it decisive in what concerns the being-verified, the being-averred, the being converted into an *object*, it does not have a horizon of brute being and of brute mind, from which the constructed objects and the significations emerge and which they do not account for.

17. TRANSLATOR: In English in the text.

Thus is specified the sense of our astonishment in face of the perceived world. It is not the Pyrrhonian doubt, it is not even the appeal to an immanent domain of positive thought of which the perceived world would be but the shadow: the shadow is in us rather than outside. In suspending the evidence of the world, in seeking recourse in our thought or our consciousness of the world, its operations and its theses, we would find nothing that surpasses or simply equals and explains the solidity of the world under our eyes and the cohesion of our life in it. By reversal of the pro and the con, we have come not only to rehabilitate negative thought as an original way of thinking, but also to formulate negatively—as that without which there is no representation—the principle of causality, and finally to conceive as negativity thought, which for Spinoza was the positive itself. Should it now be necessary to complete or rather to go beyond this reversal by saying that I am not capable of being for myself unless, at the center of myself, I am nothing at all, but that this central void must be borne by being, by a situation, a world, is never knowable except as the focus their perspectives indicate, and that in this sense there is a priority of being over thought? Thus would be brought to a close the cycle opened when Descartes showed that the thought of seeing is more certain than the thing seen or the vision—that the thought, precisely because it is nothing but absolute appearance, is absolutely indubitable and that, midway between being and nothingness, it stands more solid before the doubt than the positive and full things. To be sure, Descartes and Cartesianism had finally pushed this thinking thing which only half is over to the side of Being: since it is after all not nothing, and since nothingness has no properties, it became the sign and the trace of an infinite Being, of a spiritual positivity. But the withdrawal from the world, the return to the interior man, the *no* of reflection had all the same been installed in philosophy by the *cogito,* and had to produce in it all their consequences the day that the thought no longer believed it could grasp in itself the spontaneous genesis of a Being that is self-caused. Then negativity, which is not visible or has no properties, could no longer be borne by anything but by the world itself, could no longer be anything but a lacuna in Being. Between it and the world there would no longer even be room for the suspension of the doubt; the negativity in act would be existence itself, or at least the "there is" of the world, and philosophy would cease to be a question in order to be the consciousness of this double-faced act, of this no that is a yes, of this yes that is a no. The long evolution that had moved the positive from the world over to the side of the consciousness, which had become the correlative of the world and its connecting principle—but that at the same time prepared philosophy to install non-being as the pivot of being—would abruptly be concluded at the extremity of idealism by the rehabilitation and the primacy of the In Itself. . . .

This is what has finally appeared to us to be impossible. It seemed to us that this final avatar overcompensated for idealism rather than overcame it, that my immediate presence to the In Itself, established and undone at the same time by the infinite distance from what is nothing to what is, was, rather than a solution, a seesaw movement from realism to idealism. Philosophy is not a rupture with the world, nor a coinciding with it, but it is not the alternation of rupture and coincidence either. This double relation, which the philosophy of *Being and Nothingness* expresses so well, remains perhaps incomprehensible there because it is still a consciousness—a being that is wholly appearing—that is charged with bearing it. It has seemed to us that the task was to describe strictly our relation to the world not as an openness of nothingness upon being, but simply as openness: it is through openness that we will be able to understand being and nothingness, not through being and nothingness that we will be able to understand openness. From the point of view of *Being and Nothingness,* the openness upon being means that I visit it in itself: if it remains distant, this is because nothingness, the anonymous one in me that sees, pushes before itself a zone of void where being no longer only is, but *is seen.* It is therefore my constitutive nothingness that makes the distance from being as well as its proximity, the perspective as distinct from the thing itself, that constitutes the limits of my field into limits. It crosses these limits, this distance, by forming it; it makes perspectives arise only by first effectuating the flat projection; it goes to the *whole* because it is *nothing.* Then there is no longer any *something* and no longer openness, for there is no longer a labor of the look against its limits, there is no longer that inertia of the vision that makes us say that we have an openness upon the world. That sort of diaphragm of the vision, which through a compromise with the whole to be seen yields my point of view upon the world, is to be sure not fixed: nothing prevents us from crossing the limits with the movements of the look, but this freedom remains secretly bound; we can only displace our look, that is, transfer its limits elsewhere. But it is necessary that there be always a limit; what is won on one side must be lost from the other. An indirect and muted necessity weighs upon my vision. It is not the necessity of an objective frontier forever impassable, for the contours of my field are not lines. It is not cut out against an expanse of blackness; rather when I approach them, the things dissociate, my look loses its differentiation, and the vision ceases for lack of seer and of articulated things. Even without speaking of my motor power, I am therefore not shut up in one sector of the visible world. But I am curbed all the same, like those animals in zoological gardens without cages or bars, whose freedom gently comes to an end by some trench a little too broad for them to clear at one bound. The openness upon the world implies that the world be and remain a horizon, not because my vision would push the world back beyond itself, but because somehow he who sees is of it and is in it. Philosophy therefore does not seek to analyze our relationship with the world, to *undo* it as if it had been formed by assemblage; but it also does not terminate by an immediate and all-inclusive acknowledgment of Being, of which there would be nothing more to say. Philosophy cannot flatter itself that, by rendering explicit that relationship, it finds again in it what we would have put in it; it cannot reconstruct the thing and the world by condensing in them, in the form of implication, everything we have subsequently been able to think and say of them; rather, it remains a question, it interrogates the world and the thing, it revives, repeats, or imitates their crystallization before us. For this crystallization which is partly given to us ready-made is in other respects never terminated, and thereby we can see how the world comes about. It takes form under the domination of certain structural laws: events let rather general powers show through, powers such as the gaze or the word, which operate according to an identifiable style, according to "if . . . then . . ." relationships, according to a logic in action whose philosophical status must be defined if we wish to get out of the confusion in which the ready-made notions of thought, subject, and object throw us, and if we wish to know finally what the world is and what being is. Philosophy does not decompose our relationship with the world into real elements, or even into ideal references which would make of it an ideal object, but it discerns articulations in the world, it awakens in it regular relations of prepossession, of recapitulation, of overlapping, which are as dormant in our ontological landscape, subsist there only in the form of traces, and nevertheless continue to function there, continue to institute the new there.

The philosopher's manner of questioning is therefore not that of *cognition:* being and the world are not for the philosopher unknowns such as are to be determined through their relation with known terms, where both known and unknown terms belong in advance to the same order of *variables* which an active thought seeks to approximate as closely as possible. Nor is philosophy an *awakening of consciousness (prise de conscience)*: it is not a matter of philosophy rediscovering in a legislative consciousness the signification it would have given to the world and to being by nominal definition. Just as we do not speak for the sake of speaking but speak to someone *of* something or *of* someone, and in this initiative of speaking an aiming at the world and at the others is involved upon which is suspended all *that which* we say; so also the lexical signification and even the pure significations which are deliberately reconstructed, such as those of geometry, aim at a universe of brute being and of coexistence, toward which we were already thrown when we spoke and thought, and which, for its part, by principle does not admit the procedure of objectifying or reflective *approximation,* since it is at a distance, by way of horizon, latent or dissimulated. It is that universe that philosophy aims at, that is, as we say, *the object* of philosophy—but here never will the lacuna be filled in, the unknown transformed into known; the "object" of philosophy will never come to fill in the philosophical question, since this obturation would take from it the depth and the distance that are essential to it. The effective, present, ultimate and primary being, the thing itself, are in principle apprehended in transparency through their perspectives, offer themselves therefore only to someone who wishes not to have them but to see them, not to hold them as with forceps, or to immobilize them as under the objective of a microscope, but to let them be and to witness their continued being—to someone who therefore limits himself to giving them the hollow, the free space they ask for in return, the resonance they require, who follows their own movement, who is therefore not a nothingness the full being would come to stop up, but a question consonant with the porous being which it questions and from which it obtains not an *answer,* but a confirmation of its astonishment. It is necessary to comprehend perception as this interrogative thought which lets the perceived world be rather than posits it, before which the things form and undo themselves in a sort of gliding, beneath the yes and the no.

Our discussion of the negative announces to us another paradox of philosophy, which distinguishes it from every problem of cognition and forbids us to speak in philosophy of a *solution:* as an approach to the far-off as far-off, it is also a question put to what does not speak. It asks of our experience of the world what the world is before it is a thing one speaks of and which is taken for granted, before it has been reduced to a set of manageable, disposable significations; it directs this question to our mute life, it addresses itself to that compound of the world and of ourselves that precedes reflection, because the examination of the significations in themselves would give us the world reduced to our idealizations and our syntax. But in addition, what it finds in thus returning to the sources, it says. It is itself a human construction, and the philosopher knows very well that, whatever be his effort, in the best of cases it will take its place among the *artefacts* [18] and products of culture, as an instance of them. If this paradox is not an impossibility, and if philosophy can speak, it is because language is not only the depository of fixed and acquired significations, because its cumulative power itself results from a power of anticipation or of prepossession, because one speaks not only of what one knows, so as to set out a display of it—but also of what one does not know, in order to know it—and because language in forming itself expresses, at least laterally, an ontogenesis of which it is a part. But from this it follows that the words most charged with philosophy are not necessarily those that contain what they say, but rather those that most energetically open upon Being, because they more closely convey the life of the whole and make our habitual evidences vibrate until they disjoin. Hence it is a question whether philosophy as reconquest of brute or wild being can be accomplished by the resources of the eloquent language, or whether it would not be necessary for philosophy to use language in a way

18. TRANSLATOR: In English in the text.

that takes from it its power of immediate or direct signification in order to equal it with what it wishes all the same to say.

In sum, philosophy interrogates the perceptual faith—but neither expects nor receives an answer in the ordinary sense, because it is not the disclosing of a variable or of an unknown invariant that will satisfy this question, and because the existing world exists in the interrogative mode. Philosophy is the perceptual faith questioning itself about itself. One can say of it, as of every faith, that it is a faith *because* it is the possibility of doubt, and this indefatigable ranging over the things, which is our life, is also a continuous interrogation. It is not only philosophy, it is first the look that questions the things. We do not have a consciousness constitutive of the things, as idealism believes, nor a preordination of the things to the consciousness, as realism believes (they are indiscernible in what interests us here, because they both affirm the adequation of the thing and the mind)—we have with our body, our senses, our look, our power to understand speech and to speak, *measurants* (*mesurants*) for Being, dimensions to which we can refer it, but not a relation of adequation or of immanence. The perception of the world and of history is the practice of this measure, the reading off of their divergence or of their difference with respect to our norms. If we are ourselves in question in the very unfolding of our life, it is not because a central non-being threatens to revoke our consent to being at each instant; it is because we ourselves are one sole continued question, a perpetual enterprise of taking our bearings on the constellations of the world, and of taking the bearings of the things on our dimensions. The very questions of curiosity or those of science are interiorly animated by the fundamental interrogation which appears naked in philosophy.

> From time to time, a man lifts his head, sniffs, listens, considers, recognizes his position: he thinks, he sighs, and, drawing his watch from the pocket lodged against his chest, looks at the time. *Where am I?* and, *What time is it?* such is the inexhaustible question turning from us to the world . . .[19]

The watch and the map give here only a semblance of an answer: they indicate to us how what we are living is situated in

19. Claudel, *Art poétique* (Paris, 1951), p. 9.

relation to the course of the stars or to the course of a human day, or in relation to places that have a name. But where are these reference events and these landmarks themselves? They refer us to others, and the answer satisfies us only because we do not attend to it, because we think we are "at home." The question would arise again and indeed would be inexhaustible, almost insane, if we wished to situate our levels, measure our standards in their turn, if we were to ask: but where is the world itself? And why am I myself? [20] How old am I really? Am I really alone to be me? Have I not somewhere a double, a twin? These questions, which the sick man puts to himself in a moment of respite —or simply that glance at his watch, as if it were of great importance that the torment take place at a given inclination of the sun, at such or such hour in the life of the world—expose, at the moment that life is threatened, the underlying movement through which we have installed ourselves in the world and which recommences yet a little more time for itself. The ancients read in the heavens the hour to wage the battle. We no longer believe that it is written down anywhere. But we do and always will believe that what takes place here and now is one with the simultaneous; what takes place would not be entirely real for us if we did not know at what time. Its hour is no longer destined in advance for the event, but, whatever it be, the event appropriates it to itself; the event would not be entirely itself if we did not situate it in the immense simultaneity of the world and within its undivided thrust. Every question, even that of simple cognition, is part of the central question that is ourselves, of that appeal for totality to which no objective being answers, and which we now have to examine more precisely.

20. This is, says Alain, the question that, in *Manon Lescaut*, arises in the depths of woe. Strange caption: we have not located it in *Manon Lescaut*. One may wonder from what depth of reverie it came to Alain, and why disguised as a citation.

3 / Interrogation and Intuition [24] [Hs.]

PHILOSOPHY DOES NOT RAISE QUESTIONS and does not provide answers that would little by little fill in the blanks. The questions are within our life, within our history: they are born there, they die there, if they have found a response, more often than not they are transformed there; in any case, it is a past of experience and of knowledge that one day ends up at this open wondering. Philosophy does not take the context as given; it turns back upon it in order to seek the origin and the meaning of the questions and of the responses and the identity of him who questions, and it thereby gains access to the interrogation that animates all the questions of cognition, but is of another sort than they.

Our ordinary questions—"Where am I?" "What time is it?"— are the lack and the provisional absence of a fact or of a positive statement, holes in a fabric of things or of indicatives that we are sure is continuous, since there is a time, a space, and since the only question is at what point of this space and of this time we are. Philosophy, at first sight, only generalizes this type of question. When it asks if space, if time, if movement, if the world exist, the field of the question is more ample, but like the natural question it is still but a semi-question, included within a fundamental faith: there is something, and the only question is if it is really this space, this time, this movement, this world that we think we see or feel. The destruction of beliefs, the symbolic murder of the others and of the world, the split between vision and the visible, between thought and being do not, as they claim, establish us in the negative; when one has subtracted all that,

[105]

one installs oneself in what remains, in sensations, opinions.
And what remains is not nothing, nor of another sort than what
has been struck off: what remains are mutilated fragments of
the vague *omnitudo realitatis* against which the doubt was plied,
and they regenerate it under other names—appearance, dream,
Psyche, representation. It is in the name and for the profit of
these floating realities that the solid reality is cast into doubt.
One does not quit the something, and doubt as a destruction of
certitudes is not a doubt. It is no different when the doubt is
made methodic, when it is no longer a fluidification of the certitudes but a deliberate withdrawal, a refusal to embody them.
This time one no longer contests that there are evidences and
that for the moment they are irresistible; and if one holds them
in suspense it is for the sole motive that they are our own, caught
up in the flux of our life, and that in order to retain them more
than an instant we should have to trust in the obscure time
equipment of our internal works, which perhaps gives us only
coherent illusions. This deceiving nature, this opaque something
that would shut us up in our lights, is only a phantasm of our
rigorism, a perhaps. If this possible suffices to hold in check our
evidences, it is because we give weight to it by the decision to
tacitly presuppose nothing. If, in its name, we feign to nullify
lights we could not nullify really, take what is only conditional to
be false, make of an eventual divergence between the evident
and the true an infinite distance, and of a speculative doubt the
equivalent of a condemnation, it is because, as passive beings,
we feel ourselves caught up in a mass of Being that escapes us,
or even maneuvered by an evil agent, and we oppose to this
adversity the desire for an absolute evidence, delivered from all
facticity. Thus the methodic doubt, that which is carried out
within the voluntary zone of ourselves, refers to Being, since it
resists a factual evidence, represses an involuntary truth which
it acknowledges to be already there and which inspires the very
project of seeking an evidence that would be absolute. If it
remains a doubt, it can do so only by reviving the equivocations
of scepticism, by omitting to mention the borrowings it makes
from Being, or by evoking a falsity of Being itself, a Great
Deceiver, a Being that actively conceals itself and pushes before
itself the screen of our thought and of its evidences, as if this
elusive being were nothing. The philosophical interrogation
therefore would not go all the way through with itself if it limited

itself to generalizing the doubt, the common question of the *an sit,* to extending them to the world or to Being, and would define itself as doubt, non-knowing or non-belief. Things are not so simple. In being extended to everything, the common question changes its meaning. Philosophy elects certain beings—"sensations," "representation," "thought," "consciousness," or even a deceiving being—in order to separate itself from all being. Precisely in order to accomplish its will for radicalism, it would have to take as its theme the umbilical bond that binds it always to Being, the inalienable horizon with which it is already and henceforth circumvented, the primary initiation which it tries in vain to go back on. It would have to no longer deny, no longer even doubt; it would have to step back only in order to see the world and Being, or simply put them between quotation marks as one does with the remarks of another, to let them speak, to listen in. . . .

Then, if the question can no longer be that of the *an sit,* it becomes that of the *quid sit;* there remains only to study what the world and truth and being are, in terms of the complicity that we have with them. At the same time that the doubt is renounced, one renounces the affirmation of an absolute exterior, of a world or a Being that would be a massive individual; one turns toward that Being that doubles our thoughts along their whole extension, since they are thoughts of something and since they themselves are not nothing—a Being therefore that is meaning, and meaning of meaning. Not only that meaning that is attached to words and belongs to the order of statements and of things said, to a circumscribed region of the world, to a certain type of Being—but universal meaning, which would be capable of sustaining logical operations and language and the unfolding of the world as well. It will be *that without which* there would be neither world nor language nor anything at all— it will be the essence. When it looks back from the world to what makes it a world, from beings to what makes them be, the pure gaze, which involves nothing implicit (which does not, like the gaze of our eyes, have the darkness of a body and a past behind itself), could apply itself only to something that would be before it without restriction or condition: to what makes the world be a world, to an imperative grammar of Being, to indecomposable nuclei of meaning, systems of inseparable properties. The essences are this intrinsic sense, these necessities by principle.

However may be the realities in which they are compounded and confused (but where their implications constantly make themselves no less felt), they are the sole legitimate or authentic being, which has the pretension and the right to be and which is affirmative of itself, because it is the system of everything that is possible before the eyes of a pure spectator, the diagram or pattern of what, at all the levels, is *something*—something in general, or something material, or something spiritual, or something living.

Through the question *quid sit,* more effectively than through the doubt, philosophy succeeds in detaching itself from all beings, because it changes them into their meaning. This is already the procedure of science, when, to respond to the questions of life which are only a hesitation between the yes and the no, it casts the prevailing categories into question, invents new types of Being, a new heaven of essences. But it does not terminate this labor: it does not entirely disengage its essences from the world; it maintains them under the jurisdiction of the facts, which can tomorrow call for an other elaboration. Galileo gives but a rough draft of the material thing, and the whole of classical physics lives on an essence of *Physis* that is perhaps not the true essence: must one maintain its principles, and, by means of some auxiliary hypothesis, reduce wave mechanics to them however one can? Or, on the contrary, are we in sight of a new essence of the material world? Must we maintain the Marxist essence of history and treat the facts that seem to call it into question as empirical and confused variants, or, on the contrary, are we at a turning point where, *beneath* the Marxist essence of history, a more authentic and more complete essence shows through? The question remains unsettled in scientific knowing because in it truths of fact and truths of reason overlap and because the carving out of the facts, like the elaboration of the essences, is there conducted under presuppositions that remain to be interrogated, if we are to know fully what science means. Philosophy would be this same reading of meaning carried out to its conclusion, an exact science, the sole exact one, because it alone goes all the way in the effort to know what Nature and History and the World and Being *are,* when our contact with them is not only the partial and abstract contact of the physical experiment and calculation, or of the historical analysis, but the total contact of someone who, living in the world and in Being, means to see his life fully, particularly his life of knowledge, and who, an inhabitant of the world, tries to think himself in the world, to think the world in himself, to unravel their jumbled essences, and to form finally the signification "Being." *

When philosophy finds beneath the doubt a prior "knowing," finds around the things and the world as facts and as doubtful facts a horizon that encompasses our negations as our affirmations, and when it penetrates into this horizon, certainly it must define anew this new something. Does it define it well or sufficiently by saying that it is the *essence*? Is the question of the essence the ultimate question? With the essence and the pure spectator who sees it, are we really at the source? The essence is certainly dependent. The inventory of the essential necessities is always made under a supposition (the same as that which recurs so often in Kant): if this world is to exist for us, or if there is to be a world, or if there is to be something, then it is necessary that they observe such and such a structural law. But whence do we get the hypothesis, whence do we know that there is something, that there is a world? This knowing is beneath the essence, it is the experience of which the essence is a part and which it does not envelop. The being of the essence is not primary, it does not rest on itself, it is not it that can teach us what Being is; the essence is not *the* answer to the philosophical question, the philosophical question is not posed in us by a pure spectator: it is first a question as to how, upon what ground, the pure spectator is established, from what more profound source he himself draws. Without the necessities by essence, the unshakable connections, the irresistible implications, the resistant and stable structures, there would be neither a world, nor something in general, nor Being; but their authority as essences, their affirmative power, their dignity as principles are not self-evident. We do not have the right to say that the essences we find give the primitive meaning of Being, that they are the possible in itself, the whole possible, and to repute as impossible all that does not obey their laws, nor to treat Being and the world as their consequence: they are only its manner or its style, they are the *Sosein* and not the *Sein*. And if we are justified in saying that every thought respects them as well as does our own, if they have universal value, this is so inasmuch as another thought founded

* What is true here: what is not nothing is *something*, but: this something is not hard as a diamond, not unconditioned, *Erfahrung*.

on other principles must, if it is to make itself known to us, to enter into communication with us, adapt itself to the conditions of our own thought, of our experience, take its place in our world, and inasmuch as, finally, all the thinkers and all the essences possible open upon one sole experience and upon the same world. We are no doubt using essences in order to establish and state this; the necessity of this conclusion is a necessity of essence. But it only crosses over the limits of one thought and imposes itself upon all, it indeed only survives my own intuition of the moment and is valid for me as a durable truth because my own experience interconnects within itself and connects with that of the others by opening upon one sole world, by inscribing itself in one sole Being. It is to experience therefore that the ultimate ontological power belongs, and the essences, the necessities by essence, the internal or logical possibility, solid and incontestable as they may be under the gaze of the mind, have finally their force and their eloquence only because all my thoughts and the thoughts of the others are caught up in the fabric of one sole Being. The pure spectator in me, which elevates each thing to the essence, which produces its ideas, is assured that it touches Being with them only because it emerges within an actual experience surrounded by actual experiences, by the actual world, by the actual Being, which is the ground of the predicative Being. The possibilities by essence can indeed envelop and dominate *the facts;* they themselves derive from another, and more fundamental, possibility: that which works over my experience, opens it to the world and to Being, and which, to be sure, does not find them before itself as *facts* but animates and organizes *their facticity.* When philosophy ceases to be doubt in order to make itself disclosure, explicitation, the field it opens to itself is indeed made up of significations or of essences—since it has detached itself from the facts and the beings—but these significations or essences do not suffice to themselves, they overtly refer to our acts of ideation which have lifted them from a brute being, wherein we must find again in their wild state what answers to our essences and our significations.

When I ask myself what the something or the world or the material thing is, I am not yet the pure spectator I will become through the act of ideation; I am a field of experience where there is only sketched out the family of material things and other families and the world as their common style, the family of things said and the world of speech as their common style, and finally the abstract and fleshless style of something in general. In order to pass from this to the essences, it is necessary for me to actively intervene, to vary the things and the field, not through some manipulation, but, without touching them, by supposing changed or putting out of circuit such and such a relationship or such and such a structure, noting how this would affect the others, so as to locate those relationships and structures that are separable from the thing, and those on the contrary that one could not suppress or change without the thing ceasing to be itself. It is from this test that the essence emerges—it is therefore not a positive being. It is an in-variant, it is exactly that whose change or absence would alter or destroy the thing; and the solidity, the essentiality of the essence is exactly measured by the power we have to vary the thing. A pure essence which would not be at all contaminated and confused with the facts could result only from an attempt at total variation. It would require a spectator himself without secrets, without latency, if we are to be certain that nothing be surreptitiously introduced into it. In order to really reduce an experience to its essence, we should have to achieve a distance from it that would put it entirely under our gaze, with all the implications of sensoriality or thought that come into play in it, bring it and bring ourselves wholly to the transparency of the imaginary, think it without the support of any ground, in short, withdraw to the bottom of nothingness. Only then could we know what moments positively make up the being of this experience. But would this still be an experience, since I would be soaring over it? And if I tried to maintain a sort of adhesion to it in thought, is it properly speaking an essence that I would see? Every ideation, because it is an ideation, is formed in a space of existence, under the guarantee of my duration, which must turn back into itself in order to find there again the same idea I thought an instant ago and must pass into the others in order to rejoin it also in them. Every ideation is borne by this tree of my duration and other durations, this unknown sap nourishes the transparency of the idea; behind the idea, there is the unity, the simultaneity of all the real and possible durations, the cohesion of one sole Being from one end to the other. Under the solidity of the essence and of the idea there is the fabric of experience, this flesh of time, and this is why I am not sure of having penetrated unto the hard core of being: my incontestable power to give myself leeway (*prendre du champ*), to disengage the possible from the real, does not go as far as to dominate all the implications of the spectacle and to make of the real a simple variant of the possible; on the contrary it is the possible worlds and the possible beings that are variants and are like doubles of the actual world and the actual Being. I have leeway enough to replace such and such moments of my experience with others, to observe that this does not suppress it —therefore to determine the inessential. But does what remains after these eliminations belong necessarily to the Being in question? In order to affirm that I should have to soar over my field, suspend or at least reactivate all the sedimented thoughts with which it is surrounded, first of all my time, my body—which is not only impossible for me to do in fact but would deprive me of that very cohesion in depth (*en épaisseur*) of the world and of Being without which the essence is subjective folly and arrogance. There is therefore for me something inessential, and there is a zone, a hollow, where what is not inessential, not impossible, assembles; there is no positive vision that would definitively give me the essentiality of the essence.

Shall we say then that we *fall short of* the essence, that we have it only in principle, that it lies at the limit of an always imperfect idealization? This double thinking that opposes the principle and the fact saves with the term "principle" only a presumption of the essence, although this is the moment to decide if it is justified, and to save the presumption it entrenches us in relativism, although by renouncing the essence that is intemporal and without locality we would perhaps obtain a true thought with regard to the essence. It is on account of having begun with the antithesis of the fact and the essence, of what is individuated in a point of space and time and what is from forever and nowhere, that one is finally led to treat the essence as a limit idea, that is, to make it inaccessible. For this is what obliged us to seek the being of the essence in the form of a second positivity beyond the order of the "facts," to dream of a variation of the thing that would eliminate from it all that is not authentically itself and would make it appear all naked whereas it is always clothed—to dream of an impossible labor of experience on experience that would strip it of its facticity as if it were an impurity. Perhaps if we were to re-examine the anti-thesis of fact and essence, we would be able on the contrary to redefine the essence in a way that would give us access to it, because it would be not beyond but at the heart of that coiling up (*enroulement*) of experience over experience which a moment ago constituted the difficulty.

Only a thought that looks at being from elsewhere, and as it were head-on, is forced into the bifurcation of the essence and the fact. If I am *kosmotheoros*, my sovereign gaze finds the things each in its own time, in its own place, as absolute individuals in a unique local and temporal disposition. Since they participate in the same significations each from its own place, one is led to conceive another dimension that would be a transversal to this flat multiplicity and that would be the system of significations without locality or temporality. And then, since it is indeed necessary to connect the two and to comprehend how the two orders are connected up through us, one arrives at the inextricable problem of the intuition of essences. But am I *kosmotheoros*? More exactly: is being *kosmotheoros* my ultimate reality? Am I primitively the power to contemplate, a pure look which fixes the things in their temporal and local place and the essences in an invisible heaven; am I this ray of knowing that would have to arise from nowhere? But even while I am installing myself at this zero point of Being, I know very well that it has a mysterious tie with locality and temporality: tomorrow, in a moment, this aerial view, with everything it encompasses, will fall at a certain date of the calendar; I will assign to it a certain point of apparition on the earth and in my life. One has to believe that time has continued to flow on beneath and that the earth has continued to exist. Since, however, I had crossed over to the other side, instead of saying that I am in time and in space, or that I am nowhere, why not rather say that I am everywhere, always, by being at this moment and at this place?

For the visible present is not *in* time and space, nor, of course, *outside* of them: there is nothing before it, after it, about it, that could compete with its visibility. And yet it is not alone, it is not everything. To put it precisely, it stops up my view, that is, time and space extend beyond the visible present, and at the same time they are *behind* it, in depth, in hiding. The visible can thus fill me and occupy me only because I who see it do not see it from the depths of nothingness, but from the midst of itself; I the seer am also visible. What makes the weight, the thickness, the flesh of each color, of each sound, of each tactile texture, of the present, and of the world is the fact that he who grasps them feels himself emerge from them by a sort of coiling up or redoubling, fundamentally homogeneous with them; he feels that he is the sensible itself coming to itself and that in return the sensible is in his eyes as it were his double or an extension of his own flesh. The space, the time of the things are shreds of himself, of his own spatialization, of his own temporalization, are no longer a multiplicity of individuals synchronically and diachronically distributed, but a relief of the simultaneous and of the successive, a spatial and temporal pulp where the individuals are formed by differentiation. The things—here, there, now, then—are no longer in themselves, in their own place, in their own time; they exist only at the end of those rays of spatiality and of temporality emitted in the secrecy of my flesh. And their solidity is not that of a pure object which the mind soars over; I experience their solidity from within insofar as I am among them and insofar as they communicate through me as a sentient thing. Like the memory screen of the psychoanalysts, the present, the visible counts so much for me and has an absolute prestige for me only by reason of this immense latent content of the past, the future, and the elsewhere, which it announces and which it conceals. There is therefore no need to add to the multiplicity of spatio-temporal atoms a transversal dimension of essences— what there is is a whole architecture, a whole complex of phenomena "in tiers," a whole series of "levels of being," [1] which are differentiated by the coiling up of the visible and the universal over a certain visible wherein it is redoubled and inscribed. Fact and essence can no longer be distinguished, not because, mixed up in our experience, they in their purity would be inaccessible and would subsist as limit-ideas beyond our experience, but because—Being no longer being *before me,* but surrounding me and in a sense traversing me, and my vision of Being not forming itself from elsewhere, but from the midst of Being—the alleged facts, the spatio-temporal individuals, are from the first mounted on the axes, the pivots, the dimensions, the generality of my body, and the ideas are therefore already encrusted in its joints. There is no emplacement of space and time that would not be a variant of the others, as they are of it; there is no

1. Jean Wahl, *"Sein, Wahrheit, Welt," Revue de métaphysique et de morale,* LXV, No. 2 (April–June, 1960), 187–94.

individual that would not be representative of a species or of a family of beings, would not have, would not be a certain style, a certain manner of managing the domain of space and time over which it has competency, of pronouncing, of articulating that domain, of radiating about a wholly virtual center—in short, a certain manner of being, in the active sense, a certain *Wesen,* in the sense that, says Heidegger, this word has when it is used as a verb.[2]

In short, there is no essence, no idea, that does not adhere to a domain of history and of geography. Not that it is *confined* there and inaccessible for the others, but because, like that of nature, the space or time of culture is not surveyable from above, and because the communication from one constituted culture to another occurs through the wild region wherein they all have originated. Where in all this is the essence? Where is the existence? Where is the *Sosein,* where the *Sein?* We never have before us pure individuals, indivisible glaciers of beings, nor essences without place and without date. Not that they exist elsewhere, beyond our grasp, but because we are experiences, that is, thoughts that feel behind themselves the weight of the space, the time, the very Being they think, and which therefore do not hold under their gaze a serial space and time nor the pure idea of series, but have about themselves a time and a space that exist by piling up, by proliferation, by encroachment, by promiscuity—a perpetual pregnancy, perpetual parturition, generativity and generality, brute essence and brute existence, which are the nodes and antinodes of the same ontological vibration.

And if one were to ask what is this indecisive milieu in which we find ourselves once the distinction between fact and essence is rejected, one must answer that it is the very sphere of our life, and of our life of knowledge. Now would be the time to reject the

2. The high school building, for us who return to it, thirty years later, as for those who occupy it today, is not so much an object which it would be useful or possible to describe by its characteristics, as it is a certain odor, a certain affective texture which holds sway over a certain vicinity of space. This velvet, this silk, are under my fingers a certain manner of resisting them and of yielding to them, a rough, sleek, rasping power, which respond for an X-spot of my flesh, lend themselves to its movement of muscled flesh, or tempt it in its inertia (*Einführung in die Metaphysik* [Tübingen, 1953], p. 26). [English translation by Ralph Manheim, *Introduction to Metaphysics* (Garden City, N. Y., 1961), pp. 27–28.]

myths of inductivity and of the *Wesenschau,* which are transmitted, as points of honor, from generation to generation. It is nonetheless clear that Husserl himself never obtained one sole *Wesenschau* that he did not subsequently take up again and rework, not to disown it, but in order to make it say what at first it had not quite said. Thus it would be naïve to seek solidity in a heaven of ideas or in a *ground (fond)* of meaning—it is neither above nor beneath the appearances, but at their joints; it is the tie that secretly connects an experience to its variants. It is clear also that pure inductivity is a myth. Let us set aside the domain of physics, to show later that the psychoanalysis of objective knowledge is interminable, or rather that, like every psychoanalysis, it is destined not to suppress the past, the phantasms, but to transform them from powers of death into poetic productivity, and that the very idea of objective knowledge and the idea of algorithm as a spiritual automaton and finally the idea of an object that informs itself and knows itself are, as much as any other ideas, and more than any other, supported by our reveries. Let us leave that aside for the moment. In any case, as soon as it is a question of the living being and of the body, and a fortiori of man, it is indeed clear that no fruitful research is pure inductivity, a pure inventorying of constants in themselves, that psychology, ethnology, sociology have taught us something only by putting the morbid or archaic or simply different experience in contact with our experience, by clarifying the one by the other, criticizing the one by the other, by organizing the *Ineinander,* and finally, by practicing that eidetic variation which Husserl was wrong to reserve primarily for the solitary imagination and vision of the philosopher, whereas it is the support and the very locus of that *opinio communis* we call science. Along this route, at least, it is indeed certain that we gain access to objectivity, not by penetrating into an In Itself, but by disclosing, rectifying each by the other, the exterior datum and the internal double of it that we possess insofar as we are sensible-sentients (*sentants-sensibles*), archetypes and variants of humanity and of life, that is, insofar as we are within life, within the human being and within Being, and insofar as it is in us as well, and insofar as we live and know not halfway between opaque facts and limpid ideas, but at the point of intersection and overlapping where families of facts inscribe their generality, their kinship, group themselves about the dimensions and the site of our own existence. This environment of brute existence and essence is not something mysterious: we never quit it, we have no other environment. The facts and the essences are abstractions: what there is are worlds and a world and a Being, not a sum of facts or a system of ideas, but the impossibility of meaninglessness or ontological void, since space and time are not the sum of local and temporal individuals, but the presence and latency behind each of all the others, and behind those of still others—and what they are we do not know, but we do know at least that they are determinable in principle. This world, this Being, facticity and ideality undividedly, is not one in the sense that being one applies to the individuals it contains, and still less is it two or several in that sense. Yet it is nothing mysterious: it is, whatever we may say, this world, this Being that our life, our science, and our philosophy inhabit.[3]

We shall render explicit the cohesion of time, of space, of space and time, the "simultaneity" of their parts (literal simultaneity in space, simultaneity in the figurative sense in time) and the intertwining (*entrelacs*) of space and time. And we shall render explicit the cohesion of the obverse and the reverse of my body which is responsible for the fact that my body—which is visible, tangible like a thing—acquires this view upon itself, this contact with itself, where it doubles itself up, unifies itself, in such a way that the objective body and the phenomenal body turn about one another or encroach upon one another. For the moment it suffices to show that the unique Being, the dimensionality to which these moments, these leaves, and these dimensions belong, is beyond the classical essence and existence and renders their relationship comprehensible.

Before the essence as before the fact, all we must do is situate ourselves within the being we are dealing with, instead of looking at it from the outside—or, *what amounts to the same thing,* what we have to do is put it back into the fabric of our life, attend from within to the dehiscence (analogous to that of my own body) which opens it to itself and opens us upon it, and

3. EDITOR: Here, in the course of the text itself, are inserted these lines: "in this labor of experience on experience which is the carnal context of the essence, it is necessary to draw attention particularly to the labor of speech (take up again the paragraph under discussion, and the apprehension of the essence as a spread between words [*écart des paroles*])."

which, in the case of the essence, is the dehiscence of the speaking and the thinking. As my body, which is one of the visibles, sees itself also and thereby makes itself the natural light opening its own interior to the visible, in order for the visible there to become my own landscape, realizing (as it is said) the miraculous promotion of Being to "consciousness," or (as we prefer to say) the segregation of the "within" and the "without"; so also speech (*la parole*)—which is sustained by the thousands of ideal relations of the particular language (*la langue*), and which, therefore, in the eyes of science, is, as a constituted language (*langage*), a certain region in the universe of significations—is also the organ and the resonator of all the other regions of signification and consequently coextensive with the thinkable. Like the flesh of the visible, speech is a total part of the significations, like it, speech is a relation to Being through a being, and, like it, it is narcissistic, eroticized, endowed with a natural magic that attracts the other significations into its web, as the body feels the world in feeling itself. In reality, there is much more than a parallel or an analogy here, there is solidarity and intertwining: if speech, which is but a region of the intelligible world, can be also its refuge, this is because speech prolongs into the invisible, extends unto the semantic operations, the belongingness of the body to being and the corporeal relevance of every being, which for me is once and for all attested by the visible, and whose idea each intellectual evidence reflects a little further. In a philosophy that takes into consideration the operative world, functioning, present and coherent, as it is, the essence is not at all a stumbling block: it has its place there as an operative, functioning, essence. No longer are there essences above us, like positive objects, offered to a spiritual eye; but there is an essence beneath us, a common nervure of the signifying and the signified, adherence in and reversibility of one another—as the visible things are the secret folds of our flesh, and yet our body is one of the visible things. As the world is behind my body, the operative essence is behind the operative speech also, the speech that possesses the signification less than it is possessed by it, that does not speak *of it*, but speaks *it*, or speaks *according to it*, or lets it speak and be spoken within me, breaks through my present. If there is an ideality, a thought that has a future in me, that even breaks through my space of consciousness and has a future with the others, and finally, having become a writing, has a future in every possible reader, this can be only that thought that leaves me with my hunger and leaves them with their hunger, that betokens a generalized buckling of my landscape and opens it to the universal, precisely because it is rather an *unthought*. Ideas that are too much possessed are no longer ideas; I no longer think anything when I speak of them, as if it were essential to the essence that it be for tomorrow, as if it were only a tacking thread in the fabric of the words. A discussion is not an exchange or a confrontation of ideas, as if each formed his own, showed them to the others, looked at theirs, and returned to correct them with his own. . . . Someone speaks, and immediately the others are now but certain divergencies by relation to his words, and he himself specifies his divergence in relation to them. Whether he speaks up or hardly whispers, each one speaks with all that he is, with his "ideas," but also with his obsessions, his secret history which the others suddenly lay bare by formulating them as ideas. Life becomes ideas and the ideas return to life, each is caught up in the vortex in which he first committed only measured stakes, each is led on by what he said and the response he received, led on by his own thought of which he is no longer the sole thinker. No one thinks any more, everyone speaks, all live and gesticulate within Being, as I stir within my landscape, guided by gradients of differences to be observed or to be reduced if I wish to remain here or to go yonder. Whether in discussion or in monologue, the essence in the living and active state is always a certain vanishing point indicated by the arrangement of the words, their "other side," inaccessible, save for him who accepts to live first and always in them.

As the nervure bears the leaf from within, from the depths of its flesh, the ideas are the texture of experience, its style, first mute, then uttered. Like every style, they are elaborated within the thickness of being and, not only in fact but also by right, could not be detached from it, to be spread out on display under the gaze.

The philosophical interrogation is therefore not the simple expectation of a signification that would come to fill it. "What is the world?" or, better, "what is Being?"—these questions become philosophical only if, by a sort of diplopia, at the same time that they aim at a state of things, they aim at themselves as questions —at the same time that they aim at the signification "being,"

they aim at the being of signification and the place of signification within Being. It is characteristic of the philosophical questioning that it return upon itself, that it ask itself also what to
question is and what to respond is. Once this question to the
second power is raised, it cannot be effaced. Henceforth nothing
can continue to be as if there had never been any question. The
forgetting of the question, the return to the positive would be
possible only if the questioning were a simple absence of meaning, a withdrawal into the nothingness that is nothing. But he
who questions is not nothing, he is—and this is something quite
different—a being that questions himself; the negative in him is
borne by an infrastructure of being, it is therefore not a nothing
that eliminates itself from the account. We said that the doubt is
a clandestine positivism and that it is necessary to go beyond it
toward the something it negates and yet affirms. But conversely
if we wished to go beyond it unto a sphere of absolute certitude
that would be the sphere of significations or essences, this absolute positivism would mean that he who questions had distanced
Being and the world from himself so much that he was of them
no longer. Like the negativism of the doubt, the positivism of the
essences says secretly the contrary of what it says openly. The
intent to reach the absolutely hard being of the essence conceals
the mendacious pretension to be nothing. No question goes toward Being: if only by virtue of its being as a question, it has
already frequented Being, it is returning to it. As the view that
the question be a real rupture with Being, a lived nothingness, is
precluded, also precluded is the view that it be an ideal rupture,
an absolutely pure gaze directed upon an experience reduced to
its signification or its essence. As is precluded the view that the
question be without response, be a pure gaping toward a transcendent Being, also precluded is the view that the response be
immanent to the question and that, as Marx said, humanity raise
only the questions it can resolve. And these two views are precluded for the same reason, which is that in both hypotheses
there would finally be no question, and that in both these views
our initial situation is ignored—either, cut off from Being, we
would not even have enough of the positive to raise a question,
or, already caught up in Being, we would be already beyond
every question. The questions of essence to which one wishes to
reduce philosophy are not of themselves more philosophical than
the questions of fact, and the questions of fact, when the occa-

sion arises, no less philosophical than they. The dimension of philosophy cuts across that of the essence and the [fact].[4] To question oneself about the essence of time and of space is not yet to do philosophy, if one does not then question oneself about the relations of time itself and of space itself with their essence. And in a sense the questions of fact go further than the truths of reason.

> From time to time, a man lifts his head, sniffs, listens, considers, recognizes his position: he thinks, he sighs, and, drawing his watch from the pocket lodged against his chest, looks at the time. *Where am I?* and *What time is it?*—such is the inexhaustible question turning from us to the world. . . .[5]

Inexhaustible, because the time and the place change continually, but especially because the question that arises here is not at bottom a question of knowing in what spot of a space taken as given, at what hour of a time taken as given, we are—but first what is this indestructible tie between us and hours and places, this perpetual taking of our bearings on the things, this continual installation among them, through which first it is necessary that I be at a time, at a place, whatever they be. Positive information, a statement whatever it be, only defer that question and beguile our hunger. They refer us to some sort of law of our being that lays down that after a space there is a space, that after a time there is a time, but it is this law itself that our questions of fact are reaching for. If we could scrutinize their ultimate motivation, we would find beneath the questions *where am I?* and *what time is it?* a secret knowledge of space and time as beings to be questioned, a secret knowledge of interrogation as the ultimate relation to Being and as an ontological organ. The necessities by essence will not be the "answer" philosophy calls for, any more than are the facts. The "answer" is higher than the "facts," lower than the "essences," in the wild Being where they were, and—behind or beneath the cleavages of our acquired culture—continue to be, undivided.

What we propose here, and oppose to the search for the

4. EDITOR: We reintroduce between brackets the term "fact" erased by error.

5. Claudel, *Art poétique* (Paris, 1951), p. 9. [EDITOR: The reader will notice that the same passage from Claudel has already been cited and commented on (cf. above, pp. 103–4). The repetition is evidence of the unfinished state of the manuscript.]

essence, is not the return to the immediate, the coincidence, the effective fusion with the existent, the search for an original integrity, for a secret lost and to be rediscovered, which would nullify our questions and even reprehend our language. If coincidence is lost, this is no accident; if Being is hidden, this is itself a characteristic of Being, and no disclosure will make us comprehend it. A lost immediate, arduous to restore, will, if we do restore it, bear within itself the sediment of the critical procedures through which we will have found it anew; it will therefore not be the immediate. If it is to be the immediate, if it is to retain no trace of the operations through which we approach it, if it is Being itself, this means that there is no route from us to it and that it is inaccessible by principle. The visible things about us rest in themselves, and their natural being is so full that it seems to envelop their perceived being, as if our perception of them were formed within them. But if I express this experience by saying that the things are in their place and that we fuse with them, I immediately make the experience itself impossible: for in the measure that the thing is approached, I cease to be; in the measure that I am, there is no thing, but only a double of it in my "camera obscura." The moment my perception is to become pure perception, thing, Being, it is extinguished; the moment it lights up, already I am no longer the thing. And likewise there is no real coinciding with the being of the past: if the pure memory is the former present preserved, and if, in the act of recalling, I really become again what I was, it becomes impossible to see how it could open to me the dimension of the past. And if in being inscribed within me each present loses its flesh, if the pure memory into which it is changed is an invisible, then there is indeed a past, but no coinciding with it—I am separated from it by the whole thickness of my present; it is mine only by finding in some way a place in my present, in making itself present anew. As we never have at the same time the thing and the consciousness of the thing, we never have at the same time the past and the consciousness of the past, and for the same reason: in an intuition by coincidence and fusion, everything one gives to Being is taken from experience, everything one gives to experience is taken from Being. The truth of the matter is that the experience of a coincidence can be, as Bergson often says, only a "partial coincidence." But what is a coincidence that is only partial? It is a coincidence always past or always future, an experience that remembers an impossible past, anticipates an impossible future, that emerges from Being or that will incorporate itself into Being, that "is of it" but is not it, and therefore is not a coincidence, a real fusion, as of two positive terms or two elements of an alloyage, but an overlaying, as of a hollow and a relief which remain distinct. Coming after the world, after nature, after life, after thought, and finding them constituted before it, philosophy indeed questions this antecedent being and questions itself concerning its own relationship with it. It is a return upon itself and upon all things but not a return to an immediate—which recedes in the measure that philosophy wishes to approach it and fuse into it. The immediate is at the horizon and must be thought as such; it is only by remaining at a distance that it remains itself. There is an experience of the visible thing as pre-existing my vision, but this experience is not a fusion, a coincidence: because my eyes which see, my hands which touch, can also be seen and touched, because, therefore, in this sense they see and touch the visible, the tangible, from within, because our flesh lines and even envelops all the visible and tangible things with which nevertheless it is surrounded, the world and I are within one another, and there is no anteriority of the *percipere* to the *percipi*, there is simultaneity or even retardation. For the weight of the natural world is already a weight of the past. Each landscape of my life, because it is not a wandering troop of sensations or a system of ephemeral judgments but a segment of the durable flesh of the world, is qua visible, pregnant with many other visions besides my own; and the visible that I see, of which I speak, even if it is not Mount Hymettus or the plane trees of Delphi, is numerically the same that Plato and Aristotle saw and spoke of. When I find again the actual world such as it is, under my hands, under my eyes, up against my body, I find much more than an object: a Being of which my vision is a part, a visibility older than my operations or my acts. But this does not mean that there was a fusion or coinciding of me with it: on the contrary, this occurs because a sort of dehiscence opens my body in two, and because between my body looked at and my body looking, my body touched and my body touching, there is overlapping or encroachment, so that we must say that the things pass into us as well as we into the things. Our intuition, said Bergson, is a reflection, and he was right; his intuition shares with the philosophies of reflection a sort of supralapsarian bias: the secret of Being is in an integrity that is behind us. Like the philosophies of reflection, what Bergson lacks is the double reference, the identity of the retiring into oneself with the leaving of oneself, of the lived through with the distance. The return to the immediate data, the deepening of experience on the spot, are certainly the hallmark of philosophy by opposition to naïve cognitions. But the past and the present, the essence and the fact, space and time, are not *given* in the same sense, and none of them is given in the sense of coincidence. The "originating"[6] is not of one sole type, it is not all behind us; the restoration of the true past, of the pre-existence is not all of philosophy; the lived experience is not flat, without depth, without dimension, it is not an opaque stratum with which we would have to merge. The appeal to the originating goes in several directions: the originating breaks up, and philosophy must accompany this break-up, this non-coincidence, this differentiation. The difficulties of coincidence are not only factual difficulties which would leave the principle intact. Already with respect to the intuition of essences we have encountered this system of double truth, which is also a system of double falsity: for what is true *in principle* never being true *in fact,* and conversely the factual situation never committing the principles, each of the two instances condemns the other, and condemns it with reprieve, by leaving to it competency in its own order. If the coincidence is never but partial, we must not define the truth by total or effective coincidence. And if we have the idea of the thing itself and of the past itself, there must be something in the factual order that answers to it. It is therefore necessary that the deflection (*écart*), without which the experience of the thing or of the past would fall to zero, be also an openness upon the thing itself, to the past itself, that it enter into their definition. What is given, then, is not the naked thing, the past itself such as it was in its own time, but rather the thing ready to be seen, pregnant—in principle as well as in fact—with all the visions one can have of it, the past such as it was one day *plus* an inexplicable alteration, a strange distance—bound in principle as well as in fact to a recalling that spans that distance but does not nullify it. What there is is not a coinciding by principle or a

6. TRANSLATOR: We are translating *originaire* by "originating," to be taken in an active sense. Merleau-Ponty says it means "fundamental and inaugural" (cf. below, p. 159).

presumptive coinciding and a factual non-coinciding, a bad or abortive truth, but a privative non-coinciding, a coinciding from afar, a divergence, and something like a "good error."

It is by considering language that we would best see how we are to and how we are not to return to the things themselves. If we dream of finding again the natural world or time through coincidence, of being identical to the O-point which we see yonder, or to the pure memory which from the depths of ourselves governs our acts of recall, then language is a power for error, since it cuts the continuous tissue that joins us vitally to the things and to the past and is installed between ourselves and that tissue like a screen. The philosopher speaks, but this is a weakness in him, and an inexplicable weakness: he should keep silent, coincide in silence, and rejoin in Being a philosophy that is there ready-made. But yet everything comes to pass as though he wished to put into words a certain silence he hearkens to within himself. His entire "work" is this absurd effort. He wrote in order to state his contact with Being; he did not state it, and could not state it, since it is silence. Then he recommences. . . . One has to believe, then, that language is not simply the contrary of the truth, of coincidence, that there is or could be a language of coincidence, a manner of making the things themselves speak —and this is what he seeks. It would be a language of which he would not be the organizer, words he would not assemble, that would combine through him by virtue of a natural intertwining of their meaning, through the occult trading of the metaphor— where what counts is no longer the manifest meaning of each word and of each image, but the lateral relations, the kinships that are implicated in their transfers and their exchanges. It is indeed a language of this sort that Bergson himself required for the philosopher. But we have to recognize the consequence: if language is not necessarily deceptive, truth is not coincidence, nor mute.

We need only take language too in the living or nascent state, with all its references, those behind it, which connect it to the mute things it interpellates, and those it sends before itself and which make up the world of things said—with its movement, its subtleties, its reversals, its life, which expresses and multiplies tenfold the life of the bare things. Language is a life, is our life and the life of the things. Not that *language* takes possession of life and reserves it for itself: what would there be to say if there existed nothing but things said? It is the error of the semantic philosophies to close up language as if it spoke only of itself: language lives only from silence; everything we cast to the others has germinated in this great mute land which we never leave. But, because he has experienced within himself the need to speak, the birth of speech as bubbling up at the bottom of his mute experience, the philosopher knows better than anyone that what is lived is lived-spoken, that, born at this depth, language is not a mask over Being, but—if one knows how to grasp it with all its roots and all its foliation—the most valuable witness to Being, that it does not interrupt an immediation that would be perfect without it, that the vision itself, the thought itself, are, as has been said, "structured as a language," [7] are *articulation* before the letter, apparition of something where there was nothing or something else. Hence the problem of language is, if one likes, only a regional problem—that is, if we consider the ready-made language, the secondary and empirical operation of translation, of coding and decoding, the artificial languages, the technical relation between a sound and a meaning which are joined only by express convention and are therefore ideally isolable. But if, on the contrary, we consider the speaking word, the assuming of the conventions of his native language as something natural by him who lives within that language, the folding over within him of the visible and the lived experience upon language, and of language upon the visible and the lived experience, the exchanges between the articulations of his mute language and those of his speech, finally that operative language which has no need to be translated into significations and thoughts, that language-thing which counts as an arm, as action, as offense and as seduction because it brings to the surface all the deep-rooted relations of the lived experience wherein it takes form, and which is the language of life and of action but also that of literature and of poetry—then this logos is an absolutely universal theme, it is the theme of philosophy. Philosophy itself is language, rests on language; but this does not disqualify it from speaking of language, nor from speaking of the pre-language and of the mute world which doubles them: on the contrary, philosophy is an operative language, that language that can be known only from within, through its exercise, is open upon the things, called forth by the

7. Jacques Lacan.

voices of silence, and continues an effort of articulation which is the Being of every being.

We would err as much by defining philosophy as the search for the essences as by defining it as the fusion with the things, and the two errors are not so different. Whether we orientate ourselves upon the essences, which are the more pure in the measure that he who sees them has no part in the world, in the measure, consequently, that we look out from the depths of nothingness, or whether we seek to merge with the existing things, at the very point and at the very instant that they are, this infinite distance, this absolute proximity express in two ways—as a soaring over or as fusion—the same relationship with the thing itself. They are two positivisms. Whether one installs oneself at the level of statements, which are the proper order of the essences, or in the silence of the things, whether one trusts in speech absolutely, or whether one distrusts it absolutely —the ignorance of the problem of speech is here the ignoring of all mediation. Philosophy is flattened to the sole plane of ideality or to the sole plane of existence. On both sides one wants something—internal adequation of the idea or self-identity of the thing—to come stop up the look, and one excludes or subordinates the thought of the far-offs, the horizonal thought. That every being presents itself at a distance, which does not prevent us from knowing it, which is on the contrary the guarantee for knowing it: this is what is not considered. That the presence of the world is precisely the presence of its flesh to my flesh, that I "am of the world" and that I am not it, this is what is no sooner said than forgotten: metaphysics remains coincidence. That there is this thickness of flesh between us and the "hard core" of Being, this does not figure in the definition: this thickness is ascribed to me, it is the sheath of non-being that the subjectivity always carries about itself. Infinite distance or absolute proximity, negation or identification: our relationship with Being is ignored in the same way in both cases. In both cases, one misses it because one thinks one will ensure it more effectively by approaching the essence or the thing as closely as possible. One forgets that this frontal being before us—whether we posit it, whether it posits itself within us qua being-posited—is second by principle, is cut out upon a horizon which is not nothing, and which for its part is not by virtue of com-position. One forgets that our openness, our fundamental relationship with Being, that which makes it impossible for us to feign to not be, could not be formed in the order of the being-posited, since it is this openness precisely that teaches us that the beings-posited, whether true or false, are not nothing, that, whatever be the experience, an experience is always contiguous upon an experience, that our perceptions, our judgments, our whole knowledge of the world can be changed, crossed out, Husserl says, but not nullified, that, under the doubt that strikes them appear other perceptions, other judgments more true, because we are within Being and because there is something. Bergson had indeed said that the fundamental knowing is not that which wishes to take hold of time as between forceps, wishes to fix it, to determine it by the relations between its parts, to measure it; and that on the contrary time offers itself to him who wishes only to "see it," [8] and who, precisely because he has given up the attempt to seize it, rejoins, by vision, its internal propulsion. But more often than not the idea of fusion or of coincidence serves as a substitute for these indications, which would call for a theory of the philosophical view or vision as a maximum of true proximity to a Being in dehiscence. . . . We should have to return to this idea of proximity through distance, of intuition as auscultation or palpation in depth, of a view which is a view of self, a torsion of self upon self, and which calls "coincidence" in question.

And thereby we would see finally what the philosophical questioning is. Not the *an sit* and the doubt, where Being is tacitly understood, and not the "I know that I know nothing," where already the absolute certitude of the ideas breaks through, but a true "what do I know?" which is not quite that of Montaigne. For the "what do I know?" could be a simple appeal for the elucidation of the things that we know, without any examination of the idea of knowing. In that case it would be one of those questions of cognition (as can also be the "where am I?") where we are hesitating only about what to call entities—space, knowledge—which are taken as evident in themselves. But already when I say "what do I know?" in the course of a phrase,[9] another

8. *La Pensée et le mouvant* (Paris, 1934), p. 10. [English translation by Mabelle L. Andison, *The Creative Mind* (New York, 1946), p. 13.]

9. TRANSLATOR: *Que sais-je?*—an idiomatic exclamatory turn of phrase in French.

sort of question arises: for it extends to the idea of knowing itself; it invokes some intelligible place where the facts, examples, ideas I lack, should be found; it intimates that the interrogative is not a mode derived by inversion or by reversal of the indicative and of the positive, is neither an affirmation nor a negation veiled or expected, but an original manner of aiming at something, as it were a *question-knowing,* which by principle no statement or "answer" can go beyond and which perhaps therefore is the proper mode of our relationship with Being, as though it were the mute or reticent interlocutor of our questions. "What do I know?" is not only "what is knowing?" and not only "who am I?" but finally: "what is there?" and even: "what is the *there is?*" These questions call not for the exhibiting of something said which would put an end to them, but for the disclosure of a Being that is not posited because it has no need to be, because it is silently behind all our affirmations, negations, and even behind all formulated questions, not that it is a matter of forgetting them in its silence, not that it is a matter of imprisoning it in our chatter, but because philosophy is the reconversion of silence and speech into one another: "It is the experience . . . still mute which we are concerned with leading to the pure expression of its own meaning." [10]

10. Husserl, *Meditations cartésiennes,* French translation (Paris, 1947), p. 33. [English translation by Dorion Cairns, *Cartesian Meditations* (The Hague, 1960), pp. 38–39.]

4 / The Intertwining—The Chiasm (26)

IF IT IS TRUE that as soon as philosophy declares itself to be reflection or coincidence it prejudges what it will find, then once again it must recommence everything, reject the instruments reflection and intuition had provided themselves, and install itself in a locus where they have not yet been distinguished, in experiences that have not yet been "worked over," that offer us all at once, pell-mell, both "subject" and "object," both existence and essence, and hence give philosophy resources to redefine them. Seeing, speaking, even thinking (with certain reservations, for as soon as we distinguish thought from speaking absolutely we are already in the order of reflection), are experiences of this kind, both irrecusable and enigmatic. They have a name in all languages, but a name which in all of them also conveys significations in tufts, thickets of proper meanings and figurative meanings, so that, unlike those of science, not one of these names clarifies by attributing to what is named a circumscribed signification. Rather, they are the repeated index, the insistent reminder of a mystery as familiar as it is unexplained, of a light which, illuminating the rest, remains at its source in obscurity. If we could rediscover within the exercise of seeing and speaking some of the living references that assign them such a destiny in a language, perhaps they would teach us how to form our new instruments, and first of all to understand our research, our interrogation, themselves.

The visible about us seems to rest in itself. It is as though our vision were formed in the heart of the visible, or as though there were between it and us an intimacy as close as between the sea and the strand. And yet it is not possible that we blend into it, nor that it passes into us, for then the vision would vanish at the moment of formation, by disappearance of the seer or of the visible. What there is then are not things first identical with themselves, which would then offer themselves to the seer, nor is there a seer who is first empty and who, afterward, would open himself to them—but something to which we could not be closer than by palpating it with our look, things we could not dream of seeing "all naked" because the gaze itself envelops them, clothes them with its own flesh. Whence does it happen that in so doing it leaves them in their place, that the vision we acquire of them seems to us to come from them, and that to be seen is for them but a degradation of their eminent being? What is this talisman of color, this singular virtue of the visible that makes it, held at the end of the gaze, nonetheless much more than a correlative of my vision, such that it imposes my vision upon me as a continuation of its own sovereign existence? How does it happen that my look, enveloping them, does not hide them, and, finally, that, veiling them, it unveils them? [1]

We must first understand that this red under my eyes is not, as is always said, a *quale,* a pellicle of being without thickness, a message at the same time indecipherable and evident, which one has or has not received, but of which, if one has received it, one knows all there is to know, and of which in the end there is nothing to say. It requires a focusing, however brief; it emerges from a less precise, more general redness, in which my gaze was caught, into which it sank, before—as we put it so aptly—*fixing* it. And, now that I have fixed it, if my eyes penetrate into it, into

---

1. EDITOR: Here in the course of the text itself, these lines are inserted: "it is that the look is itself incorporation of the seer into the visible, quest for itself, which *is of it,* within the visible—it is that the visible of the world is not an envelope of *quale,* but what is between the qualia, a connective tissue of exterior and interior horizons—it is as flesh offered to flesh that the visible has its aseity, and that it is mine—The flesh as *Sichtigkeit* and generality. → whence vision is question and response. . . . The openness through flesh: the two leaves of my body and the leaves of the visible world. . . . It is between these intercalated leaves that there is visibility. . . . My body model of the things and the things model of my body: the body bound to the world through all its parts, up against it → all this means: the world, the flesh not as fact or sum of facts, but as the locus of an inscription of truth: the false crossed out, not nullified."

its fixed structure, or if they start to wander round about again, the *quale* resumes its atmospheric existence. Its precise form is bound up with a certain wooly, metallic, or porous [?] configuration or texture, and the *quale* itself counts for very little compared with these participations. Claudel has a phrase saying that a certain blue of the sea is so blue that only blood would be more red. The color is yet a variant in another dimension of variation, that of its relations with the surroundings: this red is what it is only by connecting up from its place with other reds about it, with which it forms a constellation, or with other colors it dominates or that dominate it, that it attracts or that attract it, that it repels or that repel it. In short, it is a certain node in the woof of the simultaneous and the successive. It is a concretion of visibility, it is not an atom. The red dress a fortiori holds with all its fibers onto the fabric of the visible, and thereby onto a fabric of invisible being. A punctuation in the field of red things, which includes the tiles of roof tops, the flags of gatekeepers and of the Revolution, certain terrains near Aix or in Madagascar, it is also a punctuation in the field of red garments, which includes, along with the dresses of women, robes of professors, bishops, and advocate generals, and also in the field of adornments and that of uniforms. And its red literally is not the same as it appears in one constellation or in the other, as the pure essence of the Revolution of 1917 precipitates in it, or that of the eternal feminine, or that of the public prosecutor, or that of the gypsies dressed like hussars who reigned twenty-five years ago over an inn on the Champs-Elysées. A certain red is also a fossil drawn up from the depths of imaginary worlds. If we took all these participations into account, we would recognize that a naked color, and in general a visible, is not a chunk of absolutely hard, indivisible being, offered all naked to a vision which could be only total or null, but is rather a sort of straits between exterior horizons and interior horizons ever gaping open, something that comes to touch lightly and makes diverse regions of the colored or visible world resound at the distances, a certain differentiation, an ephemeral modulation of this world—less a color or a thing, therefore, than a difference between things and colors, a momentary crystallization of colored being or of visibility. Between the alleged colors and visibles, we would find anew the tissue that lines them, sustains them, nourishes them, and which for its part is not a thing, but a possibility, a latency, and a *flesh* of things.

If we turn now to the seer, we will find that this is no analogy or vague comparison and must be taken literally. The look, we said, envelops, palpates, espouses the visible things. As though it were in a relation of pre-established harmony with them, as though it knew them before knowing them, it moves in its own way with its abrupt and imperious style, and yet the views taken are not desultory—I do not look at a chaos, but at things—so that finally one cannot say if it is the look or if it is the things that command. What is this prepossession of the visible, this art of interrogating it according to its own wishes, this inspired exegesis? We would perhaps find the answer in the tactile palpation where the questioner and the questioned are closer, and of which, after all, the palpation of the eye is a remarkable variant. How does it happen that I give to my hands, in particular, that degree, that rate, and that direction of movement that are capable of making me feel the textures of the sleek and the rough? Between the exploration and what it will teach me, between my movements and what I touch, there must exist some relationship by principle, some kinship, according to which they are not only, like the pseudopods of the amoeba, vague and ephemeral deformations of the corporeal space, but the initiation to and the opening upon a tactile world. This can happen only if my hand, while it is felt from within, is also accessible from without, itself tangible, for my other hand, for example, if it takes its place among the things it touches, is in a sense one of them, opens finally upon a tangible being of which it is also a part. Through this crisscrossing within it of the touching and the tangible, its own movements incorporate themselves into the universe they interrogate, are recorded on the same map as it; the two systems are applied upon one another, as the two halves of an orange. It is no different for the vision—except, it is said, that here the exploration and the information it gathers do not belong "to the same sense." But this delimitation of the senses is crude. Already in the "touch" we have just found three distinct experiences which subtend one another, three dimensions which overlap but are distinct: a touching of the sleek and of the rough, a touching of the things—a passive sentiment of the body and of its space —and finally a veritable touching of the touch, when my right hand touches my left hand while it is palpating the things, where the "touching subject" passes over to the rank of the touched, descends into the things, such that the touch is formed in the midst of the world and as it were in the things. Between the massive sentiment I have of the sack in which I am enclosed, and the control from without that my hand exercises over my hand, there is as much difference as between the movements of my eyes and the changes they produce in the visible. And as, conversely, every experience of the visible has always been given to me within the context of the movements of the look, the visible spectacle belongs to the touch neither more nor less than do the "tactile qualities." We must habituate ourselves to think that every visible is cut out in the tangible, every tactile being in some manner promised to visibility, and that there is encroachment, infringement, not only between the touched and the touching, but also between the tangible and the visible, which is encrusted in it, as, conversely, the tangible itself is not a nothingness of visibility, is not without visual existence. Since the same body sees and touches, visible and tangible belong to the same world. It is a marvel too little noticed that every movement of my eyes—even more, every displacement of my body—has its place in the same visible universe that I itemize and explore with them, as, conversely, every vision takes place somewhere in the tactile space. There is double and crossed situating of the visible in the tangible and of the tangible in the visible; the two maps are complete, and yet they do not merge into one. The two parts are total parts and yet are not superposable.

Hence, without even entering into the implications proper to the seer and the visible, we know that, since vision is a palpation with the look, it must also be inscribed in the order of being that it discloses to us; he who looks must not himself be foreign to the world that he looks at. As soon as I see, it is necessary that the vision (as is so well indicated by the double meaning of the word) be doubled with a complementary vision or with another vision: myself seen from without, such as another would see me, installed in the midst of the visible, occupied in considering it from a certain spot. For the moment we shall not examine how far this identity of the seer and the visible goes, if we have a complete experience of it, or if there is something missing, and what it is. It suffices for us for the moment to note that he who sees cannot possess the visible unless he is possessed by it, unless he *is of it*,* unless, by principle, according to what is required by the articulation of the look with the things, he is one of the visibles, capable, by a singular reversal, of seeing them— he who is one of them.†

We understand then why we see the things themselves, in their places, where they are, according to their being which is indeed more than their being-perceived—and why at the same time we are separated from them by all the thickness of the look and of the body; it is that this distance is not the contrary of this proximity, it is deeply consonant with it, it is synonymous with it. It is that the thickness of flesh between the seer and the thing is constitutive for the thing of its visibility as for the seer of his corporeity; it is not an obstacle between them, it is their means of communication. It is for the same reason that I am at the heart of the visible and that I am far from it: because it has thickness and is thereby naturally destined to be seen by a body. What is indefinable in the *quale,* in the color, is nothing else than a brief, peremptory manner of giving in one sole something, in one sole tone of being, visions past, visions to come, by whole clusters. I who see have my own depth also, being backed up by this same visible which I see and which, I know very well, closes in behind me. The thickness of the body, far from rivaling that of the world, is on the contrary the sole means I have to go unto the heart of the things, by making myself a world and by making them flesh.

The body interposed is not itself a thing, an interstitial matter, a connective tissue, but a *sensible for itself,* which means, not that absurdity: color that sees itself, surface that touches itself—but this paradox [?]: a set of colors and surfaces inhabited by a touch, a vision, hence an *exemplar sensible,* which offers to him who inhabits it and senses it the wherewithal to sense everything that resembles himself on the outside, such that, caught up in the tissue of the things, it draws it entirely to itself, incorporates it, and, with the same movement, communicates to the things upon which it closes over that identity without superposition, that difference without contradiction, that divergence between the within and the without that constitutes its

---

* The *Uerpräsentierbarkeit* is the flesh.

† The visible is not a tangible zero, the tangible is not a zero of visibility (relation of encroachment).

natal secret.[2] The body unites us directly with the things through its own ontogenesis, by welding to one another the two outlines of which it is made, its two laps: the sensible mass it is and the mass of the sensible wherein it is born by segregation and upon which, as seer, it remains open. It is the body and it alone, because it is a two-dimensional being, that can bring us to the things themselves, which are themselves not flat beings but beings in depth, inaccessible to a subject that would survey them from above, open to him alone that, if it be possible, would coexist with them in the same world. When we speak of the flesh of the visible, we do not mean to do anthropology, to describe a world covered over with all our own projections, leaving aside what it can be under the human mask. Rather, we mean that carnal being, as a being of depths, of several leaves or several faces, a being in latency, and a presentation of a certain absence, is a prototype of Being, of which our body, the sensible sentient, is a very remarkable variant, but whose constitutive paradox already lies in every visible. For already the cube assembles within itself incompossible *visibilia,* as my body is at once phenomenal body and objective body, and if finally it is, it, like my body, is by a tour de force. What we call a visible is, we said, a quality pregnant with a texture, the surface of a depth, a cross section upon a massive being, a grain or corpuscle borne by a wave of Being. Since the total visible is always behind, or after, or between the aspects we see of it, there is access to it only through an experience which, like it, is wholly outside of itself. It is thus, and not as the bearer of a knowing subject, that our body commands the visible for us, but it does not explain it, does not clarify it, it only concentrates the mystery of its scattered visibility; and it is indeed a paradox of Being, not a paradox of man, that we are dealing with here. To be sure, one can reply that, between the two "sides" of our body, the body as sensible and the body as sentient (what in the past we called objective body and phenomenal body), rather than a spread, there is the abyss that

2. EDITOR: Here, in the course of the text itself, between brackets, these lines are inserted: "One can say that we perceive the things themselves, that we are the world that thinks itself—or that the world is at the heart of our flesh. In any case, once a body-world relationship is recognized, there is a ramification of my body and a ramification of the world and a correspondence between its inside and my outside, between my inside and its outside."

separates the In Itself from the For Itself. It is a problem—and we will not avoid it—to determine how the sensible sentient can also be thought. But here, seeking to form our first concepts in such a way as to avoid the classical impasses, we do not have to honor the difficulties that they may present when confronted with a *cogito,* which itself has to be re-examined. Yes or no: do we have a body—that is, not a permanent object of thought, but a flesh that suffers when it is wounded, hands that touch? We know: hands do not suffice for touch—but to decide for this reason alone that our hands do not touch, and to relegate them to the world of objects or of instruments, would be, in acquiescing to the bifurcation of subject and object, to forego in advance the understanding of the sensible and to deprive ourselves of its lights. We propose on the contrary to take it literally to begin with. We say therefore that our body is a being of two leaves, from one side a thing among things and otherwise what sees them and touches them; we say, because it is evident, that it unites these two properties within itself, and its double belong-ingness to the order of the "object" and to the order of the "subject" reveals to us quite unexpected relations between the two orders. It cannot be by incomprehensible accident that the body has this double reference; it teaches us that each calls for the other. For if the body is a thing among things, it is so in a stronger and deeper sense than they: in the sense that, we said, it *is of them,* and this means that it detaches itself upon them, and, accordingly, detaches itself from them. It is not simply a thing *seen* in fact (I do not see my back), it is visible by right, it falls under a vision that is both ineluctable and deferred. Con-versely, if it touches and sees, this is not because it would have the visibles before itself as objects: they are about it, they even enter into its enclosure, they are within it, they line its looks and its hands inside and outside. If it touches them and sees them, this is only because, being of their family, itself visible and tangible, it uses its own being as a means to participate in theirs, because each of the two beings is an archetype for the other, because the body belongs to the order of the things as the world is universal flesh. One should not even say, as we did a moment ago, that the body is made up of two leaves, of which the one, that of the "sensible," is bound up with the rest of the world. There are not in it two leaves or two layers; fundamentally it is neither thing seen only nor seer only, it is Visibility sometimes wandering and sometimes reassembled. And as such it is not in the world, it does not detain its view of the world as within a private garden: it sees the world itself, the world of everybody, and without having to leave "itself," because it is wholly—because its hands, its eyes, are nothing else than—this reference of a visible, a tangible-standard to all those whose resemblance it bears and whose evidence it gathers, by a magic that is the vision, the touch themselves. To speak of leaves or of layers is still to flatten and to juxtapose, under the reflective gaze, what coexists in the living and upright body. If one wants metaphors, it would be better to say that the body sensed and the body sentient are as the obverse and the reverse, or again, as two segments of one sole circular course which goes above from left to right and below from right to left, but which is but one sole movement in its two phases. And everything said about the sensed body pertains to the whole of the sensible of which it is a part, and to the world. If the body is one sole body in its two phases, it incorporates into itself the whole of the sensible and with the same movement incorporates itself into a "Sensible in itself." We have to reject the age-old assumptions that put the body in the world and the seer in the body, or, conversely, the world and the body in the seer as in a box. Where are we to put the limit between the body and the world, since the world is flesh? Where in the body are we to put the seer, since evidently there is in the body only "shadows stuffed with organs," that is, more of the visible? The world seen is not "in" my body, and my body is not "in" the visible world ultimately: as flesh applied to a flesh, the world neither surrounds it nor is surrounded by it. A participation in and kinship with the visible, the vision neither envelops it nor is enveloped by it definitively. The superficial pellicle of the visible is only for my vision and for my body. But the depth beneath this surface contains my body and hence contains my vision. My body as a visible thing is contained within the full spectacle. But my seeing body subtends this visible body, and all the visibles with it. There is reciprocal insertion and intertwining of one in the other. Or rather, if, as once again we must, we eschew the thinking by planes and perspectives, there are two circles, or two vortexes, or two spheres, concentric when I live naïvely, and as soon as I question myself, the one slightly decentered with respect to the other. . . .

We have to ask ourselves what exactly we have found with

this strange adhesion of the seer and the visible. There is vision, touch, when a certain visible, a certain tangible, turns back upon the whole of the visible, the whole of the tangible, of which it is a part, or when suddenly it finds itself *surrounded* by them, or when between it and them, and through their commerce, is formed a Visibility, a Tangible in itself, which belong properly neither to the body qua fact nor to the world qua fact—as upon two mirrors facing one another where two indefinite series of images set in one another arise which belong really to neither of the two surfaces, since each is only the rejoinder of the other, and which therefore form a couple, a couple more real than either of them. Thus since the seer is caught up in what he sees, it is still himself he sees: there is a fundamental narcissism of all vision. And thus, for the same reason, the vision he exercises, he also undergoes from the things, such that, as many painters have said, I feel myself looked at by the things, my activity is equally passivity—which is the second and more profound sense of the narcissim: not to see in the outside, as the others see it, the contour of a body one inhabits, but especially to be seen by the outside, to exist within it, to emigrate into it, to be seduced, captivated, alienated by the phantom, so that the seer and the visible reciprocate one another and we no longer know which sees and which is seen. It is this Visibility, this generality of the Sensible in itself, this anonymity innate to Myself that we have previously called flesh, and one knows there is no name in traditional philosophy to designate it. The flesh is not matter, in the sense of corpuscles of being which would add up or continue on one another to form beings. Nor is the visible (the things as well as my own body) some "psychic" material that would be—God knows how—brought into being by the things factually existing and acting on my factual body. In general, it is not a fact or a sum of facts "material" or "spiritual." Nor is it a representation for a mind: a mind could not be captured by its own representations; it would rebel against this insertion into the visible which is essential to the seer. The flesh is not matter, is not mind, is not substance. To designate it, we should need the old term "element," in the sense it was used to speak of water, air, earth, and fire, that is, in the sense of a *general thing*, midway between the spatio-temporal individual and the idea, a sort of incarnate principle that brings a style of being wherever there is a fragment of being. The flesh is in this sense an "element" of Being. Not a fact or a sum of facts, and yet adherent to *location* and to the *now*. Much more: the inauguration of the *where* and the *when*, the possibility and exigency for the fact; in a word: facticity, what makes the fact be a fact. And, at the same time, what makes the facts have meaning, makes the fragmentary facts dispose themselves about "something." For if there is flesh, that is, if the hidden face of the cube radiates forth somewhere as well as does the face I have under my eyes, and coexists with it, and if I who see the cube also belong to the visible, I am visible from elsewhere, and if I and the cube are together caught up in one same "element" (should we say of the seer, or of the visible?), this cohesion, this visibility by principle, prevails over every momentary discordance. In advance every vision or very partial visible that would here definitively come to naught is not nullified (which would leave a gap in its place), but, what is better, it is replaced by a more exact vision and a more exact visible, according to the principle of visibility, which, as though through a sort of abhorrence of a vacuum, already invokes the true vision and the true visible, not only as substitutes for their errors, but also as their explanation, their relative justification, so that they are, as Husserl says so aptly, not erased, but "crossed out." . . . Such are the extravagant consequences to which we are led when we take seriously, when we question, vision. And it is, to be sure, possible to refrain from doing so and to move on, but we would simply find again, confused, indistinct, non-clarified, scraps of this ontology of the visible mixed up with all our theories of knowledge, and in particular with those that serve, desultorily, as vehicles of science. We are, to be sure, not finished ruminating over them. Our concern in this preliminary outline was only to catch sight of this strange domain to which interrogation, properly so-called, gives access. . . .

But this domain, one rapidly realizes, is unlimited. If we can show that the flesh is an ultimate notion, that it is not the union or compound of two substances, but thinkable by itself, if there is a relation of the visible with itself that traverses me and constitutes me as a seer, this circle which I do not form, which forms me, this coiling over of the visible upon the visible, can traverse, animate other bodies as well as my own. And if I was able to understand how this wave arises within me, how the visible which is yonder is simultaneously my landscape, I can understand a fortiori that elsewhere it also closes over upon itself and that there are other landscapes besides my own. If it lets itself be captivated by one of its fragments, the principle of captation is established, the field open for other Narcissus, for an "intercorporeity." If my left hand can touch my right hand while it palpates the tangibles, can touch it touching, can turn its palpation back upon it, why, when touching the hand of another, would I not touch in it the same power to espouse the things that I have touched in my own? It is true that "the things" in question are my own, that the whole operation takes place (as we say) "in me," within my landscape, whereas the problem is to institute another landscape. When one of my hands touches the other, the world of each opens upon that of the other because the operation is reversible at will, because they both belong (as we say) to one sole space of consciousness, because one sole man touches one sole thing through both hands. But for my two hands to open upon one sole world, it does not suffice that they be given to one sole *consciousness*—or if that were the case the difficulty before us would disappear: since other bodies would be known by me in the same way as would be my own, they and I would still be dealing with the same world. No, my two hands touch the same things because they are the hands of one same body. And yet each of them has its own tactile experience. If nonetheless they have to do with one sole tangible, it is because there exists a very peculiar relation from one to the other, across the corporeal space—like that holding between my two eyes—making of my hands one sole organ of experience, as it makes of my two eyes the channels of one sole Cyclopean vision. A difficult relation to conceive—since one eye, one hand, are capable of vision, of touch, and since what has to be comprehended is that these visions, these touches, these little subjectivities, these "consciousnesses of . . . ," could be assembled like flowers into a bouquet, when each being "consciousness of," being For Itself, reduces the others into objects. We will get out of the difficulty only by renouncing the bifurcation of the "consciousness of" and the object, by admitting that my synergic body is not an object, that it assembles into a cluster the "consciousnesses" adherent to its hands, to its eyes, by an operation that is in relation to them lateral, transversal; that "my consciousness" is not the synthetic, uncreated, centrifugal unity of a multitude of "consciousnesses of . . ." which would be centrifugal like it is, that it is sustained, subtended, by the prereflective and preobjective unity of my body. This means that while each monocular vision, each touching with one sole hand has its own visible, its tactile, each is bound to every other vision, to every other touch; it is bound in such a way as to make up with them the experience of one sole body before one sole world, through a possibility for reversion, reconversion of its language into theirs, transfer, and reversal, according to which the little private world of each is not juxtaposed to the world of all the others, but surrounded by it, levied off from it, and all together are a Sentient in general before a Sensible in general. Now why would this generality, which constitutes the unity of my body, not open it to other bodies? The handshake too is reversible; I can feel myself touched as well and at the same time as touching, and surely there does not exist some huge animal whose organs our bodies would be, as, for each of our bodies, our hands, our eyes are the organs. Why would not the synergy exist among different organisms, if it is possible within each? Their landscapes interweave, their actions and their passions fit together exactly: this is possible as soon as we no longer make belongingness to one same "consciousness" the primordial definition of sensibility, and as soon as we rather understand it as the return of the visible upon itself, a carnal adherence of the sentient to the sensed and of the sensed to the sentient. For, as overlapping and fission, identity and difference, it brings to birth a ray of natural light that illuminates all flesh and not only my own. It is said that the colors, the tactile reliefs given to the other, are for me an absolute mystery, forever inaccessible. This is not completely true; for me to have not an idea, an image, nor a representation, but as it were the imminent experience of them, it suffices that I look at a landscape, that I speak of it with someone. Then, through the concordant operation of his body and my own, what I see passes into him, this individual green of the meadow under my eyes invades his vision without quitting my own, I recognize in my green his green, as the customs officer recognizes suddenly in a traveler the man whose description he had been given. There is here no problem of the *alter ego* because it is not *I* who sees, not *he* who sees, because an anonymous visibility inhabits both of us, a vision in general, in virtue of that primordial property that belongs to the flesh, being here and now, of radiating everywhere and forever, being an individual, of being also a dimension and a universal.

What is open to us, therefore, with the reversibility of the visible and the tangible, is—if not yet the incorporeal—at least an intercorporeal being, a presumptive domain of the visible and the tangible, which extends further than the things I touch and see at present.

There is a circle of the touched and the touching, the touched takes hold of the touching; there is a circle of the visible and the seeing, the seeing is not without visible existence; [3] there is even an inscription of the touching in the visible, of the seeing in the tangible—and the converse; there is finally a propagation of these exchanges to all the bodies of the same type and of the same style which I see and touch—and this by virtue of the fundamental fission or segregation of the sentient and the sensible which, laterally, makes the organs of my body communicate and founds transitivity from one body to another.

As soon as we see other seers, we no longer have before us only the look without a pupil, the plate glass of the things with that feeble reflection, that phantom of ourselves they evoke by designating a place among themselves whence we see them: henceforth, through other eyes we are for ourselves fully visible; that lacuna where our eyes, our back, lie is filled, filled still by the visible, of which we are not the titulars. To believe that, to bring a vision that is not our own into account, it is to be sure inevitably, it is always from the unique treasury of our own vision that we draw, and experience therefore can teach us nothing that would not be outlined in our own vision. But what is proper to the visible is, we said, to be the surface of an inexhaustible depth: this is what makes it able to be open to visions other than our own. In being realized, they therefore bring out the limits of our factual vision, they betray the solipsist illusion that consists in thinking that every going beyond is a surpassing accomplished by oneself. For the first time, the seeing that I am is for me really visible; for the first time I appear to myself completely turned inside out under my own eyes. For the first time also, my movements no longer proceed unto the things to be seen, to be touched, or unto my own body occupied in seeing and touching them, but they address themselves to the body in general and for itself (whether it be my own or that of another),

---

3. EDITOR: Here is inserted between brackets, in the course of the text itself, the note: "what are these adhesions compared with those of the voice and the hearing?"

because for the first time, through the other body, I see that, in its coupling with the flesh of the world, the body contributes more than it receives, adding to the world that I see the treasure necessary for what the other body sees. For the first time, the body no longer couples itself up with the world, it clasps another body, applying [itself to it] [4] carefully with its whole extension, forming tirelessly with its hands the strange statue which in its turn gives everything it receives; the body is lost outside of the world and its goals, fascinated by the unique occupation of floating in Being with another life, of making itself the outside of its inside and the inside of its outside. And henceforth movement, touch, vision, applying themselves to the other and to themselves, return toward their source and, in the patient and silent labor of desire, begin the paradox of expression.

Yet this flesh that one sees and touches is not all there is to flesh, nor this massive corporeity all there is to the body. The reversibility that defines the flesh exists in other fields; it is even incomparably more agile there and capable of weaving relations between bodies that this time will not only enlarge, but will pass definitively beyond the circle of the visible. Among my movements, there are some that go nowhere—that do not even go find in the other body their resemblance or their archetype: these are the facial movements, many gestures, and especially those strange movements of the throat and mouth that form the cry and the voice. Those movements end in sounds and I hear them. Like crystal, like metal and many other substances, I am a sonorous being, but I hear my own vibration from within; as Malraux said, I hear myself with my throat. In this, as he also has said, I am incomparable; my voice is bound to the mass of my own life as is the voice of no one else. But if I am close enough to the other who speaks to hear his breath and feel his effervescence and his fatigue, I almost witness, in him as in myself, the awesome birth of vociferation. As there is a reflexivity of the touch, of sight, and of the touch-vision system, there is a reflexivity of the movements of phonation and of hearing; they have their sonorous inscription, the vociferations have in me their motor echo. This new reversibility and the emergence of

4. EDITOR: These words, which we reintroduce into the text, had been erased apparently by error.

the flesh as expression are the point of insertion of speaking and thinking in the world of silence.[5]

At the frontier of the mute or solipsist world where, in the presence of other seers, my visible is confirmed as an exemplar of a universal visibility, we reach a second or figurative meaning of vision, which will be the *intuitus mentis* or idea, a sublimation of the flesh, which will be mind or thought. But the factual presence of other bodies could not produce thought or the idea if its seed were not in my own body. Thought is a relationship with oneself and with the world as well as a relationship with the other; hence it is established in the three dimensions at the same time. And it must be brought to appear directly in the infrastructure of vision. Brought to appear, we say, and not brought to birth: for we are leaving in suspense for the moment the question whether it would not be already implicated there. Manifest as it is that feeling is dispersed in my body, that for example my hand touches, and that consequently we may not in advance ascribe feeling to a thought of which it would be but a mode—it yet would be absurd to conceive the touch as a colony of assembled tactile experiences. We are not here proposing any empiricist genesis of thought: we are asking precisely what is that central vision that joins the scattered visions, that unique touch that governs the whole tactile life of my body as a unit, that *I think* that must be able to accompany all our experiences. We are proceeding toward the center, we are seeking to comprehend how there is a center, what the unity consists of, we are not

Kant

5. EDITOR: Inserted here between brackets: "in what sense we have not yet introduced thinking: to be sure, we are not in the in itself. From the moment we said *seeing, visible,* and described the dehiscence of the sensible, we were, if one likes, in the order of thought. We were not in it in the sense that the thinking we have introduced was *there is,* and not *it appears to me that* . . . (appearing that would make up the whole of being, self-appearing). Our thesis is that this *there is* by inherence is necessary, and our problem to show that thought, in the restrictive sense (pure signification, thought of seeing and of feeling), is comprehensible only as the accomplishment by other means of the will of the *there is,* by sublimation of the *there is* and realization of an invisible that is exactly the reverse of the visible, the power of the visible. Thus between sound and meaning, speech and what it means to say, there is still the relation of reversibility, and no question of priority, since the exchange of words is exactly the differentiation of which the thought is the integral."

saying that it is a sum or a result; and if we make the thought appear upon an infrastructure of vision, this is only in virtue of the uncontested evidence that one must see or feel in some way in order to think, that every thought known to us occurs to a flesh.

Once again, the flesh we are speaking of is not matter. It is the coiling over of the visible upon the seeing body, of the tangible upon the touching body, which is attested in particular when the body sees itself, touches itself seeing and touching the things, such that, simultaneously, as tangible it descends among them, as touching it dominates them all and draws this relationship and even this double relationship from itself, by dehiscence or fission of its own mass. This concentration of the visibles about one of them, or this bursting forth of the mass of the body toward the things, which makes a vibration of my skin become the sleek and the rough, makes me *follow with my eyes* the movements and the contours of the things themselves, this magical relation, this pact between them and me according to which I lend them my body in order that they inscribe upon it and give me their resemblance, this fold, this central cavity of the visible which is my vision, these two mirror arrangements of the seeing and the visible, the touching and the touched, form a close-bound system that I count on, define a vision in general and a constant style of visibility from which I cannot detach myself, even when a particular vision turns out to be illusory, for I remain certain in that case that in looking closer I would have had the true vision, and that in any case, whether it be this one or another, *there is a true vision*. The flesh (of the world or my own) is not contingency, chaos, but a texture that returns to itself and conforms to itself. I will never see my own retinas, but if one thing is certain for me it is that *one* would find at the bottom of my eyeballs those dull and secret membranes. And finally, I believe it—I believe that I have a man's senses, a human body—because the spectacle of the world that is my own, and which, to judge by our confrontations, does not notably differ from that of the others, with me as with them refers with evidence to typical dimensions of visibility, and finally to a virtual focus of vision, to a detector also typical, so that at the joints of the opaque body and the opaque world there is a ray of generality and of light. Conversely, when, starting from the body, I ask how it makes itself a seer, when I examine the critical region of the aesthesiological body, everything comes to pass (as we have shown in an earlier work [6]) as though the visible body remained incomplete, gaping open; as though the physiology of vision did not succeed in closing the nervous functioning in upon itself, since the movements of fixation, of convergence, are suspended upon the advent to the body of a visible world for which they were supposed to furnish the explanation; as though, therefore, the vision came suddenly to give to the material means and instruments left here and there in the working area a convergence which they were waiting for; as though, through all these channels, all these prepared but unemployed circuits, the current that will traverse them was rendered probable, in the long run inevitable: the current making of an embryo a newborn infant, of a visible a seer, and of a body a mind, or at least a flesh. In spite of all our substantialist ideas, the seer is being premeditated in counterpoint in the embryonic development; through a labor upon itself the visible body provides for the hollow whence a vision will come, inaugurates the long maturation at whose term suddenly it will see, that is, will be visible for itself, will institute the interminable gravitation, the indefatigable metamorphosis of the seeing and the visible whose principle is posed and which gets underway with the first vision. What we are calling flesh, this interiorly worked-over mass, has no name in any philosophy. As the formative medium of the object and the subject, it is not the atom of being, the hard in itself that resides in a unique place and moment: one can indeed say of my body that it is not *elsewhere,* but one cannot say that it is *here* or *now* in the sense that objects are; and yet my vision does not soar over them, it is not the being that is wholly knowing, for it has its own inertia, its ties. We must not think the flesh starting from substances, from body and spirit—for then it would be the union of contradictories—but we must think it, as we said, as an element, as the concrete emblem of a general manner of being. To begin with, we spoke summarily of a reversibility of the seeing and the visible, of the touching and the touched. It is time to emphasize that it is a reversibility always imminent and never realized in fact. My left hand is always on the verge of touching my right hand touching the things, but I never reach coincidence; the coincidence eclipses at the moment of realization, and

6. *The Structure of Behavior* [trans. Alden L. Fisher (Boston, 1963)].

one of two things always occurs: either my right hand really passes over to the rank of touched, but then its hold on the world is interrupted; or it retains its hold on the world, but then I do not really touch *it*—my right hand touching, I palpate with my left hand only its outer covering. Likewise, I do not hear myself as I hear the others, the sonorous existence of my voice is for me as it were poorly exhibited; I have rather an echo of its articulated existence, it vibrates through my head rather than outside. I am always on the same side of my body; it presents itself to me in one invariable perspective. But this incessant escaping, this impotency to superpose exactly upon one another the touching of the things by my right hand and the touching of this same right hand by my left hand, or to superpose, in the exploratory movements of the hand, the tactile experience of a point and that of the "same" point a moment later, or the auditory experience of my own voice and that of other voices—this is not a failure. For if these experiences never exactly overlap, if they slip away at the very moment they are about to rejoin, if there is always a "shift," a "spread," between them, this is precisely because my two hands are part of the same body, because it moves itself in the world, because I hear myself both from within and from without. I experience—and as often as I wish—the transition and the metamorphosis of the one experience into the other, and it is only as though the hinge between them, solid, unshakeable, remained irremediably hidden from me. But this hiatus between my right hand touched and my right hand touching, between my voice heard and my voice uttered, between one moment of my tactile life and the following one, is not an ontological void, a non-being: it is spanned by the total being of my body, and by that of the world; it is the zero of pressure between two solids that makes them adhere to one another. My flesh and that of the world therefore involve clear zones, clearings, about which pivot their opaque zones, and the primary visibility, that of the *quale* and of the things, does not come without a second visibility, that of the lines of force and dimensions, the massive flesh without a rarefied flesh, the momentary body without a glorified body. When Husserl spoke of the horizon of the things—of their exterior horizon, which everybody knows, and of their "interior horizon," that darkness stuffed with visibility of which their surface is but the limit—it is necessary to take the term seriously. No more than are the sky or the earth is the horizon a collection of things held together, or a class name, or a logical possibility of conception, or a system of "potentiality of consciousness": it is a new type of being, a being by porosity, pregnancy, or generality, and he before whom the horizon opens is caught up, included within it. His body and the distances participate in one same corporeity or visibility in general, which reigns between them and it, and even beyond the horizon, beneath his skin, unto the depths of being.

We touch here the most difficult point, that is, the bond between the flesh and the idea, between the visible and the interior armature which it manifests and which it conceals. No one has gone further than Proust in fixing the relations between the visible and the invisible, in describing an idea that is not the contrary of the sensible, that is its lining and its depth. For what he says of musical ideas he says of all cultural beings, such as *The Princess of Clèves* and *René,* and also of the essence of love which "the little phrase" not only makes present to Swann, but communicable to all who hear it, even though it is unbeknown to themselves, and even though later they do not know how to recognize it in the loves they only witness. He says it in general of many other notions which are, like music itself "without equivalents," "the notions of light, of sound, of relief, of physical voluptuousness, which are the rich possessions with which our inward domain is diversified and adorned." [7] Literature, music, the passions, but also the experience of the visible world are—no less than is the science of Lavoisier and Ampère—the exploration of an invisible and the disclosure of a universe of ideas.[8] The difference is simply that this invisible, these ideas, unlike those of that science, cannot be detached from the sensible appearances and be erected into a second positivity. The musical idea, the literary idea, the dialectic of love, and also the articulations of the light, the modes of exhibition of sound and of touch speak to us, have their logic, their coherence, their points of intersection, their concordances, and here also the appearances are the disguise of unknown "forces" and "laws." But it is as though the secrecy wherein they lie and whence the literary expression draws them were their proper mode of existence. For these

7. *Du côté de chez Swann,* II (Paris, 1926), 190. [English translation by C. K. Scott Moncrieff, *Swann's Way* (New York, 1928), p. 503.]

8. *Ibid.,* p. 192. [Eng. trans., p. 505.]

truths are not only hidden like a physical reality which we have not been able to discover, invisible in fact but which we will one day be able to see facing us, which others, better situated, could already see, provided that the screen that masks it is lifted. Here, on the contrary, there is no vision without the screen: the ideas we are speaking of would not be better known to us if we had no body and no sensibility; it is then that they would be inaccessible to us. The "little phrase," the notion of the light, are not exhausted by their manifestations, any more than is an "idea of the intelligence"; they could not be given to us *as ideas* except in a carnal experience. It is not only that we would find in that carnal experience the *occasion* to think them; it is that they owe their authority, their fascinating, indestructible power, precisely to the fact that they are in transparency behind the sensible, or in its heart. Each time we want to get at it [9] immediately, or lay hands on it, or circumscribe it, or see it unveiled, we do in fact feel that the attempt is misconceived, that it retreats in the measure that we approach. The explicitation does not give us the idea itself; it is but a second version of it, a more manageable derivative. Swann can of course close in the "little phrase" between the marks of musical notation, ascribe the "withdrawn and chilly tenderness" that makes up its essence or its sense to the narrow range of the five notes that compose it and to the constant recurrence of two of them: while he is thinking of these signs and this sense, he no longer has the "little phrase" itself, he has only "bare values substituted for the mysterious entity he had perceived, for the convenience of his understanding." [10] Thus it is essential to this sort of ideas that they be "veiled with shadows," appear "under a disguise." They give us the assurance that the "great unpenetrated and discouraging night of our soul" is not empty, is not "nothingness"; but these entities, these domains, these worlds that line it, people it, and whose presence it feels like the presence of someone in the dark, have been acquired only through its commerce with the visible, to which they remain attached. As the secret blackness of milk, of which Valéry spoke, is accessible only through its whiteness, the idea of light or the musical idea doubles up the lights and sounds from beneath, is their other side or their depth. Their carnal texture presents to us

9. EDITOR: It: that is, the idea.
10. *Du côté de chez Swann*, II, 189. [Eng. trans., p. 503.]

what is absent from all flesh; it is a furrow that traces itself out magically under our eyes without a tracer, a certain hollow, a certain interior, a certain absence, a negativity that is not nothing, being limited very precisely to *these* five notes between which it is instituted, to that family of sensibles we call lights. We do not see, do not hear the ideas, and not even with the mind's eye or with the third ear: and yet they are there, behind the sounds or between them, behind the lights or between them, recognizable through their always special, always unique manner of entrenching themselves behind them, "perfectly distinct from one another, unequal among themselves in value and in significance." [11]

With the first vision, the first contact, the first pleasure, there is initiation, that is, not the positing of a content, but the opening of a dimension that can never again be closed, the establishment of a level in terms of which every other experience will henceforth be situated. The idea is this level, this dimension. It is therefore not a *de facto* invisible, like an object hidden behind another, and not an absolute invisible, which would have nothing to do with the visible. Rather it is the invisible *of* this world, that which inhabits this world, sustains it, and renders it visible, its own and interior possibility, the Being of this being. At the moment one says "light," at the moment that the musicians reach the "little phrase," there is no lacuna in me; what I live is as "substantial," as "explicit," as a positive thought could be— even more so: a positive thought is what it is, but, precisely, is only what it is and accordingly cannot hold us. Already the mind's volubility takes it elsewhere. We do not possess the musical or sensible ideas, precisely because they are negativity or absence circumscribed; they possess us. The performer is no longer producing or reproducing the sonata: he feels himself, and the others feel him to be at the service of the sonata; the sonata sings through him or cries out so suddenly that he must "dash on his bow" to follow it. And these open vortexes in the sonorous world finally form one sole vortex in which the ideas fit in with one another. "Never was the spoken language so inflexibly necessitated, never did it know to such an extent the pertinence of the questions, the evidence of the responses." [12] The

11. *Ibid.*
12. *Ibid.*, p. 192. [Eng. trans., p. 505.]

invisible and, as it were, weak being is alone capable of having this close texture. There is a strict ideality in experiences that are experiences of the flesh: the moments of the sonata, the fragments of the luminous field, adhere to one another with a cohesion without concept, which is of the same type as the cohesion of the parts of my body, or the cohesion of my body with the world. Is my body a thing, is it an idea? It is neither, being the measurant of the things. We will therefore have to recognize an ideality that is not alien to the flesh, that gives it its axes, its depth, its dimensions.

But once we have entered into this strange domain, one does not see how there could be any question of *leaving* it. If there is an animation *of* the body; if the vision and the body are tangled up in one another; if, correlatively, the thin pellicle of the *quale*, the surface of the visible, is doubled up over its whole extension with an invisible reserve; and if finally, in our flesh as in the flesh of things, the actual, empirical, ontic visible, by a sort of folding back, invagination, or padding, exhibits a visibility, a possibility that is not the shadow of the actual but is its principle, that is not the proper contribution of a "thought" but is its condition, a style, allusive and elliptical like every style, but like every style inimitable, inalienable, an interior horizon and an exterior horizon between which the actual visible is a provisional partitioning and which, nonetheless, open indefinitely only upon other visibles—then (the immediate and dualist distinction between the visible and the invisible, between extension and thought, being impugned, not that extension be thought or thought extension, but because they are the obverse and the reverse of one another, and the one forever behind the other) there is to be sure a question as to how the "ideas of the intelligence" are initiated over and beyond, how from the ideality of the horizon one passes to the "pure" ideality, and in particular by what miracle a created generality, a culture, a knowledge come to add to and recapture and rectify the natural generality of my body and of the world. But, however we finally have to understand it, the "pure" ideality already streams forth along the articulations of the aesthesiological body, along the contours of the sensible things, and, however new it is, it slips through ways it has not traced, transfigures horizons it did not open, it derives from the fundamental mystery of those notions "without equivalent," as Proust calls them, that lead their shadowy life in the night of the mind only because they have been divined at the junctures of the visible world. It is too soon now to clarify this type of surpassing that does not leave its field of origin. Let us only say that the pure ideality is itself not without flesh nor freed from horizon structures: it lives of them, though they be another flesh and other horizons. It is as though the visibility that animates the sensible world were to emigrate, not outside of every body, but into another less heavy, more transparent body, as though it were to change flesh, abandoning the flesh of the body for that of language, and thereby would be emancipated but not freed from every condition. Why not admit—what Proust knew very well and said in another place—that language as well as music can sustain a sense by virtue of its own arrangement, catch a meaning in its own mesh, that it does so without exception each time it is conquering, active, creative language, each time something is, in the strong sense, said? Why not admit that, just as the musical notation is a *facsimile* made after the event, an abstract portrait of the musical entity, language as a system of explicit relations between signs and signified, sounds and meaning, is a result and a product of the operative language in which sense and sound are in the same relationship as the "little phrase" and the five notes found in it afterwards? This does not mean that musical notation and grammar and linguistics and the "ideas of the intelligence"—which are acquired, available, honorary ideas—are useless, or that, as Leibniz said, the donkey that goes straight to the fodder knows as much about the properties of the straight line as we do; it means that the system of objective relations, the acquired ideas, are themselves caught up in something like a second life and perception, which make the mathematician go straight to entities no one has yet seen, make the *operative* language and algorithm make use of a second visibility, and make ideas be the other side of language and calculus. When I think they animate my interior speech, they haunt it as the "little phrase" possesses the violinist, and they remain beyond the words as it remains beyond the notes— not in the sense that under the light of another sun hidden from us they would shine forth but because they are that certain divergence, that never-finished differentiation, that openness ever to be reopened between the sign and the sign, as the flesh is, we said, the dehiscence of the seeing into the visible and of the visible into the seeing. And just as my body sees only because it is a part of the visible in which it opens forth, the sense upon which the arrangement of the sounds opens reflects back upon that arrangement. For the linguist language is an ideal system, a fragment of the intelligible world. But, just as for me to see it is not enough that my look be visible for X, it is necessary that it be visible for itself, through a sort of torsion, reversal, or specular phenomenon, which is given from the sole fact that I am born; so also, if my words have a meaning, it is not *because* they present the systematic organization the linguist will disclose, it is because that organization, like the look, refers back to itself: the operative Word is the obscure region whence comes the instituted light, as the muted reflection of the body upon itself is what we call natural light. As there is a reversibility of the seeing and the visible, and as at the point where the two metamorphoses cross what we call perception is born, so also there is a reversibility of the speech and what it signifies; the signification is what comes to seal, to close, to gather up the multiplicity of the physical, physiological, linguistic means of elocution, to contract them into one sole act, as the vision comes to complete the aesthesiological body. And, as the visible takes hold of the look which has unveiled it and which forms a part of it, the signification rebounds upon its own means, it annexes to itself the speech that becomes an object of science, it antedates itself by a retrograde movement which is never completely belied—because already, in opening the horizon of the nameable and of the sayable, the speech acknowledged that it has its place in that horizon; because no locutor speaks without making himself in advance allocutary, *be it only for himself;* because with one sole gesture he closes the circuit of his relation to himself and that of his relation to the others and, with the same stroke, also sets himself up as *delocutary,* speech of which one speaks: he offers himself and offers every word to a universal Word. We shall have to follow more closely this transition from the mute world to the speaking world. For the moment we want only to suggest that one can speak neither of a destruction nor of a conservation of silence (and still less of a destruction that conserves or of a realization that destroys—which is not to solve but to pose the problem). When the silent vision falls into speech, and when the speech in turn, opening up a field of the nameable and the sayable, inscribes itself in that field, in its place, according to its truth—in short, when it metamorphoses the structures of the visible world and makes itself a gaze of the mind, *intuitus mentis*—this is always in virtue of the same fundamental phenomenon of reversibility which sustains both the mute perception and the speech and which manifests itself by an almost carnal existence of the idea, as well as by a sublimation of the flesh. In a sense, if we were to make completely explicit the architectonics of the human body, its ontological framework, and how it sees itself and hears itself, we would see that the structure of its mute world is such that all the possibilities of language are already given in it. Already our existence as seers (that is, we said, as beings who turn the world back upon itself and who pass over to the other side, and who catch sight of one another, who see one another with eyes) and especially our existence as sonorous beings for others and for ourselves contain everything required for there to be speech from the one to the other, speech about the world. And, in a sense, to understand a phrase is nothing else than to fully welcome it in its sonorous being, or, as we put it so well, to *hear what it says* (*l'entendre*). The meaning is not on the phrase like the butter on the bread, like a second layer of "psychic reality" spread over the sound: it is the totality of what is said, the integral of all the differentiations of the verbal chain; it is given with the words for those who have ears to hear. And conversely the whole landscape is overrun with words as with an invasion, it is henceforth but a variant of speech before our eyes, and to speak of its "style" is in our view to form a metaphor. In a sense the whole of philosophy, as Husserl says, consists in restoring a power to signify, a birth of meaning, or a wild meaning, an expression of experience by experience, which in particular clarifies the special domain of language. And in a sense, as Valéry said, language is everything, since it is the voice of no one, since it is the very voice of the things, the waves, and the forests. And what we have to understand is that there is no dialectical reversal from one of these views to the other; we do not have to reassemble them into a synthesis: they are two aspects of the reversibility which is the ultimate truth.

5 / Preobjective Being:
The Solipsist World ^(?)

THE REDUCTION TO THE PREOBJECTIVE

SINCE THE ENIGMA of the brute world is finally left intact by science and by reflection, we are invited to interrogate that world without presupposing anything.[1] It is henceforth understood that in order to describe it we may not resort to any of those established "truths" which we count on each day, and which in reality teem with obscurities from which they could not be freed except precisely by conjuring up the brute world and the labor of knowledge that has posed them over it as a superstructure. For example, everything we can know through experience and science about the "causes" of perception and the action they exercise upon us will be deemed unknown. This is a precept more difficult to follow than one thinks: the temptation to construct perception out of the perceived, to construct our contact with the world out of what it has taught us about the world, is quasi-irresistible. We find authors proving that all "consciousness" is "memory," because I see today a star that perhaps has been extinct for years, and because in general every perception lags behind its object. They do not seem to notice the implications of this "proof": it supposes that the "memory" be defined not by the aspect and characteristics of the remembered but

1. EDITOR: The pagination of the manuscript clearly indicates that the chapter that begins here would not have been retained by the author. It was replaced by "Interrogation and Intuition." Since, however, it was not discarded, we thought it well to present it as an appendix.

from the outside, by the non-existence of an adequate object in the world in itself at that very moment. It therefore presupposes about us this world in itself; between this world and ourselves it presupposes relations of simultaneity and of succession that enclose us in the same objective time with this world; it presupposes a mind capable of knowing this true universe, whose relations, contracted and abbreviated by the short cut of perception, finally make of perception a case of "memory." It is the inverse route we have to follow; it is starting from perception and its variants, described as they present themselves, that we shall try to understand how the universe of knowledge could be constructed. This universe can tell us nothing (except indirectly, by its lacunae and by the aporias in which it throws us) about what is lived by us. It is not because the world called "objective" has such or such properties that we will be authorized to consider them established for the life world: at most they will be for us only a guideline for the study of the means by which we come to recognize those properties in it and encounter them in our life. And, conversely, it is not because in the "objective" world such or such a phenomenon is without visible index that we must forego making it figure in the life world. The discontinuous images of the cinema prove nothing with regard to the phenomenal truth of the movement that connects them before the eyes of the spectator—moreover, they do not even prove that the life world involves movements without a mobile: the mobile could well be projected by him who perceives. Everything that we will advance concerning the world must originate not from the habitual world —where our initiation to being and the great intellectual endeavors that have renewed it in history are inscribed only in the state of confused traces, emptied of their meaning and of their motives—but from that present world which waits at the gates of our life and where we find the means to animate the heritage and, if the occasion arises, to take it up again on our own account. We will not admit a preconstituted world, a logic, except for having seen them arise from our experience of brute being, which is as it were the umbilical cord of our knowledge and the source of meaning for us.

Moreover, we also do not allow ourselves to introduce into our description concepts issued from reflection, whether psychological or transcendental: they are more often than not only correlatives or counterparts of the *objective* world. We must, at the beginning, eschew notions such as "acts of consciousness," "states of consciousness," "matter," "form," and even "image" and "perception." We exclude the term perception to the whole extent that it already implies a cutting up of what is lived into discontinuous acts, or a reference to "things" whose status is not specified, or simply an opposition between the visible and the invisible. Not that these distinctions are definitively meaningless, but because if we were to admit them from the start, we would re-enter the impasses we are trying to avoid. When we speak of *perceptual* faith and when we assign ourselves the task of returning to the *perceptual* faith, by this we not only do not tacitly presuppose any of the physical or physiological "conditions" that delimit perception for the scientist, nor any of the postulates of a sensualist or empiricist philosophy, nor even any definition of a "first layer" of experience that would concern beings existing at a point of time and space, by opposition to the concept or the idea. We do not yet know what to see is and what to think is, whether this distinction is valid, and in what sense. For us, the "perceptual faith" includes everything that is given to the natural man in the original in an experience-source, with the force of what is inaugural and present in person, according to a view that for him is ultimate and could not conceivably be more perfect or closer—whether we are considering things perceived in the ordinary sense of the word, or his initiation into the past, the imaginary, language, the predicative truth of science, works of art, the others, or history. We are not prejudging the relations that may exist between these different "layers," nor even that they are "layers"; and it is a part of our task to decide this, in terms of what questioning our brute or wild experience will have taught us. Perception as an encounter with natural things is at the foreground of our research, not as a simple sensorial function that would explain the others but as the archetype of the originating encounter, imitated and renewed in the encounter with the past, the imaginary, the idea. We do not even know in advance what our interrogation itself and our method will be. The manner of questioning prescribes a certain kind of response, and to fix it now would be to decide our solution. For example, if we were to say that our problem here is to disengage the essence or the Εἶδος of our life in the different regions upon which it opens, this would be to presume that we will find ideal invariants whose relations will themselves be founded in essence; it would be to subordinate from the first what there might be that is fluid to what there might be that is fixed in our experience, to subject it to conditions that perhaps are the conditions not of every possible experience but only of an experience already put into words, and it would be in the end to shut ourselves up in an immanent exploration of the significations of words. Or if, in order to prejudge nothing, we take the determining of the essences in a broader sense as an effort to comprehend oneself, then it arouses no suspicion; but that is because it prescribes nothing as to the style of the results. In fact, we know what the pure questioning must not be; what it will be, we will know only by attempting it. The resolution to confine ourselves to the experience of what is in the originating or fundamental or inaugural sense presupposes nothing more than an encounter between "us" and "what is"—these words being taken as simple indexes of a meaning to be specified. The encounter is indubitable, since without it we would ask no question. We have to interpret it at the start neither as an inclusion in us of what is nor as an inclusion of us in what is. And yet in appearance we do indeed have to be "in" the world, in what is, or else what is has to be "in us." Is not the resolution to ask of experience itself its secret already an idealist commitment? We would have made ourselves badly understood if that were the conclusion drawn. It is to our experience that we address ourselves—because every question is addressed to someone or to something and because we can choose no interlocutor less compromising than *the whole of what is for us.* But the choice of this instance does not close the field of possible responses; we are not implicating in *"our experience"* any reference to an *ego* or to a certain type of intellectual relations with being, such as the Spinozist *"experiri."* We are interrogating our experience precisely in order to know how it opens us to what is not ourselves. *This does not even exclude the possibility that we find in our experience a movement toward what could not in any event be present to us in the original and whose irremediable absence would thus count among our originating experiences.* But, if only in order to see these margins of presence, to discern these references, to put them to the test, or to interrogate them, we do indeed first have to fix our gaze on what is apparently *given* to us. It is in this entirely methodic and provisional sense that the subdivisions we will presently use are to be understood. We do not have to choose between a philosophy that installs itself in the world itself or in the other and a philosophy that installs itself "in us," between a philosophy that takes our experience "from within" and a philosophy, if such be possible, that would judge it from without, in the name of logical criteria, for example: these alternatives are not imperative, since perhaps the self and the non-self are like the obverse and the reverse and since perhaps our own experience *is* this turning round that installs us far indeed from "ourselves," in the other, in the things. Like the natural man, we situate ourselves in ourselves *and* in the things, in ourselves *and* in the other, at the point where, by a sort of *chiasm,* we become the others and we become world. Philosophy is itself only if it refuses for itself the facilities of a world with one sole entry as well as the facilities of a world with multiple entries, all accessible to the philosopher. Like the natural man, it abides at the point where the passage from the self into the world and into the other is effected, at the crossing of the avenues.

I. PRESENCE

The Thing and the Something

LET US THEREFORE CONSIDER OURSELVES installed among the multitude of things, living beings, symbols, instruments, and men, and let us try to form notions that would enable us to comprehend what happens to us there. Our first truth—which prejudges nothing and cannot be contested—will be that there is presence, that "something" is there, and that "someone" is there. Before coming to the "someone," let us ask first what the "something" is.

This something to which we are present and which is present to us is, one is tempted to say, "the things"—and everyone knows, apparently, what must be understood by that. This pebble and this shell are things, in the sense that beyond what I see of them, what I touch of them, beyond their grating contact with my fingers or with my tongue, the noise they make in falling on my table, there is in them one unique foundation of these diverse "properties" (and of many others, yet unknown to me), which imposes them upon the pebble or the shell, or which, at least, contains their variations within certain limits. The power of this principle is not a factual power: I know very well that the pebble, the shell, can be crushed at once by what surrounds them. It is, so to speak, a power *de jure,* a legitimacy: beyond a certain range of their changes, they would cease to be this pebble or this shell, they would even cease to be a pebble or a shell. If they are to subsist as individuals or at least continue to bear these general denominations, they have to exhibit a certain number of properties that are in some way nuclear, that derive from one another, and, all together, emanate from this individual pebble, from this individual shell, or, in general, from every individual of the same name. When we say therefore, that there is here a pebble, a shell, and even this pebble, this shell, we mean that it fulfills these exigencies, that, at least for the moment, this unique foundation of the nuclear properties, which we call briefly "this pebble," or "a pebble," "this shell" or "a shell," manifests itself unimpeded, ready to unfold its nuclear properties under our eyes because they derive from it, because it is without restriction this pebble and this shell, or at least pebble and shell. The thing, therefore, (admitting all that can happen to it and the possibility of its destruction) is a node of properties such that each is given if one is; it is a principle of identity. What it is it is by its internal arrangement, therefore fully, without hesitation, without fissure, totally or not at all. It is what it is of itself or in itself, in an exterior array, which the circumstances allow for and do not explain. It is an ob-ject, that is, it spreads itself out before us by its own efficacy and does so precisely because it is gathered up in itself.

If that is what the thing is, for us who live among things, we have to ask if it is really ever involved originally in our contact with anything at all, if it is really through it that we can comprehend the rest, if our experience is in principle an experience of the thing, if the world, for example, is one immense thing, if our experience aims at the things directly, if we have indeed obtained from our experience its own unadulterated response, or if we have not rather introduced as essential elements that in fact are derived and are themselves in need of clarification. The thing, the pebble, the shell, we said, do not have the power to exist in face of and against everything; they are only mild forces that develop their implications on condition that favorable circumstances be assembled. But if that is so, the identity of the thing with itself, that sort of established position of its own, of rest in itself, that plenitude and that positivity that we have recognized in it already exceed the experience, are already a second interpretation of the experience. Starting with things taken in their native sense as identifiable nuclei, but without any power of their own, we arrive at the thing-object, at the In Itself, at the thing identical with itself, only by imposing upon experience an abstract dilemma which experience ignores. Perhaps the thing has no inner power of its own, but the fact remains that if it is to be able to make itself recognized by us, if it is not to disappear, if we are to be able to speak of things, it is on condition that the appearances behave as though they had an internal principle of unity. It is by opposing to the experience of things the specter of another experience that would not involve things that we force experience to say more than it said. It is by passing through the detour of *names*, by threatening the things with our non-recognition of them, that we finally accredit *objectivity*, self-identity, positivity, plenitude, if not as their own principle, at least as the condition of their possibility *for us*. The thing thus defined is not the thing of our experience, it is the image we obtain of it by projecting it into a universe where experience would not settle on anything, where the spectator would abandon the spectacle—in short, by confronting it with the possibility of nothingness. And so also when we say: even if the thing, *upon analysis*, always lies beyond proof and figures as an extrapolation, still the fact remains that we see pebbles, shells, that, at that moment at least, our exigency is satisfied, and that we have the right to define the thing as that which either is totally itself or is not—this reversal of the pro and the con, this empirical realism founded upon transcendental idealism is still a thinking of experience against the ground of nothingness. But can we think through the experience we have by profiling it over the possibility of nothingness? Is not the experience of the thing and of the world precisely the ground that we need in order to think nothingness in any way whatever? Is not thinking the thing against the ground of nothingness a double error, with regard to the thing and with regard to nothingness, and, by silhouetting it against nothingness, do we not completely denature the thing? Are not the identity, the positivity, the plenitude of the thing—reduced to what they signify in the context in which experience reaches them—quite insufficient to define our openness upon "something"?

Working Notes

Origin of Truth [1]

January, 1959

Introduction

Our state of non-philosophy——Never has the crisis been so radical——

The dialectical "solutions" = either the "bad dialectic" that identifies the opposites, which is non-philosophy—or the "embalmed" dialectic, which is no longer dialectical. End of philosophy or rebirth?

Necessity of a return to ontology——The ontological questioning and its ramifications:

the subject-object question

the question of inter-subjectivity

the question of Nature

Outline of ontology projected as an ontology of brute Being—and of logos. Draw up the picture of wild Being, prolonging my article on Husserl.[2] But the disclosure of this world, of this Being, remains a dead letter as long as we do not uproot "objective philosophy" (Husserl). An *Ursprungsklärung* is needed.

1. EDITOR: *Origin of Truth:* title the author first intended to give his work.

2. EDITOR: "The Philosopher and His Shadow," in *Edmund Husserl, 1859–1959: Recueil commemoratif* (The Hague, 1959); published in *Signes* (Paris, 1960). [English translation by Richard McCleary, *Signs* (Evanston, 1964).]

Reflection on Descartes's ontologies—the "strabism" of Western ontology [3]——

Reflection on Leibniz's ontology.

Generalization of the problem: there was a passage to the infinite as objective infinity——This passage was a thematization (and forgetting) of the *Offenheit*, of the *Lebenswelt*——We have to start anew from behind that point

Plan for Part One: to see (by immanent analysis) what "Nature" has become—and *consequently* life—and consequently man as psycho-physical subject——Circularity of the research: already what we say about Nature anticipates logic and will be taken up again in Part Two——What we say about the soul or the psycho-physical subject anticipates what we will say about reflection, consciousness, reason, and the absolute.——This circularity is no objection——We are following the order of the material, there is no order of the reasons——The order of the reasons would not give us the conviction that the order of the material gives——philosophy as center and not as construction.

Origin of Truth [4]

January, 1959

In showing the divergence between physics and the being of Physis, between biology and the being of life, what is at issue is to effect the passage from being in itself, the objective being, to

---

3. EDITOR: In the abstract of the lecture course he had given in 1957–58, the author had already written: "In Descartes, for example, the two meanings of the word nature (nature in the sense of 'natural light' and in the sense of 'natural inclination') adumbrate two ontologies (an ontology of the object and an ontology of the existent) . . ." And, further down, he asked: "Would there not be here a sort of 'ontological diplopia,' as it has been put (M. Blondel), which, after so many philosophical efforts, we can not expect to be reduced to rationality, so that the only thing to do would be to take it over fully, as the look takes over the monocular images in order to make of them one sole vision?" (*Annuaire du Collège de France*, 58° année [Paris, 1958], pp. 213, 214.)

4. EDITOR: Cf. p. 165, n. 1.

the being of the *Lebenswelt*——And this passage already indicates that no form of being can be posited without reference to the subjectivity, that the body has a *Gegenseite* of consciousness, that it is psycho-physical——

When coming to [the incarnate subjectivity of the human body, which I continue to refer to the *Lebenswelt*,] I must find something that is not the "psychic" in the sense of psychology (that is, a *Gegenabstraktion* to Nature in itself, the Nature of the *blosse Sachen*), I must reach a subjectivity and an intersubjectivity, a universe of *Geist* that, if it not be a second nature, nonetheless has its solidity and its completeness, but has this solidity and completeness still in the mode of the *Lebenswelt*——That is, I must also, across the objectifications of linguistics, of logic, rediscover the *Lebenswelt* logos.

Likewise, it would be necessary in principle to disclose the "organic history" under the historicity (*Urhistorie, erste Geschichtlichkeit*) of truth that has been instituted by Descartes as the infinite horizon of science——This historicity of truth is also what animates Marxism.

In principle it is only then that I would be in a position to define an ontology and to define philosophy. Ontology would be the elaboration of the notions that have to replace that of transcendental subjectivity, those of subject, object, meaning—— the definition of philosophy would involve an elucidation of philosophical expression itself (therefore a becoming conscious of the procedure used in what precedes "naïvely," as though philosophy confined itself to reflecting what is) as the science of pre-science, as the expression of what is before expression *and sustains it from behind*——Take as theme here the difficulty: if philosophy wishes to be absolute, it contains itself. But in reality all the particular analyses concerning Nature, life, the human body, language will make us progressively enter into the *Lebenswelt* and the "wild" being, and as I go along I should not hold myself back from entering into their positive description, nor even into the analysis of the diverse temporalities—say this already in the introduction.

1st volume of the *Origin of Truth* [5]

January, 1959

Husserl: human bodies have an "other side"—a "spiritual" side——

(cf. the mode of being of "hidden sides," hidden forever or provisionally—the mode of being of antipodes—the difference is that *by principle* the "spiritual" side of a living body can be *selbstgegeben* to me only as an absence.)

In my first volume—after physical nature and life, make a third chapter where the human body will be described as having a "spiritual" side. Show that the life of the human body cannot be described without it becoming a psycho-physical body. (Descartes—but while remaining with the compound of soul and body)——Give my equivalent of the Cartesian concept of Nature as the institution that makes us have at one stroke what a divine science would make us understand——Give an aesthesiology. A conception of time, of the "soul," in the Husserlian sense, of intercorporeity qua "natural"——But all that—which takes up again, deepens, and rectifies my first two books—must be entirely carried out within the perspective of ontology——the description of the perceived world with which this first volume concludes is considerably deepened (perception as spread [*écart*] —the body as the animal of movements and perceptions—transcendence—The order of the *urpräsentierbar*). And especially: the problem of the relation between these "truths" and philosophy as radical reflection, as reduction to transcendental immanence, is posed——The "wild" or "brute" being is introduced—the serial time, that of "acts" and decisions, is overcome—the mythical time reintroduced——The problem of the relations between rationality and symbolic function is posed: the exceeding of the signified by the signifier essential to "reason"——Critique of the reflective distinction between the interior series (the "subjective"   the "psychological") and objectivity (such as, according to Lévi-Strauss, our civilizations presuppose it)——Our relation with animality, our "kinship" (Heidegger) made explicit. All this issues in a theory of perception-imperception, and of the

5. EDITOR: Above the title, these lines: "Indicate from the start of the analysis of Nature that there is circularity: what we say here will be taken up again at the level of the logic (2d volume). No matter. One does have to begin."

Logos endiathetos (of meaning before logic)———Of the *Lebens-welt*———This new ontology must be presented in a schema in a fourth chapter (1. nature and physics; 2. life; 3. the human body; 4. "wild" being and logos). (4th chapter long, giving to the volume a "definitive" character—while initiating the transition to the study of painting, music, language.[6]

Bare all the *roots* (the "vertical" world)———Then say that the problem is posed again by the conversion of language, the passage to the "interior" man———It is only then that one will be definitively able to appraise humanism.

Being and infinity

January 17, 1959

Infinity: it is to be sure a conquest to have conceived the universe as infinity—or at least on the ground of infinity (the Cartesians)———

But have the Cartesians really done so?———Have they really seen the depth of being, which is recognized only with the notion of infinity [an inexhaustible reserve of being which is not only this and that but could have been other (Leibniz) or is effectively more than we know (Spinoza, the unknown attributes)]?

Their notion of infinity is positive. They have devaluated the closed world for the benefit of a positive infinity, of which they speak as one speaks of some thing, which they *demonstrate* in "objective philosophy"———the signs are reversed: all the determinations are negation in the sense of: are *only* negation———This is to elude infinity rather than to recognize it———Infinity congealed or given to a thought that possesses it at least enough to be able to prove it.

The veritable infinity cannot be that: it must be what exceeds us: the infinity of *Offenheit* and not *Unendlichkeit*——— Infinity of the *Lebenswelt* and not infinity of idealization——— Negative infinity, therefore———Meaning or reason which *are* contingency.

6. EDITOR: The second parenthesis opened is not closed.

The brute or wild Being (= the perceived world) and its relation with the λόγος προφορικός as *Gebilde*, with the "Logic" that we
produce——

January, 1959

The "amorphous" perceptual world that I spoke of in relation
to painting—perpetual resources for the remaking of painting
—which contains no mode of expression and which nonetheless
calls them forth and requires all of them and which arouses
again with each painter a new effort of expression—this perceptual world is at bottom Being in Heidegger's sense, which is more
than all painting, than all speech, than every "attitude," and
which, apprehended by philosophy in its universality, appears as
containing everything that will ever be said, and yet leaving us to
create it (Proust): it is the λόγος ἐνδιάθετος which calls for the λόγος
προφορικός——

[Iteration of the *Lebenswelt:* we are making a philosophy of
the *Lebenswelt,* our construction (in the mode of "logic") makes
us rediscover this world of silence. Rediscover in what sense?
Was it already there? How can we say that it was there since
nobody knew it before the philosopher said it?——But it is true
that it was there: everything we said and say did and does
involve it. It was there precisely as non-thematized *Lebenswelt.*
In a sense it is still involved as non-thematized by the very statements that describe it: for the statements as such will in their
turn be sedimented, "taken back" by the *Lebenswelt,* will be comprehended in it rather than they comprehend it—are already
comprehended in it insofar as they imply a whole *Selbst-
verständlichkeit*——But this does not prevent philosophy from
having value, from being something else than and more than the
simple partial product of the *Lebenswelt,* enclosed in a language
that leads us on. Between the *Lebenswelt* as universal Being and
philosophy as a furthermost product of the world, there is no
rivalry or antinomy: it is philosophy that discloses it]

Tacit Cogito

January, 1959

The Cogito of Descartes (reflection) is an operation on significations, a statement of relations between them (and the
significations themselves sedimented in acts of expression). It

therefore presupposes a prereflective contact of self with self (the non-thetic consciousness [of] self   Sartre) or a tacit cogito (being close by oneself)—this is how I reasoned in *Ph. P.*[7]

Is this correct? What I call the tacit cogito is impossible. To have the idea of "thinking" (in the sense of the "thought of seeing and of feeling"), to make the "reduction," to return to immanence and to the consciousness of . . . it is necessary to have words. It is by the combination of words (with their charge of sedimented significations, which are in principle capable of entering into other relations than the relations that have served to form them) that I *form* the transcendental attitude, that I *constitute* the constitutive consciousness. The words do not refer to positive significations and finally to the flux of the *Erlebnisse* as *Selbstgegeben*. Mythology of a self-consciousness to which the word "consciousness" would refer——There are only *differences* between significations.

Yet there is a world of silence, the perceived world, at least, is an order where there are non-language significations—yes, non-language significations, but they are not accordingly *positive.* There is for example no absolute flux of singular *Erlebnisse;* there are fields and a field of fields, with a *style* and a typicality ——Describe the existentials that make up the armature of the transcendental field——And which are always a relation between the agent (I can) and the sensorial or ideal field. The sensorial agent = the body——The ideal agent = speech——All this belongs to the order of the *Lebenswelt* "transcendental," that is, of transcendencies bearing "their" object

Reduction——The true transcendental——the *Rätsel Erscheinungweisen*——world

February, 1959

Wrongly presented—in particular in the *C.M.*[8]—as a suspending of the *existence of the world*——If that is what it is, it

---

7. EDITOR: *Phénoménologie de la perception* (Paris, 1945). On the notion of a tacit Cogito and the critique of the Cartesian Cogito, cf. pp. 460–68. [English translation by Colin Smith, *Phenomenology of Perception* (New York, 1962), pp. 402–9.]

8. EDITOR: Edmund Husserl, *Cartesianische Meditationen und Pariser Vorträge* (The Hague, 1950). [English translation by Dorion Cairns, *Cartesian Meditations* (The Hague, 1960).]

lapses into the Cartesian defect of being a *hypothesis of the Nichtigkeit of the world,* which immediately has as its consequence the maintenance of the *mens sive anima* (a fragment of the world) as indubitable——Every negation of the world, *but also* every neutrality with regard to the existence of the world, has as its immediate consequence that one misses the transcendental. The *epoché* has the right to be a neutralization only with regard to the world as effective in itself, to the pure exteriority: it must leave extant the phenomenon of this effective in itself, of this exteriority.

The transcendental field is a field of transcendencies. The transcendental, being a resolute overcoming of the *mens sive anima* and the psychological, *goes beyond the subjectivity* in the sense of counter-transcendence and immanence. The passage to intersubjectivity is contradictory only with regard to an insufficient reduction, Husserl was right to say. But a sufficient reduction leads beyond the alleged transcendental "immanence," it leads to the absolute spirit understood as *Weltlichkeit,* to *Geist* as *Ineinander* of the spontaneities, itself founded on the aesthesiological *Ineinander* and on the sphere of life as sphere of *Einfühlung* and intercorporeity——The notion of *species* = notion of interanimality. The intertwining of biology or psychology and philosophy = *Selbstheit* of the *world.*

Husserl himself raises the question how the world can have for me another "meaning as to its being" (*Seinssinn*) than that of *my* transcendental intentional object. *Wie kann für mich wirklich Seiendes . . . anderes sein als sozusagen Schnittpunkt meiner konstitutiven Synthesis?* (*C.M.,* § 48, p. 135).

It is in this way, says H., that is introduced the *Fremderfahrung Analyse,* which is not a temporal genesis: the objective transcendence is not *posterior* to the position of the other: the world is already there, in its objective transcendence, before this analysis, and it is its very meaning that will be rendered explicit as meaning. . . . [Hence the introduction of the other is not what produces the "objective transcendence": the other is one of its indexes, a moment of it, but it is in the world itself that the possibility of the other will be found].

The "pure others" (which are not yet "men") already introduce a Nature of which I am a part (*C.M.,* p. 137)

[margin note:] Hs. didn't list reduction properly

Einströmen—Reflection

February, 1959

Because there is Einströmen, reflection is not adequation, coincidence: it would not pass *into* the *Strom* if it placed us back at the source of the *Strom*——

Look up the passage (from *Krisis III,* I think) where it is said that the phenomenological reduction *transforms universal history*——

The *Einströmen:* a particular case of sedimentation, that is, of secondary passivity, that is, of *latent* intentionality——It is Péguy's *historical inscription*——It is the fundamental structure of *Zeitigung: Urstiftung* of a point of time——[Through?] this *latent* intentionality, intentionality ceases to be what it is in Kant: *pure actualism,* ceases to be a property of consciousness, of its "attitudes" and of its acts, to become *intentional life*——It becomes the thread that binds, for example, my present to my past in its temporal place, such as it was (and not such as I reconquer it by an *act* of evocation) the possibility of this *act* rests on the primordial structure of retention as an interlocking of the pasts in one another plus a consciousness of this interlocking as a *law* (cf. the reflective iteration: the reflection reiterated ever anew would give only "always the same thing" *immer wieder*)——Husserl's error is to have described the interlocking starting from a *Präsensfeld* considered as without thickness, as immanent consciousness: [9] it is transcendent consciousness, it is being at a distance, it is the double ground of my life of consciousness, and it is what makes there be able to be *Stiftung* not only of an instant but of a whole *system of temporal indexes*——time (already as time of the body, taximeter time of the corporeal schema) is the model of these symbolic matrices, which are openness upon being.

In OR [10] after analyses of the psychophysical body pass to analyses of memory and of the imaginary—of temporality and *from there* to the Cogito and intersubjectivity.

9. EDITOR: The author already speaks of the *Präsensfeld* or of the field of presence in the *Phénoménologie de la perception,* in the chapter devoted to Space and to Temporality. Cf. in particular pp. 307, 475, 483–84, 492. [Eng. trans., pp. 265, 415–16, 422–23, 430.] But the analysis did not at that time lead to a critique of Husserl.

10. EDITOR: *The Origin of Truth.* Cf. above, p. 165, n. 1.

Philosophy as creation (*Gebilde*), resting on itself—that cannot be the final truth.

For it would be a creation that sets as its goal to express as *Gebilde* what is *von selbst* (the *Lebenswelt*), that therefore negates itself as pure creation——

The point of view of creation, of the human *Gebilde*—and the point of view of the "natural" (of the *Lebenswelt* as Nature) are both abstract and insufficient. One cannot install oneself on either of these two levels.

What there is is a creation that is called forth and engendered by the *Lebenswelt* as operative, latent historicity, that prolongs it and bears witness to it——

(Verbal) *Wesen*——*Wesen* of history

February, 1959

Discovery of the (verbal) *Wesen:* first expression of the being that is neither being-object nor being-subject, neither essence nor existence: what *west* (the being-rose of the rose, the being-society of society, the being-history of history) answers to the question *was* as well as the question *dass;* it is not society, the rose seen by a subject, it is not a being for itself of society and of the rose (contrary to what Ruyer says): it is the roseness extending itself throughout the rose, it is what Bergson rather badly called the "images"——That in addition this roseness gives rise to a "general idea," that is, that there be several roses, a *species* rose, this is not insignificant, but results from the being-rose considered in all its implications (natural generativity)——In this way—striking all generality from the first definition of the *Wesen*—one suppresses that opposition of the fact and the essence which falsifies everything——

The being society of a society: that whole that reassembles all the views and all the clear or blind wills at grips within it, that anonymous whole which through them *hinauswollt*, that *Ineinander* which nobody sees, and which is not a group-soul either, neither object nor subject, but their connective tissue, which *west* since there will be a result, and which is the sole concession one could legitimately make to a "philosophy of several entries" (for the argument against the alternative thought of Sartre, which is that it does not make up *a world,* that it does not admit a *Weltlichkeit* of *Geist,* that it remains at the subjective spirit, must not serve to justify a philosophy where all the Egos would be on the same plane, and which thus would purely and simply ignore the problem of the other, and can be realized only as a Philosophy of the Absolute Subject)

The *Wesen* of the table ≠ a being in itself, in which the elements would be arranged ≠ a being for itself, a Synopsis = that which "tablefies" in it, what makes the table be a table.

Tacit Cogito and speaking subject

February, 1959

The dialectic become *thesis* (statement) is no longer dialectical ("embalmed" dialectic).
This is not for the profit of a *Grund* of which one could not *say* anything. The failure of the thesis, its (dialectical) reversal discloses the *Source of theses,* the physico-historical *Lebenswelt,* to which we have to return   To recommence perception, *Einfühlung,* and in particular speech, and not to eschew them. We know simply that, if it is to remain dialectical, speech can no longer be statement, *Satz,* it must be thinking speech, without reference to a *Sachverhalt,* speaking (*parole*) and not language (*langage*) (and in fact it is indeed the speaking, not the language [*la langue*] that aims at the other as a behavior, not as a "psychism," that responds to the other before he would have been understood as "psychism," in a confrontation that repels or accepts his utterances as utterances, as events——It is indeed speaking that constitutes, *in front of* myself as a signification and a subject of signification, a milieu of communication, an intersubjective diacritical system which is the spoken tongue [*la langue*] in the present, not a "human" universe, an objective spirit)——The problem is to restore this, in the present and in the past, the *Lebenswelt* history, to restore the very presence of a culture. The failure of the dialectic as thesis or "dialectical philosophy" is the discovery of this intersubjectivity which is not perspectival but vertical, which is, extended into the past, existential eternity, savage mind (*esprit sauvage*)

[margin note: *Speaking creates signification*]

The tacit Cogito does not, of course, solve these problems. In disclosing it as I did in *Ph.P.*[11] I did not arrive at a solution (my

11. EDITOR: *Phenomenology of Perception.* Cf. p. 171, n. 7.

chapter on the Cogito is not connected with the chapter on speech): on the contrary I posed a problem. The tacit Cogito should make understood how language is not impossible, but cannot make understood how it is possible——There remains the problem of the passage from the perceptual meaning to the language meaning, from behavior to thematization. Moreover the thematization itself must be understood as a behavior of a higher degree——the relation between the thematization and the behavior is a dialectical relation: language realizes, by breaking the silence, what the silence wished and did not obtain. Silence continues to envelop language; the silence of the absolute language, of the thinking language.——But for these customary developments on the dialectical relation to not be a *Weltanschauung* philosophy, unhappy consciousness, they must issue in a theory of the savage mind, which is the mind of praxis. Like all praxis, language supposes a *selbstverständlich*, an instituted, which is *Stiftung* preparing an *Endstiftung*——The problem is to grasp *what*, across the successive and simultaneous community of speaking subjects, *wishes*, *speaks*, and finally *thinks*.

Genealogy of logic
History of being
History of meaning

February, 1959

In the introduction (fundamental thought)
say that I must show that what one might consider to be "psychology" (*Phenomenology of Perception*) is in fact ontology. Do so by showing that the being of science can neither be nor be thought as *selbständig*. Whence the chapters on: Physics and Nature—animality—the human body as *nexus rationum* or *vinculum substantiale*.

But being must not only be made manifest through its divergence from the being of Science——In doing so what is at issue is to make it manifest by opposition to being as Object——I must therefore show in the introduction that the being of science is itself a part or an aspect of the objectified Infinity and that the *Offenheit* of the *Umwelt* is opposed to both of these. Whence the chapters on Descartes, Leibniz, Western ontology, which indi-

cate the historico-intentional and ontological implications of the
being of science.

In what follows (Physics and Physis—Animality—the
human body as psycho-physical), what is at issue is to operate
the reduction, that is, for me, to disclose little by little—and
more and more—the "wild" or "vertical" world. Show the intentional reference of Physics to Physis, of Physis to life, of life to
the "psycho-physical"—a reference by which one nowise passes
from the "exterior" to the "interior," since the reference is not a
reduction and since each degree "surpassed" remains in fact
presupposed (for example, the Physis of the beginning is nowise
"surpassed" by what I will say of man: it is the *correlative* of
animality as it is of man)——It is necessary then on the way to
form the theory of this "reflection" that I practice; it is not a
going back up to the "conditions of possibility"——And this is
why it is a question of an ascent on the spot (*ascension sur
place*)——Conversely everything that follows is already anticipated in what I say about Physis——This is why from the start I
must indicate the ontological import of this *Besinnung* on Physis
——We will close the circle after the study of logos and history
as Proust closes the circle when he comes to the moment where
the narrator decides to write. The end of a philosophy is the
account of its beginning.——Show this circularity, this intentional implication in a circle—and, at the same time, the *His-
tory-philosophy* circularity: * [12] I clarify my philosophical project
by recourse to Descartes and Leibniz, and that project alone will
permit knowing what history is. State all this as theses and not
only by implication.
Circularity: everything that is said at each "level" anticipates

* History-*Dichtung* thereby justified, in opposition to Gueroult.
Objective history is a dogmatic rationalism, *is a philosophy*, and not
what it claims to be, a history of what is. What is criticizable in my
history-*Dichtung* is not that it expresses *me* as a philosopher—it is
that it does not express me completely, that it also modifies me.
The history of philosophy, like science, is a *communis opinio*.

12. EDITOR: For the concept of history-*Dichtung*, cf. Husserl,
who speaks of a *Dichtung der Philosophiegeschichte*. (*Die Krisis der
Europäischen Wissenschaften und die transcendentale Phänomenologie, Husserliana,* Vol. VI [The Hague, 1954], p. 513.) The passage
concerned is copiously underlined in the copy of *Krisis* the author
owned.

and will be taken up again: for example, I make a description of the aesthesiological *Einfühlung* which is neither false, nor "true" in the absolute sense: for it is obviously a "layer" separated abstractly——It is not false either, since all the rest is anticipated in it: that is, the *Einfühlung* of the I think. What is constantly and principally implied throughout this whole first part is the λόγος: I speak of the things as if that did not call language into question! The thematization of language overcomes another stage of naïveté, discloses yet a little more the horizon of *Selbstverständlichkeiten*——the passage from philosophy to the absolute, to the transcendental field, to the wild and "vertical" being is *by definition* progressive, incomplete. This is to be understood not as an imperfection (a *Weltanschauung* philosophy, unhappy consciousness of the Encompassing) but as a philosophical *theme:* the incompleteness of the reduction ("biological reduction," "psychological reduction," "reduction to transcendental immanence," and finally "fundamental thought") is not an obstacle to the reduction, it is the reduction itself, the rediscovery of vertical being.——

There will therefore be a whole series of layers of wild being It will be necessary to recommence the *Einfühlung,* the Cogito several times.——

For example, at the level of the human body I will describe a pre-knowing; a pre-meaning, a silent knowing.

sense of the perceived: "size" before measurement, the physiognomic size of a rectangle, for example

sense of the other perceived: *Einigung* of my perception of one same man by virtue of existentials which are not literally "perceived" and yet operate in perceptions (Wolff) [13]

sense of "perceived life" (Michotte): [14] what makes an appearance *animate itself* and become "creeping" etc.

But I will then have to disclose a non-explicitated horizon: that of the language I am using to describe all that——And which co-determines its final meaning

13. EDITOR: Werner Wolff, *Selbstbeurteilung und Fremdbeurteilung im wissentlichen und unwissentlichen Versuch,* Ps. Forchung, 1932.

14. EDITOR: A. Michotte, *La Perception de la causalité* (Louvain and Paris, 1946), pp. 176–77. [English translation by T. R. Miles and Elaine Miles, *The Perception of Causality* (New York, 1963).]

Therefore very important, from the introduction on, to introduce the problem of the tacit cogito and the language cogito

Naïveté of Descartes who does not see a tacit cogito under the cogito of *Wesen,* of significations——But naïveté also of a silent cogito that would deem itself to be an adequation with the silent consciousness, whereas its very description of silence rests entirely on the virtues of language. The taking possession of the world of silence, such as the description of the human body effects it, is no longer this world of silence, it is the world articulated, elevated to the *Wesen,* spoken—the description of the perceptual λόγος is a usage of λόγος προφορικός. Can this rending characteristic of reflection (which, wishing to return to itself, *leaves itself)* come to an end? There would be needed a silence that envelops the speech anew, after one has come to recognize that speech enveloped the alleged silence of the psychological coincidence. What will this silence be? As the reduction finally is not for Husserl a transcendental immanence, but the disclosing of the *Weltthesis,* this silence will *not be the contrary* of language.

I will finally be able to take a position in ontology, as the introduction demands, and specify its theses exactly, only after the series of reductions the book develops and which are all in the first one, but also are really accomplished only in the last one. This reversal itself—*circulus vitiosus deus* [15]—is not hesitation, bad faith and bad dialectic, but return to Σιγή the abyss.[16] *One cannot make a direct ontology.* My "indirect" method (being in the beings) is alone conformed with being——"negative philosophy" like "negative theology."

15. EDITOR: The expression is in Nietzsche. *Beyond Good and Evil,* § 56, French translation (Paris, 1929), pp. 100–101. [English translation by Walter Kaufmann (New York, 1966), p. 68.]

16. EDITOR: No doubt a reminiscence of Claudel. "Time is the way offered to all that will be to be no longer. It is the *Invitation to die,* for every phrase to decompose in the explicative and total concordance, to consummate the speech of adoration addressed to the ear of *Sigè* the Abyss" (*Art poétique* [Paris, 1951], p. 57).

Weltlichkeit of *Geist*——
the *"invisible world"*
non-being in the object-Being: *Seyn*

February, 1959

One always talks of the problem of "the other," of "intersubjectivity," etc. . . . .

In fact what has to be understood is, beyond the "persons," the existentials according to which we comprehend them, and which are the sedimented meaning of all our voluntary and involuntary experiences. This unconscious is to be sought not at the bottom of ourselves, behind the back of our "consciousness," but in front of us, as articulations of our field. It is "unconscious" by the fact that it is not an *object*, but it is that through which objects are possible, it is the constellation wherein our future is read——It is between them as the interval of the trees between the trees, or as their common level. It is the *Urgemeinshaftung* of our intentional life, the *Ineinander* of the others in us and of us in them.

It is these existentials that make up the (substitutable) *meaning* of what we say and of what we understand. They are the armature of that "invisible world" which, with speech, begins to impregnate all the things we see—as the "other" space, for the schizophrenic, takes possession of the sensorial and visible space ——Not that it becomes a visible space in its turn: in the visible there is never anything but ruins of the spirit, the world will always resemble the Forum, at least before the gaze of the philosopher, who does not completely inhabit it——

Our "interior life": a world in the world, a region within it, a "place from which we speak" (Heidegger) and into which we introduce the others by true speech.

The "invisible world": it is given originally as *non-Urpräsentierbar*, as the other is in his body *given originally as absent*—as a divergence, as a transcendence (*Ideen II*)

Describe this experience of qualified non-being

Before *the other* is, the things are such non-beings, divergencies——There is an *Einfühlung* and a lateral relation with the things no less than with the other: to be sure the things are not interlocutors, the *Einfühlung* that gives them gives them as mute—but precisely: they are variants of the successful *Einfühlung*. Like madmen or animals they are *quasi-companions*.

uncs. –
as the
field wch.
makes the
objects ◇

They are lifted from my substance, thorns in my flesh——To say that there is transcendence, being at a distance, is to say that being (in the Sartrean sense) is thus inflated with non-being or with the possible, that it is not only *what it is*. The *Gestalthafte*, if one really wanted to define it, would be that. The very notion of *Gestalt*—if one wishes to define it in its own terms and not *a contrario*, as "what is not" the sum of the elements—is that.

And at the same time the *perception of* . . . the *Gestalt* cannot be a centrifugal *Sinngebung*, the imposition of an essence, a *vor-stellen*——One cannot distinguish *Empfindung* and *Empfundenes* here. It is *openness*——

If the feeling, the perceiving are understood in this way, one understands that there be *Unwahr* in the *Wahrheit*.

Science and philosophy [17]

February, 1959

The method of defining language by the pertinent; the that without which. . . . No—one locates *where* the speech passes. But this does not give speech in its full power. One would be led into error if one thought that speech *is in* these congealed relations——It is the error of scientism, which is a scientific error, and reveals itself as such (the impossibility of understanding evolutive linguistics, history——*Reduction* to synchrony——) ——What is nonetheless good and necessary in the scientific attitude: *the assuming of a position of complete ignorance with regard to language,* not presupposing our rationalization of language which is inherited. Act as if the language were not our own. Cf. Freud: the assuming of a position of ignorance before the dream, the consciousness——One will interrogate them without *Einfühlung*——Negatively, as a disclosure of the "unknown" language, this attitude is profoundly philosophical, it is constitutive of the attitude of reflection at its best. This reflection is not, and cannot be, a limitation to the phenomenology of the *Erlebnisse*. The mistrust with regard to lived experience is philosophical—one postulates that the consciousness deceives us about ourselves and about language and one is right: this is the only

17. EDITOR: This note was written after a lecture given by M. André Martinet at the Ecole Normale Supérieure on February 27, 1959.

way to *see* them. Philosophy has nothing to do with the privilege of the *Erlebnisse,* with the psychology of lived experience, etc. Similarly in history it is not a question of reinstating "decisions" as the causes of the "processes." The interiority the philosopher seeks is in any case the intersubjectivity, the *Urgemein Stiftung* which is well beyond "lived experience"——*Besinnung* versus *Erlebnisse.* But this abstention from all *Einfühlung* with language, with animals, etc. leads back to a superior *Einfühlung,* which is intended to make it possible. The search for the "wild" view of the world nowise limits itself to a return to precomprehension or to prescience. "Primitivism" is only the counterpart of scientism, and is still scientism. The phenomenologists (Scheler, Heidegger) are right in pointing out this precomprehension which precedes inductivity, for it is this that calls in question the ontological value of the *Gegen-stand.* But a return to pre-science is not the goal. The reconquest of the *Lebenswelt* is the reconquest of a *dimension,* in which the objectifications of science themselves retain a meaning and are to be understood as *true* (Heidegger himself says this: every *Seinsgeschick* is true, is part of the *Seinsgeschichte*)—the pre-scientific is only an invitation to comprehend the meta-scientific and this last is not non-science. It is even disclosed *through* the constitutive movements of science, on condition that we reactivate them, that we see that left to themselves they *verdecken.* For example, the structuralist attitude = the verbal chain, language as recreating itself entirely under our eyes in each act of speech, the intent to circumscribe the act of speaking where *it is formed,* is the intent to return to the originating, to the *Ursprung*—on condition that one not shut oneself up in the factual, synchronic determination—is the intent to grasp the cohesion of the synchronic-diachronic whole within speech, the *monumental* speech, therefore, mythical, if one likes——Ambiguity of the constitutive act of science: the exclusive attention to the verbal chain, to phonics and semantics *intertwined,*

is: 1st, the exigency to grasp the *Ursprung*   *Entdeckung* of the *Ursprung.*

    2d, the reduction to the *Gegenstand,* i.e. *Verdeckung* of the *Ursprung.*

February, 1959

Make Part One: first outline of ontology——

Start from the present: contradictions etc.
ruin of philosophy——
Show that that calls in question not only the classical philosophy, but also the philosophies of the dead god (Kierkegaard—Nietzsche—Sartre) inasmuch as they are its contrary. (and also, of course, the dialectic as a "maneuver")

Take up again the whole philosophical movement in a "fundamental thought"——

Results of *Ph.P.*[18]——Necessity of bringing them to ontological explicitation:

the thing—the world—Being
the negative—the cogito—the Other—language.

The problems that remain after this first description: they are due to the fact that in part I retained the philosophy of "consciousness"
Disclosure of the wild or brute Being by way of Husserl and the *Lebenswelt* upon which one opens. What is Philosophy? The domain of the *Verborgen* (philosophy and occultism)
Once this whole outline is made, say what an outline is, why an outline is needed and why it is only an outline. It is the beginning necessary and sufficient to see well what is at stake: Being—but not yet to ensure our steps in this land——A *wiederholung* is necessary:
"destruction" of the objectivist ontology of the Cartesians
Rediscovery of φύσις, then of λόγος and the vertical history starting from our "culture" and the *Winke* of our "science"——
My whole first part to be conceived in a very direct, contemporary manner, like the *Krisis* of Husserl: show our non-philosophy, then seek its origin in a historical *Selbstbesinnung* and in a *Selbstbesinnung* on our culture which is science: in it will be sought the *Winke*

18. EDITOR: *Phenomenology of Perception.*

Time——

[undated, probably February or March, 1959]

The upsurge of time would be incomprehensible as the *creation* of a supplement of time that would push the whole preceding series back into the past. That passivity is not conceivable.

On the other hand every analysis of time that views it from above is insufficient.

Time must *constitute itself*—be always seen from the point of view of someone who *is of it*.

But this seems to be contradictory, and would lead back to one of the two terms of the preceding alternative.

The contradiction is lifted only if the new present is itself a transcendent: one knows that it is not there, that it was just there, one never coincides with it——It is not a segment of time with defined contours that would come and set itself in place. It is a cycle defined by a central and dominant region and with indecisive contours—a swelling or bulb of time——A creation of this sort alone makes possible 1) the influence of the "contents" on time which passes "more quickly" or "less quickly," of *Zeitmaterie* on *Zeitform;* 2) the acceptance of the truth of the transcendental analysis: time is not an absolute series of events, a tempo—not even the tempo of the consciousness—it is an institution, a system of equivalences

March, 1959

Leray's report at the C.d.F.: [19] the "strange" particles
The "existence" of a particle that would endure but a billionth of a second. . . .
What does such an *existence* mean?
One conceives it after the model of macroscopic existence: with an enlargement, an adequate temporal magnifying glass, this brief duration would be like one of the durations we do have experience of.
And since the enlargement can always be conceived still greater —one postulates at the same time the *there is* of a minimum

19. EDITOR: Refers to the report of the work of M. Louis Leprince-Ringuet presented by M. Jean Leray to the Assembly of the Professors of the Collège de France, March 15, 1959.

(without which one would not seek the microscopical, under the macroscopical), and that it is always beneath, in horizon. . . . It is the very structure of a horizon—but it is evident that this structure means nothing in the in itself—that it has meaning only in the *Umwelt* of a carnal subject, as *Offenheit*, as *Verborgenheit* of Being. As long as one does not establish oneself in this ontological order, one has a top-heavy thought, an empty or contradictory thought. . . .
Kant's or Descartes's analysis: the world is neither finite nor infinite, it is indefinite—i.e. it is to be thought as *human* experience—of a finite understanding faced with an infinite Being (or: Kant: with an *abyss* of human thought)
This is not at all what Husserl's *Offenheit* or Heidegger's *Verborgenheit* means: the ontological milieu is not thought of as an order of "human representation" in contrast with an order of the in itself——It is a matter of understanding that truth itself has no meaning outside of the relation of transcendence, outside of the *Ueberstieg* toward the horizon—that the "subjectivity" and the "object" are one sole whole, that the subjective "lived experiences" count in the world, are part of the *Weltlichkeit* of the "mind," are entered in the "register" which is Being, that the object is nothing else than the *tuft* of these *Abschattungen*. . . . It is not we who perceive, it is the thing that perceives itself yonder—it is not we who speak, it is truth that speaks itself at the depths of speech——Becoming-nature of man which is the becoming-man of nature——The world is a *field*, and as such is always open.

[margin note: wld as field.]

Resolve similarly the problem of the unicity or plurality of times (Einstein): by return to the idea of horizon——

Visible and invisible, 2d Part

May, 1959

(Being and the world:
on Descartes, Leibniz, etc.)

Say: what we say there, is it the thing itself? No, there are historical motivations. the *Lebenswelt* is "subjective"——How disclose them? The history of philosophy will be only the projection of these views—or will be meaningless by dint of wanting to be "objective." *Our* problems and the problems immanent in *a* philosophy: can one pose the first to the second? (Gouhier) [20] There is but one solution: show that there is transcendence, to be sure, between the philosophies, not reduction to one unique plane, but that, in this spread staggered out in depth, they nevertheless refer to one another, it is nevertheless a question of the same Being——Show between the philosophies a perceptual relation or a relation of transcendence. Hence a vertical history, which has its rights alongside of the "objective" history of philosophy——Apply here the very conception of perceptual being and *Offenheit* that has been developed in Part One——Study how this is different from relativism, how the "projection" of one thought in the other lets a "nucleus of being" appear nevertheless (cf. Lefort's exposition on Machiavelli: [21] how, in what sense, can one claim to go to the things themselves while refusing this right to the others? It is necessary to account for their views and for oneself—but it is in addition necessary that what is aimed at be interrogation, *Befragung*).

Philosophy: circles that include one another: this Part One is already an exercise of history, it arises from the historical *Lebenswelt*——And conversely the history of philosophy that we will evoke was already a certain kind of *Umwelt*——Concept of ontological history. The rendering explicit of the *Umwelt* of Western ontology, when confronted with our beginning, is to give it solidity, rectify it—(connection of the concepts: Being Nature Man) Of course this will not be exhaustive: they are threads of vertical history, disheveled, they are not essences.

So also the analysis of Nature will be a way to find the beginning again and to rectify it (alleged contact with the thing itself); one rediscovers the originating *a contrario* across the movements of the collective scientific thought.

The recourse to the history of philosophy is already a theory of history, of language, etc.

20. EDITOR: Allusion to M. Henri Gouhier's *L'Histoire et sa philosophie* (Paris, 1952). The question is raised in particular with regard to Hamelin's interpretation of Descartes. Cf. pp. 18–20.
21. EDITOR: Unpublished lecture given at the Institut Français de Sociologie in May, 1959.

The visible and the invisible

May, 1959

Part one: Ontological outline
    Chapter I   The world and being
    Chapter II   Being and the world

(Show that metaphysics is a naïve ontology, *is* a sublimation of the Entity (*Etant*)————But this is evidently a transposition of metaphysics, interpreted according to the views of Chapter I.

It is necessary to establish the *right* to this transposition. Is it a "putting into perspective" that would be forever indemonstrable? Does one remain in dialectical empiricism and the reciprocity of the perspectives?

No. It is not a matter of "history of philosophy." The history of philosophy always involves this subjectivity. Show that the interpretation of Descartes by Gueroult, for example, always involves a subjective bringing into perspective (the "subjective" is here precisely the presupposition that philosophy is made of "*problems*"————cf. the inaugural lecture: that is what he opposes to Bergson [22]).————What I propose is not a "view" of history of philosophy. Or else it is history, but structural: i.e. not the event of such and such a philosophy as a *creation* and a *solution* of "problems," but this philosophy situated within the hieratic ensemble of Being and the existential eternity, i.e. within an *interrogative* ensemble which, like Lefort's *Machiavelli*,[23] is not a dogmatism.

Cf. Pingaud, *Madame de La Fayette:* [24] Madame de La Fayette's book *is* a Court book (*appearance, restraint*) But, once the Court had disappeared, the book, detached from these historical roots, gives rise to a myth from 1808 onwards. The (mythical) significance would be *created* through ignorance of the social background.

In a sense, the signification is always the divergence: what the other says appears to me to be full of meaning because his *lacunae* are never where mine are. Perspective multiplicity.

22. EDITOR: Inaugural lecture given at the Collège de France on December 4, 1951, by M. Martial Gueroult upon assuming the chair of the history and technology of philosophical systems.
23. EDITOR: Reference to a work in preparation.
24. EDITOR: *Mme. de La Fayette par elle-même* (Paris, 1959).

But this reduction to the myth presupposes a ground of non-mythical positivity which is another myth. One has to understand that *myth, mystification, alienation* etc. are second-order concepts.

Madame de La Fayette is a myth, but not in the sense that the myth is a construction. In the sense that (Lévi-Strauss) every usage of the symbolic function is a myth.

It is not just any text that can acquire this mythical power. Beware of the new *Aufklärung*.

What there is in *The Princess of Clèves* that makes it capable of becoming a myth.

So also Descartes, metaphysics: I do not mean to say that these are myths in the sense of: artifices without truth, a confused view of what ontology *should* be today——There is the truth of Descartes, but on condition that one reads it between the lines; the atmosphere of Descartes's thought, the Cartesian functioning; and this is not the imposition of an exterior point of view upon Descartes, of a *question* that is not his own upon his philosophy. Show that there is an absolute, a philosophy, which is immanent in the history of philosophy, and which nonetheless is not a reabsorption of all the philosophies into one sole philosophy, nor eclecticism and scepticism either. One sees it if one succeeds in making of philosophy a perception, and of the history of philosophy a perception of history——Everything comes down to this: form a theory of perception and of comprehension that shows that to comprehend is not to constitute in intellectual immanence, that to comprehend is to apprehend by coexistence, laterally, *by the style,* and thereby to attain at once the far-off reaches of this style and of this cultural apparatus.

What I will say there about the history of philosophy anticipates what I will say about the Cogito and logos——So also what I say in the first chapter anticipates the conception of the history of philosophy of Chapter II. And likewise all that anticipates the comprehension of science (of Nature) given in the following chapters. There are only anticipations, *Vorhabe.* Philosophy as concentric problems. But it is so—

Perception——unconscious——One [25]——retrograde movement
of the true——sedimentation (of which the retrograde movement of the true is a part)

May 2, 1959

The taxi driver at Manchester, saying to me (I understood
only a few seconds later, so briskly were the words "struck off"):
I will ask the police where *Brixton Avenue* is.——Likewise, in
the tobacco shop, the woman's phrase: *Shall I wrap them
together?* [26] which I understood only after a few seconds—and
all at once——cf. recognizing someone from a description, or
the event from a schematic prevision: once the meaning is given
the signs take on the full value of "signs." But first the meaning
must be given. But then *how* is it given? Probably a chunk of the
verbal chain is identified, projects the meaning which returns
upon the signs——It is not enough to say (Bergson): a coming
and going. It is necessary to understand between what and what,
and what makes up the interval between them. It is not a series
of inductions——It is *Gestaltung* and *Rückgestaltung*. "Retrograde movement of the true" that phenomenon that one can no
longer undo oneself from what has once been thought, that one
finds it again in the materials themselves. . . .

The meaning is "perceived" and the *Rückgestaltung* is a "perception." This means: there is a *germination* of what *will have
been* understood. (*Insight* and *Aha Erlebnis*)——And that
means: the perception (the first one) is *of itself* an openness
upon a field of *Gestaltungen*——And that means: perception is
unconsciousness. What is the unconscious? What functions as a
pivot, an existential, and in this sense, is and is not perceived.
For one perceives only figures upon levels——And one perceives
them only by relation to the level, which therefore is unper-
ceived.——The perception of the level: always *between* the objects, it is that about which. . . .

The occult in psychoanalysis (the unconscious) is of this
sort (cf. a woman in the street feeling that they are looking at
her breast, and checking her clothing. Her corporeal schema is
for itself—for the other——It is the *hinge* of the for itself and
the for the other——To have a body is to be looked at (it is not
only that), it is to be *visible*——Here the impression of telepa-

25. TRANSLATOR: *On*—the indefinite pronoun.
26. TRANSLATOR: In English in the text.

thy, of the occult = vivacity in reading the look of the other in a flash——Should we say *reading*? It is on the contrary by means of this phenomenon that one comprehends reading——To be sure, if a woman of good faith who closes her coat (or the contrary), were questioned, she would not *know* what she has just done. She would not know it in the language of conventional thought, but she would know it as one knows the repressed, that is, not as a figure on a ground, but as ground. A detail perception: a wave that runs on in the field of the *In der Welt Sein*——

The speaking-understanding relation: the moving oneself-perceiving the goal relation, i.e.: the goal is not posed, but it is what I am lacking, what marks a certain deflection on the dial of the corporeal schema. Likewise I speak by rejoining such and such a modulation of the linguistic space with the linguistic apparatus——the words bound to their sense as the body to its goal.

I do not perceive any more than I speak——Perception has me as has language——And as it is necessary that all the same *I* be there in order to speak, *I* must be there in order to perceive——But in what sense? As *one*[27]——What is it that, from my side, comes to animate the perceived world and language?

Husserl *Zeitbewusstsein*——

May, 1959

1. What is the "receptive" element of the absolute consciousness?——H. is right to say that it is not I who constitute time, that it constitutes itself, that it is a *Selbsterscheinung*——But the term "receptivity" is improper precisely because it evokes a Self distinct from the present and who *receives* it——It must be understood simply by opposition to spontaneous acts (thought, etc.)

2. Is it the new present, in its individuality, that pushes the preceding one into the past, and that *fills* a part of the future? In that case there would not be *time*, but times——Time must be

27. TRANSLATOR: *On*—the indefinite pronoun. ". . . I ought to say that *one* perceives in me, and not that I perceive. Every sensation bears within itself the germ of a dream or depersonalization . . ." (*Phenomenology of Perception*, p. 215 [French text, p. 249].)

understood as a system that embraces everything——Although
it is graspable only for him who *is there,* is at a present

3. What is the impressional consciousness, the |Urerlebnis?|
Like the *Selbstgegebenheit* of the exterior thing, it is in reality
not a term *effectively* untraversable (temporal knob), but a
transcendent, an optimum, an *etwas . . .* (a *Gestalt* and not an
individual)——And the "to be conscious" of this *Urerlebnis* is
not coincidence, fusion with . . . nor is it an act or *Auffassung*
(this Husserl said), nor is it a nihilating (Sartre), it is separation (*écart*), such as the corporeal schema, which is the foundation of space *and of time,* makes comprehensible——It is a
perception-imperception, i.e. an operative and not thematized
meaning   (this is at bottom what Husserl means when he
considers retention to be fundamental: that means that the
absolute present which I am is as if it were not)——

4. All this still leaves untouched the question: what is "to
know," "to be conscious," "to perceive," "to think" in the Cartesian sense——A question never raised——One discusses
around theses such as "connection" (*liaison*), "thought of seeing
and of feeling" in the sense of presumption, "meaning"——One
shows that a binding (*liant*) is needed, that a "pure *denken*" is
necessary, or a *Selbsterscheinung,* an auto-apparition, an apparition that is pure apparition. . . . But all this presupposes the
idea of the for itself and in the end cannot explain transcendence——Look in a completely different direction: the for itself
itself as an incontestable, but derived, characteristic: it is the
culmination of separation (*écart*) in *differentiation*——Self-
presence *is* presence to a differentiated world——The perceptual separation (*écart*) as making up the "view" such as it is
implicated in the reflex, for example—and enclosing being for
itself by means of language as differentiation. To be conscious =
to have a figure on a ground—one cannot go back any further.

Transcendence of the thing and transcendence of the phantasm
May, 1959

The transcendence of the thing compels us to say that it is
plenitude only by being inexhaustible, that is, by not being all
actual under the look—but it promises this total actuality, since
it *is there.* . . .

When we say that—on the contrary—the phantasm is not observable, that it is empty, non-being, the contrast with the sensible is therefore not absolute. The senses are apparatus to form concretions of the inexhaustible, to form existent significations——But the thing is not really *observable:* there is always a skipping over in every observation, one is never at the thing itself. What we call the *sensible* is only the fact that the indefinite [succession] of *Abschattungen precipitates*——But, conversely, there is a precipitation or crystallization of the imaginary, of the existentials, of the symbolic matrices——

[on the same page]

"Thought," "consciousness," and being at . . .

Retention (inasmuch as it does not posit, does not aim at the immediate past, and only *has it* behind itself), the perceptual presence (for example, the presence of what is behind my back), the presence of my whole past sedimented into existentials, my reference to what I mean in speech, and to the diacritical apparatus of the available significations, my motor reference to the spot I want to go to, the *Vorhabe* (the *Stiftung* of a field or an idea), the installation in a space by the corporeal schema, and the founding of a time in the embryology of behavior—all this turns around the problem of an existence that is not a *thought* of existing—and which Husserl finds again in the heart of the psychological reflection as an absolute retentional flux (but in Husserl there is here the idea of a time of *Empfindung* which is not good: the present in the broad sense is a symbolic matrix and not only *a* present that breaks up toward the past)——I.e. of a Self-presence that is not an *absence from oneself,* a contact with Self *through* the divergence (*écart*) with regard to Self——The figure on a ground, the simplest "*Etwas*"——the *Gestalt* contains the key to the problem of the mind

see Wertheimer's *Productive Thinking* [28] to determine in what sense the *Gestalt* contains and does not contain the significations of the highest degree

28. EDITOR: New York and London, 1945.

The looks that cross = *eine Art der Reflexion*

May, 1959

It is already the flesh of things that speaks to us of our own flesh, and that speaks to us of the flesh of the other——My "look" is one of those givens of the "sensible," of the brute and primordial world, that defies the analysis into being and nothingness, into existence as consciousness and existence as a thing, and requires a complete reconstruction of philosophy. The analytics of being and nothingness at the same time discloses and masks this order: it discloses it as a menace of being on nothingness and of nothingness on being, it masks it because the entity and the negentity remain in principle isolable.

the look that kills
decentering, not annihilation.
to call into question for Sartre (nothingness)
= to kill; to be in question = to cease to be

(Bergson) Transcendence——*forgetting*——time

May 20, 1959

I said: the openness to the world such as we rediscover it in ourselves and the perception we divine within life (a perception that at the same time is spontaneous being (thing) and being-self ("subject")——Bergson once explicitly said, in the text of *La Pensée et le mouvant* where he speaks of the consciousness seeking to see time and not to measure it, that there is a consciousness that is *at the same time spontaneous and reflected* [29]) intertwine, encroach upon, or cling to one another.

29. EDITOR: The author refers to this passage: "But this duration which science eliminates, and which is so difficult to conceive and express, is what one feels and lives. Suppose we try to find out what it is? How would it appear to a consciousness which desired only to see it without measuring it, which would then grasp it without stopping it, which in short, would take itself as object, and which, spectator and actor alike, at once spontaneous and reflective, would bring ever closer together—to the point where they would coincide—the attention which is fixed, and the time which passes?" (*La Pensée et le mouvant* [Paris, 1934], p. 10.) [English translation by Mabelle L. Andison, *The Creative Mind* (New York, 1946), p. 13.]

Make clear what that means.

That evokes, beyond the "point of view of the object" and the "point of view of the subject," a common nucleus which is the "winding" (*serpentement*),[30] being as a winding (what I called "modulation of the being in the world"). It is necessary to make understood how that (or any *Gestalt*) is a perception "being formed in the things." This is still only an approximative expression, in the subject-object language (Wahl, Bergson) of what there is to be said. That is, that the things have us, and that it is not we who have the things. That the being that has been cannot stop having been. The "Memory of the World." That language has us and that it is not we who have language. That it is being that speaks within us and not we who speak of being.*

 (margin note: Things have us — not we them —)

But then how understand the subjectivity? Inadequacy of the Bergsonian representation of a soul that conserves everything (this makes it impossible that the perceived-imaginary difference be a difference in nature). Insufficiency also of the Malebranche representation of a vision in god: that is the equivalent of the transcendental consciousness, it is "conservation" in the form of "signification." The solution is to be sought in vision itself: memory will be understood only by means of it. Vision has to be already a modulation or a winding in the one, a variant of a perceptual system of the world, in order that memory can be and can involve forgetting. The description of retention in Husserl (and that of subjectivity as time, of the absolute flux, of the pre-intentional retention) is a start, but leaves open the question: whence comes the "shrinking" of the temporal perspective, the passage of the remote retentions into the horizon, the forgetting?

The problem of forgetting: lies essentially in the fact that it is discontinuous. If at each phase of the *Ablaufphänomen*, a segment of the past would fall into oblivion, we would have a field of the present like a diaphragm of an objective, and forgetting would be occultation resulting from the removal of the efficacious stimuli, it would be the point where the *clear image* is no longer produced because the corporeal trace is effaced. Or again, in idealist language: forgetting would be a part of the

---

30. EDITOR: *Ibid.*, p. 293. [Eng. trans., p. 229.]

* Finally there is something profound in Ruyer when he says that the in itself and the for itself are the same thing. But not to be understood as: the things are souls.

present-past system, in exact correspondence with a new segment of present descended from the future.

But it is not so: there are retentions that are not forgotten,
even very remote ones. There are fragments "perceived" just
now, that disappear (have they been perceived? And what exactly is the relation between the perceived and the *imper-
ceived?*)———And besides there is no objective segment of the
present that descends from the future. Husserl's diagram is dependent on the convention that one can represent the series of
nows by points on a line.[31] To be sure, Husserl at this point adds
the whole recasting of the retentions and the retentions of retentions that result therefrom, and it is in this that he does not conceive of time as serial and as a succession of punctual events. But
even complicated in this fashion, the representation of the phenomenon of flow is faulty. Not inasmuch as it is spatial. For in
fact space does not comprise *points*, *lines* any more than time
does. Understand that the *Gestalt* is already transcendence: it
makes me understand that a line is a vector, that a point is a center of forces———There are neither absolute lines nor points nor
colors in the things. The field vision and the field notion———Bergson saying that the winding perhaps reproduces no *real* line.[32]
But there is no line that would be *"real."* Hence space is not to be
blamed, as Bergson does. And correlatively it does not suffice to
pass to time as fusion to have the solution———That is a false
antithesis———We have to pass from the thing (spatial or temporal) as identity, to the thing (spatial or temporal) as difference, i.e. as transcendence, i.e. as always "behind," beyond,
far-off . . . the present itself is not an absolute coincidence without transcendence; even the *Urerlebnis* involves not total coincidence, but partial coincidence, because it has horizons and
would not be without them———the present, also, is ungraspable
from close-up, in the forceps of attention, it is an encompassing.
Study exactly the *Erfüllung* of the present: the danger of this
metaphor: it makes me think that there is a *certain void* that has

31. EDITOR: Husserl, "Vorlesungen zur Phänomenologie der
inneren Zeitbewusstseins," *Jahrbuch für Philosophie und Phänomen-
ologische Forschung,* IX (1928), 22. See the exposition and discussion
of the analysis of Husserl's diagram in *Phénoménologie de la perception*, pp. 477 ff. [Eng. trans., pp. 417 ff.]

32. EDITOR: *La Pensée et le mouvant*, p. 294. [Eng. trans., p.
230.]

its own dimensions and that is filled by a defined quantity of the present (it is always a field defined by the objective diaphragm). When Husserl speaks of a "norm," he means precisely that one cannot presuppose such a norm as given. It is a question of a *Normierung.* I.e. (Heidegger) of the positing of a *measurant* (*mesurant*). One sees then that the norm and the diaphragm, etc. *derive* from a total phenomenon which is finally the "world" (cf. Manchester lecture: [33]) (each perception is a "thought," but the whole is *"inscribed"* in the world——Every event belongs to the type of historical event that Péguy speaks of, "a rhythm of the event of the world"—again the winding——the problems of knowing what is the subject of the State, of war, etc. are exactly of the same type as the problem of knowing what is the subject of perception: one will not clear up the philosophy of history except by working out the problem of perception)

Whence the impossibility of a philosophy of *Being and Nothingness:* the future is not nothingness, the past is not the imaginary in the sense Sartre takes it——To be sure *there is* the present, but the transcendence of the present makes it precisely able to connect up with a past and a future, which conversely are not a nihilation——

In short: nothingness (or rather non being) is hollow and not *hole.* The open, in the sense of a *hole,* that is Sartre, is Bergson, is negativism or ultra positivism (Bergson)—indiscernible. There is no *nichtiges Nichts.* Bring to a focus my discussion of Bergson's ideas on nothingness: I am right in saying that Bergson proves too much, but wrong in seeming to conclude from that that Sartre is right. The negintuition of nothingness is to be rejected because nothingness also is always *elsewhere.* The true solution: *Offenheit* of the *Umwelt, Horizonhaftigkeit.*

The problem of forgetting: it comes, I said, from the fact that forgetting is discontinuous. It must be conceived not as an occultation (Bergson), not as a passage into nothingness, annihilation—and not as a positive function that envelops a knowledge of what it hides (Freud—Sartre),[34] but as a manner of being to . . . in turning away from . . .——The to-be-conscious itself is

33. EDITOR: Lecture given by the author at the University of Manchester, May 1, 1959.
34. EDITOR: Under the parenthesis, between the lines, as according to the author's habit, these words appear: *positivism, negativism.* The first manifestly refers to Freud and the second to Sartre.

to be conceived as transcendence, as to be surpassed by . . . and hence as ignorance But still there is the perceptual [?]?——Yes, but it is not an immediation in the sense of *contact*. (And it is not a distance in the way Sartre means it: a *nothing that is me,* and that separates me from the thing)——It is true that it is not in "blending" perception and imperception that one will explain forgetting.

It is in better understanding perception (and hence imperception)—i.e.: understand perception as differentiation, forgetting as undifferentiation. The fact that one no longer sees the memory = not a destruction of a psychic *material* which would be *the* sensible, but its disarticulation which makes there be no longer a *separation* (*écart*), a *relief*. This is the night of forgetting. Understand that the "to be conscious" = to have a figure on a ground, and that it disappears by disarticulation——the figure-ground distinction introduces a third term between the "subject" and the "object." It is *that separation* (*écart*) first of all that is the perceptual *meaning*.

[margin note: To be G = to have figure on a ground]

Philosophy and Literature

[undated, probably June, 1959]

[margin note: Φ = Being speaking w/in us = Creation]

Philosophy, precisely as "Being speaking within us," expression of the mute experience by itself, is creation. A creation that is at the same time a reintegration of Being: for it is not a creation in the sense of one of the commonplace *Gebilde* that history fabricates: it knows itself to be a *Gebilde* and wishes to surpass itself as *pure Gebilde,* to find again its origin. It is hence a creation in a radical sense: a creation that is at the same time an adequation, the only way to obtain an adequation.

This considerably deepens Souriau's views on philosophy as supreme art: [35] for art and philosophy *together* are precisely not arbitrary fabrications in the universe of the "spiritual" (of "culture"), but contact with Being precisely as creations. Being is *what requires creation of us* for us to experience it.

[margin note: Being - what requires creation of us for us to expert -]

Make an analysis of literature in this sense: as *inscription* of Being.

35. EDITOR: At the head of the note, this reference: "see Souriau. *L'Instauration philosophique* (Paris, 1939); Gueroult, 'La Voie de l'objectivité esthétique,' *Mélanges Souriau* (Paris, 1952)."

Being and World, chapter III [36]

> [undated, probably June, 1959]

Tr. —thought by divergence.

In accordance with the idea of transcendence (as thought by divergence [*pensée d'écart*], not possession of the object) seek to define a history of philosophy that would not be a flattening of history into "my" philosophy—and that would not be idolatry: a recovery or repetition of Descartes, the sole means of rendering to him *his own* truth, by thinking it once again, that is, starting from ourselves——Intelligible world in facets——The history of philosophy as a *perception* of other philosophers, intentional encroachment upon them, a thought of one's own that does not kill them, either by overcoming them, or by copying them. Follow them in their problems (Gueroult [37])—but their problems are within the problem of Being: this they all profess, and hence we can, we must think them in this horizon.

Say all that at the beginning of chapter III

And also: this ontological outline is an anticipation of philosophy—and hence of the history of philosophy (it implies the use of language, the use of the history operative within us). It is necessary to disclose the presuppositions. And to do so is moreover to do philosophy and not history.

Mark the relation between chapter III and chapter IV on Nature and science: what will be examined with it is a certain ontology (objectivist).

the dilemma: how to rely on the consciousness?
> how to challenge the consciousness?
> to be surmounted by the idea of consciousness as *Offenheit*——

Understanding and the implied [38]——History of philosophy
> June, 1959

The history of philosophy that would have to be made (alongside of Gueroult's) is the history of implication. For example: Descartes's theses on the distinction of the soul and the body

36. EDITOR: *Being and World:* first title given by the author to the first part of his work.
37. EDITOR: Inaugural Lecture. Cf. n. 22, p. 187.
38. TRANSLATOR: *"Entendement et sous-entendu."*

Reversal —

and on their union cannot be exposed on the plane of the under-standing, and justified together by a continuous movement of thought. They can be affirmed together only if one takes them with their *implication*——In the order of implication, the search for the essence and the search for existence are not opposed, are the same thing——Consider language, even philosophical lan-guage, not as a sum of statements or of "solutions," but as a veil lifted, a verbal chain woven. . . .

June 4, 1959

Hegel's expression: *an sich oder für uns* = there is a thought (the reflective thought) that, precisely because it would like to grasp the thing in itself immediately, falls back on the subjectiv-ity——And which, conversely, because it is haunted by the being for us, does not grasp it and grasps only the thing "in itself," in signification.

The true philosophy = apprehend what makes the leaving of oneself be a retiring into oneself, and vice versa.

Grasp this chiasm, this reversal. That is the mind.

Philosophy. To define its milieu, start from Gouhier's ques-tion: can one put to a philosophy questions that it has not put to itself? To answer no is to make of philosophy separate works, is to deny *philosophy*.[39] To answer yes is to reduce history to philos-ophy.[40]

My point of view: a philosophy, like a work of art, is an object that can arouse more thoughts than those that are "con-tained" in it (can one enumerate them? Can one count up a language?), retains a meaning outside of its historical context, even *has* meaning only outside of that context. Give an example of this vertical or philosophical history: Descartes, Malebranche. Is it not necessary to distinguish their problems such as they thought them and the problems that really move them, and that *we* formulate.——Does this lead to conclusions that are always relativistic? that is, that will be overthrown by another time? No,

39. TRANSLATOR: "*La* philosophie."
40. EDITOR: *L'Histoire et sa philosophie* [Gouhier]. It seems the author refers more particularly to the last chapter, where the difference between a history of philosophy and a history of philoso-phies is emphasized. Cf. pp. 136–39.

if the philosophies in their integrality are a *question,* the interrogative thought which makes them speak is not overcome by what will come later (Lefort on Machiavelli [41]).

Dualism——Philosophy

July, 1959

The problems posed in *Ph.P.*[42] are insoluble because I start there from the "consciousness"-"object" distinction——

Starting from this distinction, one will never understand that a given fact of the "objective" order (a given cerebral lesion) could entail a given disturbance of the relation with the world— a massive disturbance, which seems to prove that the whole "consciousness" is a function of the objective body——It is these very problems that must be disqualified by asking: *what* is the alleged *objective* conditioning? Answer: it is a way of expressing and noting an event of the order of brute or wild being which, ontologically, is primary. This event is that a given *visible* properly disposed (a body) hollows itself out an invisible sense—— The common stuff of which all the structures are made is the *visible,* which, for its part, is nowise of the objective, of the in itself, but is of the transcendent—which is not opposed to the for Itself, which has cohesion only for a Self——the Self to be understood not as nothingness, not as something, but as the unity by transgression or by correlative encroachment of "thing" and "world" (the time-thing, the time-being)

August, 1959

Show 1. that the modern theory of perception is a phenomenology (Michotte [43]) and discloses brute being, the "vertical" world——

2. that information theory applied to perception, and operationalism applied to behavior—is in fact, confusedly glimpsed at, the idea of meaning as a view of the organism, the idea of the flesh

41. EDITOR: Allusion to a work being prepared.
42. EDITOR: *Phenomenology of Perception.*
43. EDITOR: *The Perception of Causality.*

age analogy (coding and
on condition that one dis-
neath the discriminating
d its "comprehensible" dia-
the information.

thinking subject
September, 1959

cit, silent *Being-at* (*Etre-à*),
if blindly identified, which is
pect to it—the *self* of percep-
Ulysses, as the anonymous one
not yet traced its path. Percep-
non-possession: it is precisely
one is dealing with that one has
Anonymity and generality. That
means: not a *nichtiges Nichts*, but a "lake of non-being," a
certain nothingness sunken into a local and temporal *openness*
—vision and feeling in fact, and not thought of seeing and of
feeling——If it is said that the thought of seeing and of feeling
sustains this vision and this feeling, the world and Being will
only be an ideate, the vertical or wild Being will never be able to
be rediscovered, the teleology of the "natural light" is converted
into ideality.

Speaking subject: it is the subject of a *praxis*. It does not
hold before itself the words said and understood as objects of
thought or ideates. It possesses them only by a *Vorhabe* which is
of the same type as the *Vorhabe* of place by my body that betakes
itself unto that place. That is: it is a certain lack of . . . such or
such a signifier, which does not construct the *Bild* of what it
lacks. There is therefore here a neo-teleology, which no more
permits being supported by a *consciousness of* . . . , nor by an
ec-stasy, a constructive project, than does the perceptual teleology. The Saussurean analysis of the relations between signifiers
and the relations from signifier to signified and between the
significations (as differences between significations) confirms
and rediscovers the idea of perception as a *divergence* (*écart*) by
relation to a *level*, that is, the idea of the primordial Being, of the
Convention of conventions, of the speech before speech.

What is to be elucidated: it is the upheaval that speech introduces in pre-linguistic Being. It does not modify it first, it is first itself an "egocentric language." But nevertheless it brings a ferment of transformation that will give the operative signification; then the question is: what is this ferment? This praxisthought? Is it the same being that perceives and that speaks? Impossible that it not be the same. And if it is the same, is this not to re-establish the "thought of seeing and of feeling," the Cogito, the consciousness of . . . ?

September, 1959

Take up again the analysis of the cube. It is true that the cube itself, with six equal faces, is only for an unsituated gaze, for an *operation* or inspection of the mind seating itself at the center of the cube, for a field of *Being*——And everything one can say about the perspectives upon the cube do not concern it.

But the cube itself *by opposition* to the perspectives—is a negative determination. Here Being is what excludes all non-being, all appearance; the in itself is what is not simply *percipi*. The mind as bearer of this Being is what is nowhere, what envelops every *where*

Hence this *analysis* by the reflective thought, this *refinement* of Being (the wax "all naked" Descartes) by-passes the Being already there, pre-critical——How to describe that Being? No longer by what it *is not*, but by what it *is*. One has then: an openness upon the cube itself by means of a view of the cube which is a distancing, a transcendence—to say that I have a view of it is to say that, in perceiving it, I go from myself unto it, I go out of myself into it. I, my *view*, are caught up in the same carnal world with it; i.e.: my view and my body themselves emerge from the *same* being which is, among other things, a *cube*——The reflection that qualifies them as subjects of vision is that same dense reflection that makes me touch myself touching, i.e. that *the same* in me be seen and seer: I do not even see myself seeing, but *by encroachment* I complete my visible body, I prolong my being-seen beyond my being-visible for myself. And it is for my flesh, my body of vision, that there can be the cube itself which closes the circuit and completes my own being-seen. It is hence finally the massive unity of Being as the encompassing of myself and of the cube, it is the wild, non-refined, "vertical" Being that makes there be a cube.

With this example grasp the upsurge of the pure "signification"———the "signification" cube (such as the geometer defines it), the essence, the Platonic idea, the object are the concretion of the *there is*, are *Wesen*, in the verbal sense, i.e., *ester* [44]———
Every *that* [45] involves a *what* [46] because the *that* is not nothing, hence is *etwas*, hence *west*———
Study the way that language and the way that algorithm arouse signification

The problem of analysis

September, 1959

Do we have the right to comprehend the time, the space of the child as an undifferentiation of *our* time, of *our* space, etc. . . . ? This is to reduce the child's experience to our own, at the very moment one is trying to respect the phenomena. For it is to think it as the *negation* of *our* differentiations. It would be necessary to go all the way to thinking it *positively*, unto phenomenology.

But the same question arises with regard to every *other*, to the alter ego in particular———And *to that other than me who is the I reflected on*, for myself who reflects.

Solution: recapture the child, the alter ego, the unreflected within myself by a lateral, pre-analytic participation, which is perception, *ueberschreiten* by definition, intentional transgression. When I perceive the child, he is given precisely in a certain divergence (*écart*) (*originating presentation of the unpresentable*) and the same for my perceptual lived experience for myself, and the same for my alter ego, and the same for the pre-analytic thing. Here is the common tissue of which we are made. The wild Being. And the perception of this perception (the phenomenological "reflection") is the inventory of this originating depar-

44. EDITOR: *Ester*, as a French translation of *Wesen*, is a term borrowed from Gilbert Kahn. Cf. Martin Heidegger, *Introduction à la métaphysique*, French translation (Paris, 1958), p. 239 (Glossary of German terms).
45. TRANSLATOR: In English in the text.
46. TRANSLATOR: In English in the text.

ture whose documents we carry in ourselves, of this *Ineinander* that awakens to itself, it is the usage of the *immer wieder* which is the sensible, the carnal itself (for every reflection is after the model of the reflection of the hand touching by the hand touched, open generality, a prolongation of the body's reserve [*volant*]), hence reflection is not an identification with oneself (thought of seeing or of feeling) but non-difference with self = silent or blind identification. And when the reflection wishes to be done with this horizonal openness, when it wishes to apprehend itself no longer across a horizon and in virtue of an institution of nature, but directly and without anything left over, then all it can do is to sublimate itself in verbalization, give itself a body that would not be natural only, make a language germinate, a "transparent" apparatus that gives the illusion of a pure or empty presence to oneself, and which nonetheless attests only a determined void, empty of this or that . . .

The essential is to describe the vertical or wild Being as that pre-spiritual milieu without which nothing is thinkable, not even the spirit, and by which we pass into one another, and ourselves into ourselves in order to have *our own* time. It is philosophy alone that gives it——

Philosophy is the study of the *Vorhabe* of Being, a *Vorhabe* that is not *cognition*, to be sure, that is wanting with regard to cognition, to operation, but that envelops them as Being envelops the beings.

Piaget's logicism is an absolutization of our culture—so also his psychology which opens upon his logic. Incompatible with an ethnological experience. Psychology, logic, ethnology are rival dogmatisms that destroy one another; philosophy alone, precisely because it aims at the total domain of Being, renders them compatible by relativizing them. The regions of knowledge, left to themselves, are in conflict and in contradiction.

Gestalt

September, 1959

What is a *Gestalt*? A whole that does *not* reduce itself to the sum of the parts—a negative, exterior definition——A designation of the *Gestalt* by contrast with the domain of the in itself in which one is installed——the *Gestalthafte,* says Heidegger, is here left aside——

From within, then, (that is: not by *interior observation,* but by approaching the *Gestalt* as much as possible, by communicating with it, which can be done by considering the others or the visible as well as by considering "states of consciousness") what is a *Gestalt*? What is a contour, what is a segregation, what is a circle or a line? Or an organization in depth, a relief?

These are *not* psychic elements (sensation), assembled psychic spatio-temporal individuals. But what then? To have the experience of a *Gestalt* is not to sense by coincidence, but what then?

It is a principle of distribution, the pivot of a system of equivalencies, it is the *Etwas* of which the fragmentary phenomena will be the manifestation——But is it then an essence, an idea? The idea would be free, intemporal, aspatial. The *Gestalt* is not a spatio-temporal individual, it is ready to integrate itself into a constellation that spans space and time—but it is not free in regard to space and time, it is not aspatial, atemporal, it only escapes the time and space conceived as a series of events in themselves, it has a certain weight that doubtless fixes it not in an objective site and in a point of objective time, but in a region, a domain, which it dominates, where it reigns, where it is everywhere present without one ever being able to say: it is here. It is transcendence. This is what one expresses again in speaking of its generality, of its *Transponierbarkeit*——It is a double ground of the lived.

And who experiences it? A mind that would grasp it as an idea or a signification? No. It is a body——In what sense? My body *is* a *Gestalt* and it is co-present in every *Gestalt*. It is a *Gestalt;* it also, and eminently, is a heavy signification, it is flesh; the system it constitutes is ordered about a central hinge or a pivot which is openness to . . . , a bound and not a free possibility——And at the same time it is a component of every *Gestalt.* The flesh of the *Gestalt* (the grain of the color, the indefinable something that animates the contour or which, in Michotte's experiments, animates the rectangle that "creeps" [47]) is what

47. EDITOR: *The Perception of Causality.*

responds to its inertia, to its insertion in a "world," to its *field* biases

The *Gestalt* therefore implies the relation between a perceiving body and a sensible, i.e. transcendent i.e. horizonal i.e. vertical and not perspectival world——
It is a diacritical, oppositional, relative system whose pivot is the *Etwas*, the thing, the world, and not the idea——
The idea is the *Etwas* upon which the body is centered no longer qua *sensible* but qua *speaking*——
Every Psychology that places the *Gestalt* back into the framework of "cognition" or "consciousness" misses the meaning of the *Gestalt*——

There remains to understand precisely what the being for itself of the *Gestalt* experience is——It is being for X, not a pure agile nothingness, but an inscription in an open register, in a lake of non being, in an *Eröffnung*, in an *offene*.

Pregnancy, transcendence——

September, 1959

Show that these notions * represent a getting into contact with being as pure *there is*. One witnesses that event by which there is something. Something rather than nothing and this rather than something else. One therefore witnesses the advent of the positive: this rather than something *else*.
This advent is not a self-realization of a being that would be the cause of itself, identical, objective——And not even the self-realization of a preponderant possible in the sense of the logical possible (Leibniz). The ideology of the logical possible is no different from the ideology of the necessary: the necessary is simply the unique possible; the possible already contains the idea of intrinsic existence; if there is a conflict between several possibles with regard to existence, it is because, by virtue of a veritable mystery (Leibniz), the possibles are not compossible.

Hence the *gestaltung* is not being by definition, essentialization——It is [verbal) *Wesen*, the operation of *ester*, the appari-

* Pregnancy, *Gestalt*, phenomenon.

tion of an *Etwas* existing by radiation——*Warum ist etwas eine gestalt?* Why is this rather than that a "good" form, or a *strong form,* or an orientation toward a possibility? [see Egon Brunswik [48] and show that the effort of the *New Look* [49] and of information theory is to find an operational, scientific expression of what is not the being-object, the in itself]——[reproduce here my critique of Lévi-Strauss's explanation of the *gestaltung* by the pooling of "chances," by *combination* [50]——yes a combination is needed, but what is elaborated through this combination, the symbolic matrix of the West is not a *product* of causality] Show that since the *Gestalt* arises from polymorphism, this situates us entirely outside of the philosophy of the subject and the object.

Empirical   pregnancy   and   geometrical   pregnancy   (E. Brunswik [51])

September, 1959

Profound idea of a pregnancy that is not only that of the forms privileged for reasons of geometrical equilibrium—but also according to an intrinsic regulation, a *Seinsgeschick* of which the geometrical pregnancy is but one aspect. It is in this way that I want to understand "empirical pregnancy"——Understood in this way, it consists in defining each perceived being by a structure or a system of equivalencies about which it is disposed, and of which the painter's stroke—the flexuous line—or

48. EDITOR: Cf. *Perception and the Representative Design of Psychological Experiments* (Berkeley, 1956).

49. TRANSLATOR: In English in the text.

50. EDITOR: We have no knowledge of such a critique; doubtless it was formulated in a course or in a personal note. M. Lévi-Strauss, we recall, had posed in new terms the problem of the cumulative or non-cumulative history of cultures in comparing non-comulative cultures to players trying for series in roulette. He showed that the collaboration of cultures, voluntary or involuntary, had had an effect analogous to that which would be obtained by "a coalition of gamblers betting on the same series at several different tables, with an agreement that they would pool the numbers which each of them might require to proceed with his series." Cf. *Race and History,* UNESCO (Paris, 1952), pp. 37–38.

51. EDITOR: The problem of empirical pregnancy and geometrical pregnancy is dealt with by Egon Brunswik in *Experimentelle Psychologie in Demonstrationen* (Vienna, 1935).

the sweep of the brush is the peremptory evocation. It is a question of that λόγος that pronounces itself silently in each sensible thing, inasmuch as it varies around a certain type of message, which we can have an idea of only through our carnal participation in its sense, only by espousing by our body its manner of "signifying"—or of that λόγος uttered whose internal structure sublimates our carnal relation with the world.

To criticize the "little man inside the man"—perception as cognition of an ob-ject—to rediscover man finally face to face with the world *itself*, to rediscover the pre-intentional present—is to rediscover that vision of the origins, which sees itself within us, as poetry rediscovers what articulates itself within us, unbeknown to us (Max Ernst in Charbonnier's book [52]).

The principle of ontology: being in indivision

September, 1959

Hence every painting, every action, every human enterprise is a crystallization of time, a cipher of transcendence——At least if one understands them as a certain spread (*écart*) between being and nothingness, a certain proportion of white and black, a certain sampling of the Being in indivision, a certain manner of modulating time and space

Pregnancy: the psychologists forget that this means a power to break forth, productivity (*praegnans futuri*), fecundity——Secondarily: it means "typicality." It is the form that has arrived at itself, that *is itself*, that poses itself by its own means, is the equivalent of the cause of itself, is the *Wesen* that is because it *este,*[53] auto-regulation, cohesion of self with self, identity in depth (dynamic identity), transcendence as being-at-a-distance, there is——

52. EDITOR: Georges Charbonnier: *Le Monologue du peintre I* (Paris, 1959), p. 34. During an interview, Max Ernst recalls the terms in which he had once defined the painter's role: "Just as, ever since the celebrated Letter of the Seer, the poet's role consists in writing under the dictation of what thinks itself, what articulates itself within him, the painter's role is to circumscribe and to project forth what sees itself within him."

53. EDITOR: Cf. p. 203, n. 44.

The pregnancy is what, in the visible, requires of me a *correct* focusing, defines its correctness. My body *obeys* the pregnancy, it "responds" to it, it is what is suspended on it, flesh responding to flesh. When a "good" form appears, either it modifies its surroundings by radiation, or it obtains from my body a movement until . . .

This definition of pregnancy as implying motivity a fortiori places it entirely outside of Piaget's alternatives: field effects or sensori-motor activity? When one says that the form is "pre-empirical," "innate," whether with regard to the perceived or to what is thought, what one means in fact is that there is here *Urstiftung* and not simply subsumption, a sense by transcendence and not a recognition of the concept.

September, 1959

Finally one has to admit a sort of truth in the naïve descriptions of perception: εἴδωλα or *simulacra,* etc. the thing of itself giving perspectives, etc. But all that takes place in an order that is no longer that of objective Being, that is the order of the lived or of the phenomenal which is precisely to be justified and rehabilitated as the foundation of the objective order.

One can claim that the order of the phenomenal is second by reference to the objective order, is but a province of it, when one considers only the intra-mundane relations between objects. But as soon as one introduces the other and even the living body, the work of art, the historical milieu, one realizes that the order of the phenomenal must be considered as autonomous and that, if one does not recognize this autonomy in it, it is definitively *impenetrable.*

The other, not as a "consciousness," but as an inhabitant of a body, and consequently of the world. Where is the other in this body that I see? He is (like the meaning of the sentence) immanent in this body (one cannot detach him from it to pose him apart) and yet, more than the sum of the signs or the significations conveyed by them. He is that of which they are always the partial and non-exhaustive image—and who nonetheless is attested wholly in each of them. Always in process of an unfinished incarnation———Beyond the objective body as the sense of the painting is beyond the canvas.

September, 1959

Descartes (*Dioptrics*): *who* will see the image painted in the eyes or in the brain? Therefore finally a *thought* of this image is needed———Descartes already sees that we always put a little man in man, that our objectifying view of our own body always obliges us to seek *still further inside* that *seeing man* we thought we had under our eyes.

But what he does not see is that the primordial vision that one must indeed come to cannot be the *thought of seeing*——— This thought, this disclosure of being which finally is *for* someone, is still the little man inside man, but this time contracted into a metaphysical point. For finally we know no vision but that by a composite substance, and it is this subtilized vision that we call thought———If being is to disclose itself, it will do so before a transcendence, and not before an intentionality, it will be the engulfed brute being that returns to itself, it will be the *sensible* that hollows itself out———

Ontology—

October, 1959

Take topological space as a model of being. The Euclidean space is the model for perspectival being, it is a space without transcendence, positive, a network of straight lines, parallel among themselves or perpendicular according to the three dimensions, which sustains all the possible situations———Underlying appropriateness of this idea of space (and of velocity, movement, time) with the classical ontology of the *Ens realissimum*, of the infinite entity. The topological space, on the contrary, a milieu in which are circumscribed relations of proximity, of envelopment, etc. is the image of a being that, like Klee's touches of color, is at the same time older than everything and "of the first day" (Hegel), that the regressive thought runs up against without being able to deduce it directly or indirectly (by "choice of the best") from Being by itself, that is a perpetual *residue*——It is encountered not only at the level of the physical world, but again it is constitutive of life, and finally it founds the *wild* principle of Logos——It is this wild or brute being that intervenes at all levels to overcome the problems of the classical ontology (mechanism, finalism, in every case: artificialism)— —the *Theodicy* of Leibniz sums up the effort of Christian theology to find a route between the necessitarian conception of Being, alone possible, and the unmotivated upsurge of brute Being, which latter is finally linked up with the first by a compromise, and, to this extent, the hidden god sacrificed to the *Ens realissimum.*

Sunday, October 10, 1959

Malraux asks why, how, one painter learns from another, of whom he makes copies (Van Gogh of Millet)—to be *himself,* learn himself in the other, with and against him.

Likewise one can ask why he who knows how to handle colors knows also how to handle the pencil or sometimes to sculpture——What there is in *common*——

All this is indeed obscure as long as one thinks that to sketch or to paint is to produce something positive out of nothing. Then the act of sketching and of painting—the act of painting like oneself and that of painting like the other are isolated from one another, and one no longer sees any relation between them. But we would see a relation if we understood that to paint, to sketch, is not to produce something from nothing, that the drawing, the touch of the brush, and the visible work are but the trace of a total movement of Speech, which goes unto Being as a whole, and that this movement contains the expression with lines as well as the expression with colors, *my* expression as well as that of the other painters. We dream of systems of equivalen*cies,* and indeed they do function. But their logic, like the logic of a phonematic system, is summed up in one sole tuft, in one sole gamut, they are all animated with one sole movement, they each and all are one sole vortex, one sole contraction of Being. What is needed is to make explicit this horizonal totality which is not a *synthesis*   — Anti- Kantian

Wild perception——The Immediate——Cultural perception——learning.[54]

October 22, 1959

I say that the Renaissance perspective is a cultural fact, that perception itself is polymorphic and that if it becomes Euclidean, this is because it allows itself to be oriented by the system.

Whence the question: how can one return from this perception fashioned by culture to the "brute" or "wild" perception? What does the informing consist in? By what act does one undo it (return to the phenomenal, to the "vertical" world, to lived experience)?

Whence also the question: does this informing of perception by culture, this descent of the invisible into the visible, oblige us to say, as does Egon Brunswik, for example, that the perceptual pregnancy is a *learning* [55] of the ecological milieu, that the auto-constitutional *Gestalten* of the Berlin school are derived from the "empirical *Gestalten*"? [56]

What I maintain is that: 1. there is an informing of perception by culture which enables us to say that culture is perceived ——There is a dilatation of perception, a carrying over of the *Aha Erlebnis* of "natural" perception to instrumental relations for example (chimpanzees) which obliges us to put in continuity the perceptual openness to the world (λόγος ἐνδιάθετος) and the openness to a cultural world (acquisition of the use of instruments).

2. this original layer above *nature* shows that *learning* [57] is *In der Welt Sein,* and not at all that *In der Welt Sein* is *learning,*[58] in the American sense or in the cognitive sense of Brunswik.

My position in the problem of the "return to the immediate" to be defined: the perceptual in the sense of the non-projective, vertical world—is always given with sense experience (*le sen-*

---

54. TRANSLATOR: In English in the text.
55. TRANSLATOR: In English in the text.
56. EDITOR: Cf. *Perception and the Representative Design of Psychological Experiments* (Berkeley, 1956). For the discussion of the *Gestalten* of the Berlin school, cf. pp. 132–34; for perception as learning, cf. pp. 122–23.
57. TRANSLATOR: In English in the text.
58. TRANSLATOR: In English in the text.

tir), with the phenomenal, with the silent transcendence. And yet someone like Piaget ignores this absolutely, has totally converted his perception into a cultural-Euclidean perception. What right have I therefore to call immediate this original that can be forgotten to such an extent?

Describe very precisely the way perception masks itself to itself, makes itself Euclidean. Show that the pregnancy of the geometrical forms is grounded intrinsically (not culturally) in that they, better than others, allow an ontogenesis (they stabilize being. What Piaget expresses—badly—in saying that in them the "deformations" annul one another [59]), but that this intrinsic pregnancy, in order to retain all its meaning, must be maintained within the zone of transcendence, within the context of the pre-Being, of the *Offenheit* of the *Umwelt,* and not dogmatically considered self-evident——the Euclidean perception has a privilege, but it is not an absolute privilege, and it is contested as absolute by the transcendence—which demands the Euclidean world as one of its aspects——

With life, natural perception (with the savage mind) is perpetually given to us the wherewithal to set up the universe of immanence——And yet, this universe tends of itself to become autonomous, realizes of itself a repression of transcendence—— *The key is in this idea that perception qua wild perception is of itself ignorance of itself, imperception,* tends of itself to see itself as an *act* and to forget itself as latent intentionality, as *being at*——

Same problem: how every philosophy is language and nonetheless consists in rediscovering silence.

Perception and language

October 27, 1959

I describe perception as a diacritical, relative, oppositional system—the primordial space as topological (that is, cut out in a

---

59. EDITOR: Cf. in particular, *La Perception,* Symposium de l'Association psychologique scientifique de langue française (Louvain, 1953; Paris, 1955). Piaget discusses geometrical pregnancy and empirical pregnancy, and writes: "Likewise, we think that a good form is that which, within perceptual structures where everything is deformation, gives rise to maximum compensations, hence to minimum deformations" (p. 19).

total voluminosity which surrounds me, in which I am, which is behind me as well as before me . . .)

This is right. But there is all the same this difference between perception and language, that I *see* the perceived things and that the significations on the contrary are invisible. The natural being is at rest in itself, my look can stop on it. The Being whose home is language cannot be fixed, looked at, it is only from afar   Hence it is necessary to account for this relative positivity of the perceived (even if it is only non-negation, even if it does not resist *observation,* even if every crystallization is illusory in some respect), especially since it is upon it that the positivity of the invisible rests. There is no intelligible world, *there is* the sensible world.

(But also what is this *there is* of the sensible world, of nature?)

The sensible is precisely that medium in which there can be *being* without it having to be posited; the sensible appearance of the sensible, the silent persuasion of the sensible is Being's unique way of manifesting itself without becoming positivity, without ceasing to be ambiguous and transcendent. The sensible world itself in which we gravitate, and which forms our bond with the other, which makes the other be for us, is not, precisely qua sensible, "given" except by allusion——The sensible is that: this possibility to be evident in silence, to be understood implicitly, and the alleged positivity of the sensible world (when one scrutinizes it unto its roots, when one goes beyond the empirical-sensible, the secondary sensible of our "representation," when one discloses the Being of Nature) precisely proves to be an *ungraspable,* the only thing finally that is seen in the full sense is the totality wherein the sensibles are cut out. Thought is only a little further still from the *visibilia.*

The chiasm

November 1, 1959

—the cleavage, in what regards the essential, is not *for Itself for the Other,* (subject-ob-ject) it is more exactly that between someone who goes unto the world and who, from the exterior, seems to remain in his own "dream." *Chiasm* by which what announces itself to me as being appears in the eyes of the others to be only "states of consciousness"——But, like the chiasm of the eyes, this one is also what makes us belong to the same world —a world which is not projective, but forms its unity across incompossibilities such as that of *my* world and the world of the other——By reason of this mediation through reversal, this chiasm, there is not simply a for-Oneself for-the-Other antithesis, there is Being as containing all that, first as sensible Being and then as Being without restriction——

Chiasm, instead of the For the Other: that means that there is not only a me-other rivalry, but a co-functioning. We function as one unique body

The chiasm is not only a me other exchange (the messages he receives reach me, the messages I receive reach him), it is also an exchange between me and the world, between the phenomenal body and the "objective" body, between the perceiving and the perceived: what begins as a thing ends as consciousness of the thing, what begins as a "state of consciousness" ends as a thing.

One cannot account for this double "chiasm" by the cut of the For Itself and the cut of the In Itself. A relation to Being is needed that would form itself *within Being*——This at bottom is what Sartre was looking for. But since for him there is no *interior* except me, and every *other* is exteriority, Being for him remains intact after this decompression that occurs in it, it remains pure positivity, object, and the For Itself participates in it only through a sort of folly——

November, 1959

. . . .
Meaning is *invisible*, but the invisible is not the contradictory of the visible: the visible itself has an invisible inner framework (*membrure*), and the in-visible is the secret counterpart of the visible, it appears only within it, it is the *Nichturpräsentierbar* which is presented to me as such within the world—one cannot see it there and every effort to *see it there* makes it disappear, but it is *in the line* of the visible, it is its virtual focus, it is inscribed within it (in filigree)——

The *comparisons* between the invisible and the visible (the *domain*, the *direction* of thought . . .) are not *comparisons* (Heidegger), they mean that the visible is pregnant with the invisible, that to comprehend fully the visible relations (house) one must go unto the relation of the visible with the invisible. . . . The other's visible is my invisible; my visible is the other's invisible; this formula (that of Sartre) is not to be retained. We have to say: Being is this strange encroachment by reason of which my visible, although it is not superposable on that of the other, nonetheless opens upon it, that both open upon the same sensible world——And it is the same encroachment, the same junction at a distance, that makes the messages from my organs (the monocular images) reassemble themselves into one sole vertical existence and into one sole world.

Hence meaning is not nihilation, nor a sacrifice of the For Itself to the In Itself——To envisage such a sacrifice, such a *creation* of the truth, is still to think according to the model of the In Itself, on the basis of the In Itself, and, since it escapes, to confide in the For Itself the heroic mission of making it be—— To envisage that is still to think the *Weltlichkeit* of minds according to the model of that of Cartesian space. Lacking an In Itself of the For Itselfs, the For Itself is charged with the task of *making* it. But I do not think the *Weltlichkeit* of minds in terms of the In Itself—and it is chimerical to seek in the future what is not. The *Weltlichkeit* of minds is ensured by the roots they push forth, not in the Cartesian space, to be sure, but in the aesthetic world. The aesthetic world to be described as a space of transcendence, a space of incompossibilities, of explosion, of dehiscence, and not as objective-immanent space. And then thought, the subject, to be described as a spatial situation also, with its own "locality"   And hence the spatial "metaphors" to be understood as an indivision of being and nothingness. And hence meaning is not nihilation——

This *separation* (*écart*) which, in first approximation, forms meaning, is not a no I affect *myself* with, a lack which I constitute as a lack by the upsurge of an *end* which I give myself—it is a *natural* negativity, a first institution, always already there——

Consider the right, the left: these are not simply contents within a relational spatiality (i.e. *positive*): they are not *parts* of space (Kant's reasoning is valid here: the whole is primary),

they are total parts, cuts in an encompassing, topological space
——Consider the *two*, the *pair*, this is not *two acts, two syntheses*, it is a fragmentation of being, it is a possibility for separation (two eyes, two ears: the possibility for *discrimination*, for the use of the diacritical), it is the advent of difference (on the ground of *resemblance* therefore, on the ground of the ὁμοῦ ἦν πάντα).

. . . .

The visible and the invisible

November, 1959

Must one not say that
the idea of transcendence = adjourns ad infinitum all *that which* we think we touch or see?

No, however: the visible, which is always "further on," is *presented* as such. It is the *Urpräsentation* of the *Nichturpräsentierbar*——*To see* is precisely, in spite of the infinite analysis always possible, and although no *Etwas* ever remains *in our hands*, to have an *Etwas*.

Is this then a pure and simple contradiction? Not at all: the visible ceases to be an inaccessible if I conceive it, not according to the proximal thought, but as an encompassing, lateral investment, *flesh*.

The "senses"—dimensionality—Being

November, 1959

Each "sense" is a "world," i.e. absolutely incommunicable for the other senses, and yet constructing a *something* which, through its structure, is from the first *open* upon the world of the other senses, and with them forms one sole Being. Sensoriality: for example, a color, yellow; it surpasses itself of itself: as soon as it becomes the color of the illumination, the dominant color of the field, it ceases to be such or such a color, it has therefore of itself an ontological function, it becomes apt to represent all things (like engravings, *Dioptrics*, Discourse IV). With one sole movement it imposes itself as particular and ceases to be visible as particular. The "World" is this whole where each "part," when one takes it for itself, suddenly opens unlimited dimensions—becomes a *total part.*

Now this particularity of the color, of the yellow, and this universality are not a *contradiction,* are *together* sensoriality itself: it is by the same virtue that the color, the yellow, at the same time gives itself as a *certain* being and as a *dimension,* the expression *of every possible being*——What is proper to the sensible (as to language) is to be representative of the whole, not by a sign-signification relation, or by the immanence of the parts in one another and in the whole, but because each part is *torn up* from the whole, comes with its roots, encroaches upon the whole, transgresses the frontiers of the others. It is thus that the parts overlap (transparency), that the present does not stop at the limits of the visible (behind my back). Perception opens the world to me as the surgeon opens a body, catching sight, through the window he has contrived, of the organs in full functioning, taken *in their activity,* seen sideways. It is thus that the sensible initiates me to the world, as language to the other: by encroachment, *Ueberschreiten.* Perception is not first a perception of *things,* but a perception of *elements* (water, air . . .) of *rays of the world,* of things which are dimensions, which are worlds, I slip on these "elements" and here I am in the *world,* I slip from the "subjective" to Being.

The alleged "contradiction" between the yellow as some thing and the yellow as the title of a world: this is not a contradiction, for it is precisely within its particularity as yellow and through it that the yellow becomes a universe or an *element*——That a color can become a level, a fact become a category (exactly as in music: describe a note as particular, i.e. in the field of another *tone*—and "the same" note that has become that within whose key a music is written) = the veritable movement toward the universal. The universal is not above, it is beneath (Claudel), it is not before, but *behind* us——atonal music = the equivalent of the philosophy of Being in indivision. Like paintings without identifiable things, without the *skin* of things, but giving their *flesh*——The *Transponierbarkeit* is a particular case of a more general transposition of which atonal music is the thematization   All this implies the Being in indivision——

This universality of the sensible = *Urpräsentation* of what is not *Urpräsentierbar* = the sensible hollowed out in the being without restriction, that Being which is *between* my perspective and that of the other, my past and my present.

What is proper to the perceived: to be already there, to not be *through* the act of perception, to be the reason for that act, and not the reverse. Sensoriality = transcendence, or a mirror of transcendence.

Depth

November, 1959

Depth and "back" (and "behind")——It is pre-eminently the dimension of the hidden——(every dimension is of the hidden)——
There must be depth since there is a point whence I see—since the world surrounds me——
Depth is the means the things have to remain distinct, to remain things, while not being what I look at at present. It is pre-eminently the dimension of the simultaneous. Without it, there would not be a world or Being, there would only be a mobile zone of distinctness which could not be brought here without quitting all the rest—and a "synthesis" of these "views." Whereas, by virtue of depth, they coexist in degrees of proximity, they slip into one another and integrate themselves. It is hence because of depth that the things have a flesh: that is, oppose to my inspection obstacles, a resistance which is precisely their reality, their "openness," their *totum simul*. The look does not overcome depth, it goes round it.
Depth is *urstiftet* in what I see in clear vision as the retention is in the present—without "intentionality"——
cf. Metzger saying that it arises at the moment when it was going to be impossible to have a distinct vision of 2 points at the same time. Then, the two images that are out of phase and not superposable "take" suddenly as profiles *of* the same thing in depth [60]——This is not an *act* or an intentionality (which would

60. EDITOR: Wolfgang Metzger, *Gesetze des Sehens* (Frankfurt, 1936; 2d ed. expanded, 1953), p. 285.

go to an *in itself* and would give only juxtaposed in itselfs)——
It is in general, and by virtue of a field property, that this
identification of two incompossible views is made, and because
depth is open to me, because I have this dimension so as to move
my look in it, *this openness*——

November, 1959

Say that the things are structures, frameworks, the stars of
our life: not before us, laid out as perspective spectacles, but
gravitating about us.

Such things do not presuppose man, who is made of their
flesh. But yet their eminent being can be understood only by him
who enters into perception, and with it keeps in distant-contact
with them——

The essence, the *Wesen*. Underlying kinship between the
essence and perception: the essence, likewise, is an inner framework, it is not above the sensible world, it is beneath, or in its
depth, its thickness. It is the secret bond—the Essences are
*Etwas*es at the level of speech, as the things are Essences at the
level of Nature. Generality of the things: why are there several
samples of each thing? This is imposed by the very definition of
the things as field beings: how could there be a field without
generality?

With transcendence I show that the visible is invisible, *that
vision is in principle what convinces me by an appearance al-
ready-there that there is no room to seek a proximal being*
perception, what assures me of an inapperceived (of a hidden-
revealed: transparency, encroachment)   This invisible of the
visible is then what enables me to rediscover in productive
thought all the structures of vision, and to radically distinguish
thought from operation, from logic.

I-the other, an inadequate formula

November, 1959

The I-other relation to be conceived (like the intersexual
relation, with its indefinite substitutions cf. Schilder *Image and*

Appearance, p. 234 [61]) as complementary roles one of which cannot be occupied without the other being also: masculinity implies femininity, etc. Fundamental polymorphism by reason of which I do not have to constitute the other *in face of* the Ego: he is already there, and the Ego is conquered from him. Describe the pre-egology, the "syncretism," indivision or transitivism. What is it that *there is* at this level? There is the vertical or carnal universe and its polymorphic matrix. Absurdity of the *tabula rasa* on which *cognitions* would be arranged: not that there be cognitions before cognitions, but because there is the *field.* The I-other problem—a *Western* problem.

November, 1959

Philosophy has never spoken—I do not say of *passivity:* we are not effects—but I would say of the passivity of our activity, as Valéry spoke of a *body of the spirit:* new as our initiatives may be, they come to birth at the heart of being, they are connected onto the time that streams forth in us, supported on the pivots or hinges of our life, their *sense* is a "direction"——The soul always thinks: this is in it a property of its state, it cannot not think because a *field* has been opened in which *something* or the *absence* of something is always inscribed. This is not an *activity* of the soul, nor a production of thoughts in the plural, and I am not even the author of that hollow that forms within me by the passage from the present to the retention, it is not I who makes myself think any more than it is I who makes my heart beat. From there leave the philosophy of *Erlebnisse* and pass to the philosophy of our *Urstiftung*

. . . .

November 26, 1959

A "direction" of thought——This is not a *metaphor*—— There is no *metaphor* between the visible and the invisible (the invisible: either my thought for myself or the sensible given to

61. EDITOR: P. Schilder, *The Image and Appearance of the Human Body* (London, 1955).

the other for me): *metaphor* is too much or too little: too much if the invisible is really invisible, too little if it lends itself to transposition——

There is no metaphor: 1) because thought involves a quasi-locality that has to be described (locality not by inherence in a spatio-temporal point—but locality by elastic tie: one cannot say that a mind is here, but one can say that it is *not there*—this negation little by little extends to all parts of the world and of the lived body (*corps propre*)—and yet there is a locality by investment, and, when all that is said, there is a theater of apparition of the other)

2) because the originating locality, even in what concerns the "things" or the "direction" of a movement of things is not identifiable in ob-jective space either, not a relation *in* ob-jective space——A *direction* is not *in* space: it is in filigree across it——It is therefore transposable to thought——

The mind is neither here, nor here, nor here. . . . And yet it is "attached," "bound," it is *not without bonds*——Negation of negation and position: one does not have to choose between them. The mind is in no objective site, and yet it is invested in a site which it rejoins by its environs, which it circumvents, as my locality for myself is the point that all the vanishing lines of my landscape designate to me, and which is itself *invisible*.

Leibniz

December, 1959

In denying the conception of perception-reproduction (on my body in itself of the exterior thing in itself), I open up access to a brute Being with which I would not be in the *subject and object* relation, and still less in the relation of effect with cause. The *In der Welt Sein* relation will take the place held in Leibniz by the relation of reciprocal expression of the perspectives taken on the world, and hence god as the unique author of these diverse perspectives which emanate from him as thoughts. The Being thus discovered is to be sure not the god of Leibniz, the "monadology" thus disclosed is not the system of monads—substances; but certain Leibnizian descriptions—that each of the views of the world is a world apart, that nonetheless "what is particular to one would be public to all," that the monads would be in a relation of expression between themselves and with the world, that they differ from one another and from it as perspectives—are to be maintained entirely, to be taken up again in the brute Being, to be separated from the substantialist and ontotheological elaboration Leibniz imposes upon them——

The expression of the universe in us is certainly not the harmony between our monad and the others, the presence of the ideas of all things in it—but it is what we see in perception, to be taken as such instead of *explaining* it. Our soul has no windows: that means *In der Welt Sein*——

The pre-established harmony (like occasionalism) always maintains the in itself and simply connects it with what we experience through a relation from substance to substance founded in god—instead of making of it the cause of our thoughts——but it is precisely a question of rejecting entirely the idea of the In Itself——

It is the recovery of the theme of perception that transforms the significance of the Leibnizian idea of expression.

Vertical world and vertical history

"World"

December, 1959

A "world" (it is a whole world, the world of sound, of color, etc. . . .) = an organized ensemble, which is *closed*, but which, strangely, is representative of all the rest, possesses its symbols, its equivalents for everything that is not itself. Painting for space, for example.

A "world" has dimensions. By definition they are not the sole possible ones (by passage to a 3rd dimension, spatial beings separated in the first two can be connected). But by definition also they have the value of an inner framework, they are more than singularities of content: the values in a pencil sketch are representative of the whole.

Thus the painting is a "world" by opposition to the unique and "real" world——In any case, it forms a world with all the other paintings——The *same* sensible elements signify something else there than in the prosaic world.

Replace the notions of concept, idea, mind, representation with the notions of *dimensions,* articulation, level, hinges, pivots, configuration——The point of departure = the critique of the usual conception of the *thing* and its *properties* → critique of the logical notion of the subject, and of logical inherence → critique of the *positive* signification (differences between significations), signification as a separation (*écart*), theory of predication—founded on this diacritical conception

The passage to a superior dimension = *Urstiftung* of a meaning, reorganization. In what sense is it prepared for in the given structure? As the sensible structure can be understood only through its relation to the body, to the flesh—the invisible structure can be understood only through its relation to logos, to speech——The invisible meaning is the inner framework of speech——The world of perception encroaches upon that of movement (which also is *seen*) and inversely movement has [eyes?] Likewise the world of ideas encroaches upon language (one thinks it) which inversely encroaches upon the ideas (one thinks because one speaks, because one writes)——

The others' words make me speak and think because they create within me an other than myself, a divergence (*écart*) by relation to . . . what I see, and thus designate it to me myself. The other's words form a grillwork through which I see my thought. Did I have it before this conversation? Yes, as a unique fundamental tone, *Weltthesis,* not as *thoughts,* significations or statements——To be sure, it is necessary to think in order to speak, but to think in the sense of being in the world (*être au monde*) or in the vertical Being of *Vorhabe.* Thoughts are the coinage of this total being——Delimitations—within it.

Husserl *lebendige Gegenwart* [62]

December, 1959

My body is never *in movement perspektivisch,* as are the other things——

62. EDITOR: Reference to an unpublished text of Husserl, classified as D.12.IV, and reproduced under the title "Die Welt der lebendigen Gegenwart und die Konstitution der ausserleiblichen Umwelt," in *Philosophy and Phenomenological Research,* Vol. 6, No. 3 (March, 1946).

It is not *in rest* either like some of them. It is beneath objective rest and movement——

The movements it will perform by the *Ich gehe* (and which are not "perspectival") will always be *possible rests* at each moment——*Possible* in what sense? It is certainly not a question of a certain *Ort in which* my body *could* be, i.e. of the evocation of a logical possibility of being there. It is a question of a power—of an I can.

Veränderung and *Unveränderung*—Build a doctrine of the negative on these phenomena. The positive and the negative are the two "sides" of a Being; in the *vertical* world, every being has this structure (To this structure is bound the ambiguity of the consciousness, and even a sort of blindness of the consciousness, of imperception in perception——To see is to not see—to see the other is essentially to see my body as an object, so that the other's body object could have a psychic "side." The experience of my own body and the experience of the other are themselves the two sides of one same Being: where I say that I see the other, in fact it especially happens that I objectify my body, the other is the horizon or other side of this experience——It is thus that one speaks *to the other* although one has only to do with oneself).

Against the doctrine of contradiction, absolute negation, the *either or*——Transcendence is identity within difference.

Science and ontology

Monday, January 4, 1960

Justify science as an operation within the given situation of knowledge—and thereby make apparent the necessity of the ontology "complementary" with this operational science——

Characterize the scientific treatment of being, time, evolution, etc., as a locating of "features" of the Universe or of "features" of Beings, a systematic explanation of what they imply in virtue of their role as *hinges. By principle* science is not an *exhausting,* but a physiognomic portrait——Its freedom of manipulation, its operational freedom is immediately synonymous with an intra-ontology. The equivalence that analytic geometry establishes between space and number to be understood, not as a spiritualization of space (Brunschvicg), but indeed as a spatialization of the understanding, as an intuition of the ontological equivalence of space and number before a subject of knowledge that is *of the world.*

The scientific deduction-experimental fact parallelism is neither to be contested, nor to be understood as a proof of a *realism* of science. It is founded on the fact that the deductive science renders explicit the structures, the *pivots,* certain traits of the inner framework of the world. This *truth* of science, far from making a philosophy useless, is founded and guaranteed only by a relation of transcendence with Being, an inherence of the subject and the object of science in a preobjective Being.

Scale—Ontological significance of this notion.
Endo-ontology cf. Husserl's phenomenological absolute.

January 20, 1960

It is a going beyond the ontology of the In itself—and expresses this overcoming in terms of the in itself——Scale: a *projective* notion: one imagines a being in itself marked on a map in itself, where it appears transposed according to a given ratio of sizes, so that the representations on different scales are different "visual pictures" of the same in itself——One goes one step further in suppressing the *model In itself:* there is no longer anything but representations on different scales. But they remain of the order of the "visual picture" or of the in itself by an inevitable inconsistency as long as one has not reached the problematic of philosophy.——It is a question of understanding that the "views" at different scales are not projections upon corporeities—screens of an inaccessible In itself, that they and their lateral implication in one another are the reality, exactly: that the reality is their common inner framework (*membrure*), their nucleus, and not something *behind them:* behind them, there are only other "views" still conceived according to the in itself-projection schema. The real is *between them,* this side of them. The macrophenomenon and the microphenomenon are not two more or less enlarged projections of a real in itself *behind them:* the macrophenomena of evolution are not less real, the microphenomena *not more* real. There is no hierarchy between them.

The content of my perception, microphenomenon, and the large-scale view of the enveloping phenomena are not two projections of the In itself: Being is their common inner framework. Each field is a dimensionality, and Being is dimensionality itself. It is therefore accessible indeed by my perception. It is even my perception that presents to me in a spectacle the reference of lateral transcendence from the "appearances" to the essence as a nucleus of (verbal) *Wesen*——The cognitions at a $>$ or $<$ scale (microphysical-macrophenomena) are a determination in dotted lines (by mathematical instruments, i.e. inventory of the structures) of nuclei of being whose actuality perception alone gives me, and which can be conceived only by derivation from its inner framework.

It is necessary to suppress the causal thought which is always: view of the world from without, from the point of view of a Kosmotheoros with, in anti-thesis, the antagonistic and inseparable movement of the reflective recuperation——I must no longer think myself *in the world* in the sense of the ob-jective spatiality, which amounts to autopositing myself and installing myself in the *Ego uninteressiert*——What replaces causal thought is the idea of transcendence, that is, of a world seen within inherence in this world, by virtue of it, of an Intra ontology, of a Being encompassing-encompassed, of a vertical, dimensional Being, dimensionality——And what replaces the antagonistic and solidary reflective movement (the immanence of the "idealists") is the fold or hollow of Being having by principle an *outside,* the architectonics of the configurations. There is no

longer $\begin{cases} \text{—consciousness} \\ \text{—projections} \\ \text{—In itself or object} \end{cases}$

There are fields in intersection, in a field of fields wherein the "subjectivities" are integrated, as Husserl indicates in the unpublished text on teleology and the phenomenological absolute, since they bear in their intrastructure a *leistende subjectivität* which is wholly *supported* on them.

The Invisible, the negative, vertical Being

January, 1960

A certain relation between the visible and the invisible, where the invisible is not only non-visible [63] (what has been or

63. Or *possibly* visible (in different degrees of possibility: the past has been, the future will be able to be seen).

will be seen and is not seen, or what is seen by an other than me, not by me), but where its absence counts in the world (it is "behind" the visible, imminent or eminent visibility, it is *Urpräsentiert* precisely as *Nichturpräsentierbar*, as another dimension) where the lacuna that marks its place is one of the points of passage of the "world." It is this negative that makes possible the *vertical* world, the union of the incompossibles, the being in transcendence, and the topological space and the time in joints and members, in dis-junction and dis-membering [64]—and the possible as a claimant of existence (of which "past" and "future" are but partial expressions)—and the male-female relation (the two pieces of wood that children see fitting together of themselves, irresistibly, because each is the *possible of the other*)—and the "divergence," and the totality above the divergencies—and the thought-unthought relation (Heidegger)—and the relation of *Kopulation* where two intentions have *one sole Erfüllung*

January, 1960

Husserl too thinks that one sole world is possible, this one (cf. unpublished texts at the Sorbonne: [65] unicity of the world, *like of God*). The "other possible worlds" are ideal variants of this one.——But this unique possible which our world is is not, in its very fabric, made of actuality——The Leibnizian notion of the possible as non-contradictory, as not involving negativity, is not the contrary of actualism: it is its counterpart, it is positivist like it. And finally the actual for Leibniz is only the limiting case of that possibility, the full possibility, it is what does not involve moral contradiction, what is not bad or what is *the best possible* in the twofold sense of: as good as can be, and the very best one of the possibles. With Husserl, the unicity of the world means not that it is actual and that every other world is imaginary, not that it is in itself and every other world for us only, but that it is at the root of every thought of possibles, that it even is surrounded with a halo of possibilities which are its attributes, which are *Möglichkeit an Wirklichkeit* or *Weltmöglichkeit*, that, taking on the form of the world of itself, this singular and

64. It is the same thing: the [?] is *Kopulation* (Husserl).
65. EDITOR: Unpublished text, 1930, classified E.III.4.

perceived being has a sort of natural destination to be and to embrace every possible one can conceive of, to be *Weltall*. Universality of our world, not according to its "content" (we are far from knowing it entirely), not as recorded fact (the "perceived") but according to its configuration, its ontological structure which envelops every possible and which every possible leads back to. The eidetic variation, therefore, does not make me pass to an order of separated essences, to a logical possible, the invariant that it gives me is a structural invariant, a Being in intrastructure which in the last analysis has its *Erfüllung* only in the *Weltthesis* of this world.

Problematic of the visible and the invisible

January, 1960

Principle: not to consider the invisible as an *other visible* "possible," or a "possible" visible for an other: that would be to destroy the inner framework that joins us to it. Moreover since this "other" who would "see" it—or this "other world" it would constitute would necessarily be connected to our own, the true possibility would necessarily reappear within this connection——The invisible is *there* without being an *object*, it is pure transcendence, without an ontic mask. And the "visibles" themselves, in the last analysis, they too are only centered on a nucleus of absence——

Raise the question: the invisible life, the invisible community, the invisible other, the invisible culture.
Elaborate a phenomenology of "the other world," as the limit of a phenomenology of the imaginary and the "hidden"——

Perception——Movement——Primordial unity of the sensible field——Transcendence synonym of incarnation——Endo-ontology——Soul and body——Qualitative integration and differentiation——

January, 1960

When I move myself, the perceived things have an apparent displacement that is inversely proportional to their distance—

the closest move more———The extent of the displacement can serve as an index for the distance.

Fundamental: it is absolutely *artificial* to recompose the phenomenon as geometrical optics does, to construct it on the basis of the angular displacement on the retina of images corresponding to *such* or *such* a point. I am ignorant of this geometry, and what is given to me phenomenally is not a set of *displacements* or *non-displacements* of this kind, it is the *difference* between what takes place at one distance and at another distance, it is the integral of those differences; the "points" that the optico-geometric analysis *gives* itself are, phenomenally, not points, but very small structures, monads, *metaphysical* points or transcendences. How name this system of differentiation of *Veränderung* and *Unveränderung*? In fact, to designate it thus, to describe it thus, is already to substitute for it its "projection" on a space for objective analysis. To tell the truth, movements, rests, distances, apparent sizes, etc., are only different indexes of refraction of the transparent medium that separates me from the *things themselves*, different expressions of that coherent distention across which Being shows itself and conceals itself. To pose the problem on the strength of such or such an index of distance as psychology does is already to break the structural unity of the world and to engage in the isolating attitude. Absolute primacy of the World and of Being for a "vertical" philosophy which really takes perception in the present———

For this same philosophy, therefore, the "partial" phenomena (here *Veränderung*, there *Unveränderung*), are not to be considered as positive, to be represented by a geometrical diagram where positive *lines* on a neutral *ground* connect positive *points*. On the contrary, each of these points result, by differentiation and objectification, from the movement of *Übergang* and from the intentional encroachment that sweeps the field. Absolute primacy of movement, not as *Ortsveränderung*, but as instability instituted by the organism itself (cf. F. Meyer [66]), as *fluctuation organized by it*, and, consequently, dominated. My mobility is the means of compensating for the mobility of the things, and hence of comprehending it and of surveying it from above (*survoler*).

66. EDITOR: François Meyer, *Problématique de l'évolution*, (Paris, 1954).

It is by principle that every perception is movement. And the unity of the world, the unity of the perceiver are this living unity of displacements compensated for. There is a point of fixation that does not budge in the movements of my body (compensated for by those of the eyes); on this side of that point there are apparent displacements of the objects when my head moves, beyond that point there are apparent displacements in the inverse direction: both are plus or minus variants of the *Unveränderung* of the fixed point (which results from the fact that my eyes move, compensating for the movements of my head)——The fixity of the fixed point and the mobility of what is this side of it and beyond it are not partial, local phenomena, and not even a set of phenomena: it is one sole transcendence, one sole graduated series of *divergencies*——The structure of the visual field, with its near-bys, its far-offs, its horizon, is indispensable for there to be *transcendence,* the model of every transcendence. Apply to the perception of space what I said about the perception of time (in Husserl): Husserl's diagram as a *positivist* projection of the vortex of temporal differentiation.[67] And the *intentional* analysis that tries to compose the field with intentional threads does not see that the threads are emanations and idealizations of one fabric, differentiations of the fabric.

If this vertical-perceptual view of the world and of being is recovered, there is no reason to seek to construct in the objective body, as the physiology of the nervous system does, a whole mass of hidden nervous phenomena by which the stimuli defined objectively would be *elaborated* into the total perception. The same critique applies to these physiological reconstructions and to the intentional analysis: neither sees that never will one construct perception and the perceived world with these *positive* terms and relations. The endeavor is *positivist:* with something *innerweltlich,* with traits of the world, to *fabricate* the architectonics of the *Welt.* It is a thought that acts as if the world wholly positive were given, and as if the problem were to make the perception of the world first considered as nonexisting arise therefrom. This problematic is of the type: why is there a perception of the world and *not no perception.* It is causal, positivist, negativist thought. Starting from the positive, it is obliged to hollow out lacunae in it (the organism as a *cavity,* the subjectiv-

67. EDITOR: Cf. above, p. 195, n. 31.

ity as the retreat of for Itself) and paradoxically wants these lacunae to be apparatus, dispositions of nervous functionings. . . . That's a case of trying to drink up the sea. And it entails the false idea that we have only the result of these complicated operations, that we exist on a sea of processes of which we know nothing. The postulate that the sole *Weltlichkeit* of the mind is of the type of the *Weltlichkeit* by end-to-end causality, the kind that reigns between the Cartesian *Blosse Sachen*——That, whether one [?] the psychological processes (unconscious) or the physiological processes ("mystery" of the brain). Criticize Freud's unconscious in this manner: as it is necessary to return to the phenomenal in order to understand the so-called play of perceptual "indexes"—which is clarified at once when we rediscover the evidence of the equivalencies of the *world*—so also the overdetermination, the ambiguity of the motivations must be understood by rediscovering our quasi-perceptual relationship with the human world through quite simple and nowise hidden existentials: only they are, like all structures, *between* our acts and our aims and not behind them——Redescribe the whole interhuman and even spiritual life in these terms, the *Weltlichkeit* of the mind, its non-insularity, its bonds with other minds and with truth also to be understood as differentiations of a spatio-temporal architectonics——

Once that is done, there is no more cause to pose the problem of the relations between the *soul* and the *body* as between two positive substances, nor to introduce an "institution of nature" that compels the soul to function according to the apparatus of the body and also the body to furnish ready-made thoughts to the soul—nor to envisage a *parallelism* which is a complete misconception, since it presupposes that the soul and the body contain respectively a bound series of phenomena or of ideas each rigorously continuous. The bond between the soul and the body is not a parallelism (and finally an identity in an ob-jective infinite Being, of which the totality body and the totality soul are two expressions)—nor is it the absolute opacity of an institution that reconnects by the efficacity of decision two orders each of which would suffice to itself——It is to be understood as the bond between the convex and the concave, between the solid vault and the hollow it forms——No correspondence (parallelist or of pure occasionalism) is to be sought between what takes place "in

the body" and what takes place "in the soul" in perception: it is
the same misconception to seek in the physical world an exact
equivalent of the organisms or in the organisms an integral
microcausal explanation——The soul is *planted* in the body as
the stake in the ground, without point by point correspondence
between ground and stake—or rather: the soul is the hollow of
the body, the body is the distention of the soul. The soul adheres
to the body as their signification adheres to the cultural things,
whose reverse or other side it is——

But this (plenum and hollow) does not suffice: for idealism
also says that, and we do not say it in the same sense. The soul,
the for itself is *a hollow and not a void,* not absolute non-being
with respect to a Being that would be plenitude and hard core.
The sensibility of the others is "the other side" of their aesthesio‑
logical body. And I can surmise this other side, *nichturprä‑
sentierbar,* through the articulation of the other's body on *my
sensible,* an articulation that does not empty me, that is not a
hemorrhage of my "consciousness," but on the contrary redoubles
me with an *alter ego.* The other is born in the body (of the other)
by an overhanging of that body, its investment in a *Verhalten,* its
interior transformation which I witness. The coupling of the
bodies, that is, the adjustment of their intentions to *one sole
Erfüllung,* to one sole wall they run into from two sides, is latent
in the consideration of one sole sensible world, open to participa‑
tion by all, which is given to each. The unicity of the visible
world, and, by encroachment, the invisible world, such as it
presents itself in the rediscovery of the vertical Being, is the
solution of the problem of the "relations between the soul and
the body"——

What we have said at the start concerning my perception as
integration-differentiation, my being set up on a universal diacrit‑
ical system, makes of my incarnation no longer a "difficulty," a
fault in the clear diamond of philosophy—but the typical fact,
the essential articulation of my constitutive transcendence: it is
necessary that a body perceive bodies if I am to be able to be not
ignorant of myself——

When the embryo's organism starts to perceive, there is not a
creation of a For itself by the body in itself, and there is not a
descent into the body of a pre-established soul, it is that the
vortex of the embryogenesis suddenly centers itself upon the

interior hollow it was preparing——A certain fundamental divergence, a certain constitutive dissonance emerges——The mystery is the same as that by which a child slides into language,
learns, as that by which an absent *arrives*, becomes (again)
present. The absent also is of the in itself; no longer counts in
the relief of the "vertical." [68] It is in the universal structure
"world"—encroachment of everything upon everything, a being
by promiscuity—that is found the reservoir whence proceeds
this new absolute life. All verticality comes from the vertical
Being——

We must accustom ourselves to understand that "thought"
(*cogitatio*) is not an invisible contact of self with self, that it
lives outside of this intimacy with oneself, *in front of* us, not in
us, always eccentric. Just as we rediscover the field of the sensible world as interior-exterior (cf. at the start: as global adhesion
to the infinity of motor indexes and motivations, as my belongingness to this *Welt*), so also it is necessary to rediscover as the
reality of the inter-human world and of history a surface of separation between me and the other which is also the place of our
union, the unique *Erfüllung* of his life and my life. It is to this
surface of separation and of union that the existentials of my
personal history proceed, it is the geometrical locus of the projections and introjections, it is the invisible hinge upon which my
life and the life of the others turn to rock into one another, the
inner framework of intersubjectivity

Human body   Descartes

February 1, 1960

The Cartesian idea of the human body as human *non-closed*,
open inasmuch as governed by thought—is perhaps the most
profound idea of the union of the soul and the body. It is the
soul intervening in a body that is *not of the in itself*, (if it were,
it would be closed like an animal body), that can be a body
and living—human only by reaching completion in a "view of
itself" which is thought——

68. Cf. Freud, mourning.

Husserl: the *Erwirken* of Thought and historicity
"*Vertical*" conception of Thought

February, 1960

Husserl: the *Gebilde* whose *Seinsart* is *Gewordenheit aus menschlichen Aktivität* are *originär* "*erfasst*" in a pure *Erwirken* (Text of *Ursprung* given by Fink,[69] which was not taken up by Louvain)

Extraordinary: the consciousness I have of *producing* my thoughts, my significations, is identical with my consciousness of their "human" origin——It is precisely as a step into the invisible, outside of all nature, of all Being, radical freedom, therefore, that thought is a bond with a human activity——I rejoin *man* precisely in my absolute non being. Humanity is invisible society. The self-consciousness forms a system with the self-consciousness of the other, precisely through its absolute solitude——

I don't like that——It is very close to Sartre——but it presupposes an activity-passivity *split* which Husserl himself knows does not exist since there is a secondary passivity, since every *Vollzug* is a *Nachvollzug* (even the first: language and its reference to a *Vollzug* before every *Vollzug*), since sedimentation is the sole mode of being of ideality——

I would like to develop that in the sense: the invisible is a hollow in the visible, a fold in passivity, not pure production. For that make an analysis of language, showing to what extent it is a quasi-natural displacement.

But what is fine is the idea of taking literally the *Erwirken* of thought: it is really *empty*, is of the *invisible*——All the positivist bric-a-brac of "concepts," "judgments," "relations" is eliminated, and the mind quiet as water in the fissure of Being——We must not look for spiritual things, there are only structures of the void——But I simply wish to plant this void in the visible Being, show that it is its *reverse side*—in particular the reverse side of language.

69. EDITOR: Edmund Husserl, "Die Frage nach dem Ursprung der Geometrie als intentional-historisches Problem," *Revue internationale de philosophie* (January 15, 1939), p. 209.

Just as it is necessary to restore the *vertical* visible world, so also there is a *vertical* view of the mind, according to which it is not made of a multitude of memories, images, judgments, it is one sole movement that one can coin out in judgments, in memories, but that holds them in one sole cluster as a spontaneous *word* contains a whole becoming, as *one sole grasp* of the hand contains a whole chunk of space.

Essence———Negativity.

February, 1960

I do not oppose quality to quantity, nor perception to idea———I seek in the perceived world nuclei of meaning which are in-visible, but which simply are not invisible in the sense of the absolute negation (or of the absolute positivity of the "intelligible world"), but in the sense of the *other dimensionality*, as depth hollows itself out behind height and breadth, as time hollows itself out behind space———The other dimensionality grafts itself onto the preceding ones starting from a *zero of* depth for example. But this too is contained in Being as universal dimensionality.

Husserl's eidetic variation, and its in-variant, designates only these *hinges* of Being, these structures accessible through quality as well as through quantity———

In order to study the insertion of every dimensionality in Being—study the insertion of depth in perception, and that of language in the world of silence———

Show that there is no eidetic variation without *speech;* show this starting from the *imaginary* as support of the eidetic variation, and speech as support of the imaginary

Problem of the negative and of the concept
Gradient

February, 1960

The problem of negativity is the problem of depth. Sartre speaks of a world that is not vertical, but in itself, that is, flat, and for a nothingness that is absolute abyss. In the end, for him depth does not exist, because it is bottomless——For me, the negative means absolutely nothing, and the positive neither (they are synonymous) and that not by appeal to a vague "compound" of being and nothingness, the structure is not a "compound." I take my starting point where Sartre ends, in the Being taken up by the for Itself——It is for him the finishing point because he starts with being and negentity and *constructs* their union. For me it is structure or transcendence that explains, and being and nothingness (in Sartre's sense) are its two abstract properties. For an ontology from within, transcendence does not have to be constructed, from the first it is, as Being doubled with nothingness, and what is to be explained is its doubling (which, moreover, is never finished)——Describe structure, everything is there, and the integration of structures in *Sein*, and meaning as meaning by investment (the meaning of the words I say to someone "hits him" ("*tombe sur la tête*"), *takes hold* of him before he has understood, draws the response from him——We are in humanity as a horizon of Being, because the horizon is what *surrounds* us, us no less than the things. But it is the horizon, not humanity, that is being——*Like humanity (Mensch-heit) every concept is first a horizonal generality, a generality of style*——There is no longer a problem of the concept, generality, the idea, when one has understood that the sensible itself is *invisible*, that the *yellow* is capable of setting itself up as a level or a horizon——

For Sartre, it is always *I* who forms depth, who hollows it out, who does everything, and who closes from within my prison in upon myself——

For me, on the contrary, even the most characterized acts, the decisions (a Communist's break with the Party), *this is not a non-being that makes itself be* (*to be a Communist, or to be a non-Communist*)——These decisions that *settle* are for me ambiguous (Communist outside of communism, if I break, non-Communist within communism, if once again I rally to it), and this ambiguity, it must be admitted, said, is of the same sort as the impartiality of past history, when it puts our former choices or the former doctrines beyond the true and the false   for me the truth is this beyond the truth, this depth where there are still *several relationships* to be considered.

The concept, the signification are the singular *dimensionalized*, the *formulated* structure, and there is no vision of this invisible hinge; nominalism is right: the significations are only *defined separations (écarts)*——

The gradient: not linear being, but structured being

The "representational" acts and the others——Consciousness and existence

February, 1960

Husserl admitted (L.U.[70]) that the representational acts are always founding with respect to the others—and that the others are not reducible to them——the consciousness was defined by priority as cognition—but it is admitted that *Werten* is original——

This is the sole possible position in a Philosophy of consciousness——

Is it still maintained in the unpublished texts where, for example, sexual instinct is considered "from the transcendental point of view"? [71] Does that not mean that non-representational "acts" (?) have an ontological function? But how could they, with the same rights as cognition, since they do not give "objects" and are *fungierende* rather than *acts*? (like time)

In fact, the solution of the L.U. is provisional, bound to the omnipotence of the eidetic method, that is, of reflexivity——It corresponds to a period when Husserl calmly distinguished the reflected and the unreflected (language that functions and language as ideality) as *Wesen* and *Tatsache*——If one remained with that, the intervention of "non-objectifying acts," their ontological function would be purely and simply the overthrow of the consciousness, irrationalism.

One does not get out of the rationalism-irrationalism dilemma as long as one thinks "consciousness" and "acts"——The decisive step is to recognize that in fact a consciousness is intentionality without acts, *fungierende*, that the "objects" of con-

70. EDITOR: Edmund Husserl, *Logische Untersuchungen*, 1st ed., 2 vols. (Halle, 1900–1901); 2d ed., 3 vols. (Halle, 1913–21).

71. EDITOR: Unpublished text entitled *Universale Teleologie*, classified E.III.5, published and translated into Italian in the volume *Tempo e Intentionalità*, in Archivio di Filosofia, Organo dell' Instituto di Studi filosofici (Padua, 1960).

sciousness themselves are not something positive *in front of* us, but nuclei of signification about which the transcendental life pivots, specified voids—and that the consciousness itself is an *Urpräsentierbar* for Itself which is presented as *Nichturprä-sentierbar* for the other, that sense experience (*le sentir*) is an *Urpräsentation* of what by principle is *Nichturpräsentierbar,* the transcendent, the thing, the "quale" become "level" or dimension —that the chiasm, the intentional "encroachment" are irreducible, which leads to the rejecting of the notion of subject, or to the defining of the subject as a field, as a hierarchized system of structures opened by an inaugural *there is.*

As a result of this reform of the "consciousness," immediately the non-objectifying intentionalities are no longer in the alternative of being *subordinate* or *dominant,* the structures of the affectivity are constitutive with the same right as the others, for the simple reasons that they are already the structures of knowledge being those of *language.* We must no longer ask why we have *affections* in addition to "representative sensations," since the representative sensation also (taken "vertically" to its insertion in our life) is affection, being a presence to the world through the body and to the body through the world, being *flesh,* and language is also. Reason too is *in* this horizon—promiscuity with Being and the world

Philosophy of speech and malaise of culture

March, 1960

There is a danger that a philosophy of speech would justify the indefinite proliferation of writings—and even of pre-writings (working notes—Husserl's *Forschungsmanuskript.* With him notion of the *Arbeitsprobleme*——*Arbeit:* that impossible enterprise of grasping the transcendental consciousness in the act)— the habit of speaking without knowing what one is saying, the confusion of style and of thought etc.

Yet: 1) it has always been that way in fact—the works that escape this profusion are *"academic"* works

2) there is a remedy, which is not to return to the American analytic-academic method—which would be to retreat from the problem—but to proceed over and beyond by facing the things again

Rays of past
of world

March, 1960

The interior monologue—the "consciousness" itself to be understood not as a series of individual (sensible or non sensible) *I think that*'s, but as openness upon *general* configurations or constellations, rays of the past and rays of the world at the end of which, through many "memory screens" dotted with lacunae and with the imaginary, pulsate some almost sensible structures, some individual memories. It is the Cartesian idealization applied to the mind as to the things (Husserl) that has persuaded us that we were a flux of individual *Erlebnisse*, whereas we are a field of Being. Even in the present, the landscape is a configuration.

The "associations" of psychoanalysis are in reality "rays" of time and of the world.

For example the memory screen of a yellow-striped butterfly (Freud, The Wolf Man [72]) reveals upon analysis a connection with yellow-streaked pears that in Russian call to mind *Grusha* which is the name of a young maid. There are not here three memories: the butterfly—the pear—the maid (of the same name) "associated." There is a certain play of the butterfly in the colored *field*, a certain (*verbal*) *Wesen* of the butterfly and of the pear—which communicate with the language *Wesen* Grusha (in virtue of the force of incarnation of language)——There are three *Wesen* connected by their center, belonging to the same ray of being. The analysis shows in addition that the maid spread open her legs like the butterfly its wings. Hence there is an *overdetermination* of the association——Perhaps valid in general: there is no association that comes into play unless there is overdetermination, that is, a relation of relations, a coincidence that cannot be fortuitous, that has an *ominal* sense. The tacit Cogito "thinks" only overdeterminations. I.e. symbolic matrices ——Overdetermination *always* occurs: the retrograde movement of the true (= the pre-existence of the ideal) (i.e. according

72. EDITOR: Sigmund Freud, *Cinq Psychanalyses*, French translation (Paris, 1954). [English translation by James Strachey, *An Infantile Neurosis*, Vol. XVII of *The Standard Edition of the Complete Psychological Works of Sigmund Freud* (London, 1955), p. 90.]

to Husserl the very fact of Speech as invocation of the nameable) furnishes always still other reasons for a given association——

For this see The Psychopathology of Everyday Life——(cf.
in *Cinq Psychanalyses*,[73] p. 397: subject dreams of an *Espe*
whose wings are torn out—but it is *Wespe*—but his initials are
SP—he is the castrated one——Analyze this operation of verbal
castration which is also a displaying of his initials (overdetermination)——The "castrating subject" is not a Thinker who knows
the true and who strikes it out. It is lateral junction of SP and
castration)——In general: Freud's *verbal* analyses appear in-
credible because one realizes them in a Thinker. But they must
not be *realized* in this way. Everything takes place in non-con-
ventional thought.

Notion of "ray of the world" (Husserl—Unpublished texts) (or
line of the universe)

                                    March, 1960

It is the idea not of a slice of the objective world between me
and the horizon, and not of an objective ensemble organized
synthetically (under an idea), but of an axis of equivalencies—
of an axis upon which all the perceptions that can be met with
there are equivalent, not with respect to the objective conclusion
they authorize (for in this respect they are quite different) but in
that they are all under the power of my vision of the moment
    elementary example: all the perceptions are implicated in
my actual I can——

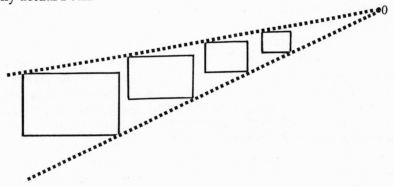

73. Eng. trans., *An Infantile Neurosis*, p. 94.

what is seen can be an object near and small or large and far-off.

The ray of the world is not represented here: what I represent here is a series of "visual pictures" and their law——The ray of the world is neither this series of logical possibles, nor the *law* that defines them—(interobjective relation)——It is the gaze within which they are all simultaneous, fruits of my I can——It is the very vision of depth——The ray of the world does not admit of a noema-noesis analysis. This does not mean that it presupposes *man*. It is a leaf of Being.

The "ray of the world" is not a synthesis and not "reception," but *segregation* i.e. implies that one is already *in the world or in being*. One carves in a being that remains in its place, of which one does not make a *synopsis*—and which is not in itself——

The visible and the invisible

April, 1960

The second part of the book (which I am beginning) with my description of the visible as in-visible, must lead in the third to a confrontation with the Cartesian ontology (finish Gueroult's Descartes—read his Malebranche—see Leibniz and Spinoza). The confrontation directed by this idea: Descartes = no *Weltlichkeit* of the mind, the mind consigned to the side of a god who is beyond thought——This leaves open the problem of the communication of the substances (occasionalism, harmony, parallelism)——My descriptions, my rehabilitation of the perceived world with all its consequences for the "subjectivity," in particular my description of corporeity and the "vertical" Being, all this is to lead to a mind-body, mind-mind communication, to a *Weltlichkeit* that would not be the *Weltlichkeit* of Nature simply transposed as in Leibniz, where the little perceptions and God as flat projection re-establish, on the side of the mind, a continuity symmetrical with that of Nature. This continuity, no longer existing even in Nature, a fortiori does not exist on the side of the mind. And yet there is a *Weltlichkeit* of the mind, it is not insular. Husserl showing that the mind is that milieu where there is *action at a distance* (memory) (text published in Cahiers Internationaux de Sociologie [74])   The Leibnizian postulate of

74. EDITOR: *"L'Esprit collectif,"* an unedited text of Husserl, trans. R. Toulemont, *Cahiers Internationaux de Sociologie,* XXVII (July–Dec., 1959), 128.

a projection of Nature in the monads (punctual correspondence) is typically a postulate of the "visual picture," an unconsciousness of the "wild" or perceived world

"Indestructible" past,
and intentional analytic—and ontology

April, 1960

The Freudian idea of the unconscious and the past as "indestructible," as "intemporal" = elimination of the common idea of time as a "series of *Erlebnisse*"——There is an architectonic past. cf. Proust: the *true* hawthorns are the hawthorns of the past——Restore this life without *Erlebnisse,* without interiority —which is what Piaget calls, badly indeed, egocentrism—which is, in reality, the "monumental" life, *Stiftung,* initiation.

This "past" belongs to a mythical time, to the time before time, to the prior life, "farther than India and China"——

What is the *intentional analysis* worth in regard to it? It gives us: every past *sinngemäss* has been present, i.e. its past being has been founded in a presence——And, certainly, that is so true [of ?] it that it *is still present.* But precisely there is here something that the intentional analytic cannot grasp, for it cannot rise (Husserl) to this "simultaneity" which is meta-intentional (cf. Fink article on the *Nachlass* [75]). The intentional analytic tacitly assumes a place of absolute contemplation *from which* the intentional explicitation is made, and which could embrace present, past, and even openness toward the future——It is the order of the "consciousness" of significations, and in this order there is no past-present "simultaneity," there is the evidence of their divergence——Whereas the *Ablaufsphäno-men* that Husserl describes and thematizes contains in itself something quite different: it contains the "simultaneity," the *passage,* the *nunc stans,* the Proustian corporeity as guardian of the past, the immersion in a Being in transcendence not reduced to the "perspectives" of the "consciousness"—it contains an intentional reference which is not only from the past [76] to the

75. EDITOR: E. Fink, "Die Spätphilosophie Husserls in der Freiburger Zeit," in *Edmund Husserl, 1859–1959* (The Hague, 1960), pp. 99–115.
76. EDITOR: Above the word "past," the author notes between parentheses, "subordinated."

factual, empirical present, but also and inversely from the factual present to a dimensional present or *Welt* or Being, where the past is "simultaneous" with the present in the narrow sense. This *reciprocal* intentional reference marks the limit of the intentional analytic: the point where it becomes a philosophy of transcendence. We encounter this *Ineinander* each time the intentional reference is no longer that from a *Sinngebung* to a *Sinngebung* that *motivates* it but from a "noema" to a "noema." And in fact here it is indeed the past that adheres to the present and not the *consciousness* of the past that adheres to the *consciousness* of the present: the "vertical" past contains in itself the exigency to have been perceived, far from the consciousness of having perceived bearing that of the past. The past is no longer here a "modification" or modalization of the *Bewusstsein von*. . . . Conversely it is the *Bewusstsein von*, the having perceived that is borne by the past as massive Being. I have perceived it *since it was*. The whole Husserlian analysis is blocked by the framework of *acts* which imposes upon it the philosophy of *consciousness*. It is necessary to take up again and develop the *fungierende or latent* intentionality which is the intentionality within being. That is not compatible with "phenomenology," that is, with an ontology that obliges whatever is not nothing to *present* itself to the *consciousness* across *Abschattungen* and as deriving from an originating donation which is an *act,* i.e. one *Erlebnis* among others (cf. Fink's critique of Husserl in the early article from the colloquium on phenomenology [77]). It is necessary to take as primary, not the consciousness and its *Ablaufsphänomen* with its distinct intentional threads, but the vortex which this *Ablaufsphänomen* schematizes, the spatializing-temporalizing vortex (which is flesh and not consciousness facing a noema)

Telepathy——Being for the other——Corporeity

April, 1960

Organs to be seen (Portmann [78])——My body as an organ to be seen——I.e.: to perceive a part of my body is also to perceive

77. EDITOR: E. Fink, "L'Analyse intentionnelle," in *Problèmes actuels de la phénoménologie* (Bruges, 1952).

78. EDITOR: A. Portmann, *Tiergestalt.* [English translation, *Animal Forms and Patterns: A Study of the Appearance of Animals*

it as *visible,* i.e. *for the other.* And to be sure it assumes this character because in fact someone does look at it——But this *fact* of the other's presence would not itself be possible if antecedently the part of the body in question were not *visible,* if there were not, around each part of the body, a halo of *visibility*—— But this visible not actually seen is not the Sartrean *imaginary:* presence to the absent or of the absent. It is a presence of the imminent, the latent, or the hidden——Cf. Bachelard saying that each sense has its own imaginary.

This visibility of my body (for me—but also *universal* and, eminently, for the other) is what is responsible for what is called telepathy. For a minute indication of the other's behavior suffices to activate this danger of visibility. For example, a woman feels her body desired and looked at by imperceptible signs, and without even herself looking at those who look at her. The "telepathy" here is due to the fact that she anticipates the other's effective perception (nymphomania) cf. *Psychoanalysis and the Occult* [79] ——One feels oneself looked at (burning neck) not because something passes from the look to our body to burn it at the point seen, but because to feel one's body is also to feel its aspect for the other. One would here have to study in what sense the other's sensoriality is implicated in my own: to feel my eyes is to feel that they are threatened with being seen——But the correlation is not always thus of the seer with the seen, or of speaking with hearing: my hands, my face also are of the visible. The case of reciprocity (seeing seen), (touching touched in the handshake) is the major and perfect case, where there is *quasi-reflection (Einfühlung), Ineinander;* the general case is the adjustment of a visible for me to a tangible for me and of this visible for me to a visible for the other—(for example, my hand)

(London, 1952).] The author is applying to the human body certain of Portmann's remarks concerning the animal organism. Cf. notably p. 113: the body patterns of certain animals "must be appraised as a special organ of reference in relationship to a beholding eye and to the central nervous systems. The eye and what is to be looked at form together a functional unit which is fitted together according to rules as strict as those obtaining between food and digestive organs."

79. EDITOR: Georges Devreux, *Psychoanalysis and the Occult* (New York, 1953).

'Εγώ and οὖτις

April, 1960

The I, really, is nobody, is the anonymous; it must be so, prior to all objectification, denomination, in order to be the Operator, or the one to whom all this occurs. The named I, the I named (*Le Je dénommé, le dénommé Je*), is an object. The primary I, of which this one is the objectification, is the unknown *to whom* all is given to see or to think, to whom everything appeals, before whom . . . there is something. It is therefore negativity—ungraspable in person, of course, since it is *nothing*.

But is this *he who thinks*, reasons, speaks, argues, suffers, enjoys, etc.? Obviously not, since it is nothing——He who thinks, perceives, etc. is this negativity as openness, by the body, to the world——Reflexivity must be understood by the body, by the relation to self of the body, of speech. The speaking-listening duality remains at the heart of the I, its negativity is but the *hollow* between speaking and hearing, the point where their equivalence is formed——The body-negative or language-negative duality *is* the subject——the body, language, as alter ego——The "among ourselves" (*entre-nous*) (Michaux) of my body and me—my duplication—which does not prevent the passive-body and the active-body from being welded together in *Leistung*—from *overlapping*, being non-different——This, even though every *Leistung* accomplished (animated discussion, etc.), always gives me the impression of having "left myself"——

Visible—Invisible

May, 1960

When I say that every visible: 1) involves a ground which is not visible in the sense the figure is

2) even in what is figural or figurative in it, is not an ob-jective *quale*, an in Itself surveyed from above, but slips under the gaze or is swept over by the look, is born in silence under the gaze (when it arises straight ahead, it comes from the horizon, when it comes on the scene laterally, it does so "noiselessly"—in the sense that Nietzsche says great ideas are born *noiselessly*)—hence, if one means by visible the

objective *quale*, it is in this sense not visible, but *Unverborgen*

When I say then that every visible is invisible, that perception is imperception, that consciousness has a *"punctum cae-cum,"* that to see is always to see more than one sees—this must not be understood in the sense of a *contradiction*——It must not be imagined that I add to the visible perfectly defined as in Itself a non-visible (which would be only objective absence) (that is, objective presence *elsewhere*, in an *elsewhere* in itself)——One has to understand that it is the visibility itself that involves a non-visibility——In the very measure that I see, I do not know *what* I see (a familiar person is not defined), which does not mean that there would be *nothing* there, but that the *Wesen* in question is that of a ray of the world tacitly touched——The perceived world (like painting) is the ensemble of my body's routes and not a multitude of spatio-temporal individuals——The invisible of the visible. It is its belongingness to a ray of the world——There is a *Wesen* of red, which is not the *Wesen* of green; but it is a *Wesen* that in principle is accessible only through the seeing, and is accessible as soon as the seeing is given, has then no more need to be *thought*: seeing is this sort of thought that has no need to think in order to possess the *Wesen* —It *este* [80] in the red like the memory of the high school building in its odor [81]——Understand this active *Wesen*, coming from the red itself, perhaps as the articulation of the red upon the other colors or under the lighting. From this, understand that the red has in itself the possibility to become neutral (when it is the color of the lighting), dimensionality——This becoming-neutral is not a change of the red into "another color"; it is a modification of the red by its own duration (as the impact of a figure or a line on my vision tends to become dimensional, and to give it the value of an index of the curvature of space)——And since there are such structural modifications of the quality by space (transparency, constancies) as well as by the other qualities, we must understand that the *sensible world* is this perceptual logic, this system of equivalencies, and not a pile of spatio-temporal individuals. And this logic is neither *produced* by our psychophysical constitution, nor produced by our categorial equipment, but

80. EDITOR: See above, p. 203, n. 44.
81. EDITOR: Allusion to Heidegger, *Einführung in die Metaphysik* (Tübingen, 1953), pp. 25–26. [English translation, *Introduction to Metaphysics* (Garden City, N. Y., 1961), pp. 27–28.]

lifted from a *world* whose inner framework our categories, our constitution, our "subjectivity" render explicit——

Blindness (*punctum caecum*) of the "consciousness"

May, 1960

What it does not see it does not see for reasons of principle, it is because it is consciousness that it does not see. *What* it does not see is what in it prepares the vision of the rest (as the retina is blind at the point where the fibers that will permit the vision spread out into it). *What* it does not see is what makes it see, is its tie to Being, is its corporeity, are the existentials by which the world becomes visible, is the flesh wherein the *object* is born. It is inevitable that the consciousness be mystified, inverted, indirect, in principle it sees the things *through the other end*, in principle it disregards Being and prefers the object to it, that is, a Being with which it has broken, and which it posits beyond this negation, by negating this negation——In it it ignores the non-dissimulation of Being, the *Unverborgenheit*, the non-mediated presence which is not something positive, which is being of the far-offs (*être des lointains*)

Flesh of the world—Flesh of the body—Being

May, 1960

Flesh of the world, described (apropos of time, space, movement) as segregation, dimensionality, continuation, latency, encroachment——Then interrogate once again these phenomena-questions: they refer us to the perceiving-perceived *Einfühlung*, for they mean that we are already *in* the being thus described, that we *are of it*, that between it and us there is *Einfühlung*

That means that my body is made of the same flesh as the world (it is a perceived), and moreover that this flesh of my body is shared by the world, the world *reflects* it, encroaches upon it and it encroaches upon the world (the felt [*senti*] at the same time the culmination of subjectivity and the culmination of materiality), they are in a relation of transgression or of overlapping——This also means: my body is not only one perceived among others, it is the measurant (*mesurant*) of all, *Nullpunkt* of all the dimensions of the world. For example, it is not one mobile or moving among the mobiles or movings, I am not conscious of its movements as *a distance taken by relation to me*, it *sich bewegt* whereas the things *are moved*. This means a sort of "reflectedness" (*sich bewegen*), it thereby constitutes itself *in itself*——In a parallel way: it touches *itself*, sees *itself*. And consequently it is capable of *touching or seeing* something, that is, of being open to the things in which (Malebranche) it reads its own modifications (because we have no idea of the soul, because the soul is a being of which there is no idea, a being *we are* and do not see). The touching oneself, seeing oneself, a "knowing by sentiment"——

The *touching itself, seeing itself* of the body is itself to be understood in terms of what we said of the seeing and the visible, the touching and the touchable.   I.e. it is not an act, it is a being at (*être à*). To touch *oneself*, to see *oneself*, accordingly, is not to apprehend oneself as an ob-ject, it is to be open to oneself, destined to oneself (narcissism)——Nor, therefore, is it to reach *oneself*, it is on the contrary to escape *oneself*, to be ignorant of *oneself*, the self in question is by divergence (*d'écart*), is *Unverborgenheit of the Verborgen* as such, which consequently does not cease to be hidden or latent——

The feeling that one feels, the seeing one sees, is not a thought of seeing or of feeling, but vision, feeling, mute experience of a mute meaning——

The quasi "reflective" redoubling, the reflexivity of the body, the fact that it touches itself touching, sees itself seeing, does not consist in surprising a connecting activity behind the connected, in reinstalling oneself in this constitutive activity; the self-perception (sentiment of oneself, Hegel would say) or perception of perception does not convert what it apprehends into an object and does not coincide with a constitutive source of perception: in fact I do not entirely succeed in touching myself touching, in seeing myself seeing, the experience I have of myself perceiving does not go beyond a sort of *imminence*, it terminates in the invisible, simply this invisible is *its* invisible, i.e. the reverse of *its* specular perception, of the concrete vision I have of my body in the mirror. The self-perception is still a perception, i.e. it gives me a *Nicht Urpräsentierbar* (a non-visible, myself), but this it gives me through an *Urpräsentierbar* (my tactile or visual appearance) in transparency (i.e. as a latency)——My invisibility for myself does not result from my being a *positive* mind, a *positive* "consciousness," a *positive* spirituality, an existence as consciousness (i.e. as pure *appearing to self*), it comes from the fact that I am he who: 1) has a visible world, i.e. a dimensional body, and open to participation; 2) i.e. a body visible for itself; 3) and therefore, finally, a self-presence that is an absence from self——The progress of the inquiry toward the *center* is not the movement from the conditioned unto the condition, from the founded unto the *Grund:* the so-called *Grund* is *Abgrund.* But the abyss one thus discovers is not such *by lack of ground,* it is upsurge of a *Hoheit* which supports from above (*tient par le haut*) (cf. Heidegger, *Unterwegs zur Sprache* [82]), that is, of a negativity that *comes to the world.*

The flesh of the world is not explained by the flesh of the body, nor the flesh of the body by the negativity or self that inhabits it—the 3 phenomena are *simultaneous*——

The flesh of the world is not *self-sensing* (*se sentir*) as is my flesh——It is sensible and not sentient——I call it flesh, nonetheless (for example, the relief, depth, "life" in Michotte's experiments [83]) in order to say that it is a *pregnancy* of possibles, *Weltmöglichkeit* (the possible worlds variants of this world, the world beneath the singular and the plural) that it is therefore absolutely not an ob-ject, that the *blosse Sache* mode of being is but a partial and second expression of it. This is not hylozoism: inversely, hylozoism is a conceptualization——A false thematization, in the order of the explicative-Entity, of our experience of carnal presence—It is by the flesh of the world that in the last analysis one can understand the lived body (*corps propre*)—— The flesh of the world is of the Being-seen, i.e. is a Being that is *eminently percipi,* and it is by it that we can understand the *percipere:* this perceived that we call my body applying itself to the rest of the perceived, i.e. treating itself as a perceived by itself and hence as a perceiving, all this is finally possible and means something only because *there is* Being, not Being in itself,

82. EDITOR: *Unterwegs zur Sprache* (Tübingen, 1959), p. 13. "Die Sprache ist: Sprache. Die Sprache spricht. Wenn wir uns in den Abgrund, den dieser Satz nennt, fallen lassen, stürzen wir nicht ins Leere weg. Wir fallen in die Höhe. Deren Hoheit öffnet eine Tiefe."
83. EDITOR: Cf. above, p. 178, n. 14.

identical to itself, in the night, but the Being that also contains
its negation, its *percipi*——cf. Bergson saying: we have already
given ourselves the consciousness by positing the "images," and
therefore we do not have to deduce it at the level of the "conscious" living being, which is *less* and not more than the universe of images, which is one concentration or abstraction of
them——It was meaningless to thus realize the consciousness
before the consciousness. And this is why we say, for our part,
that what is primary is not the diffuse "consciousness" of the "images" (a diffuse consciousness which is nothing, since Bergson
explains that there is consciousness only through the "camera
obscura" of the centers of indetermination and the bodies [84]), it
is Being

Metaphysics—Infinity
World—*Offenheit*

May, 1960

World and Being:
their relation is that of the visible with the invisible (latency) the invisible is not another visible ("possible" in the logical sense) a positive only *absent*

It is *Verborgenheit* by principle i.e. invisible *of the visible,*
Offenheit of the *Umwelt* and not *Unendlichkeit*——*Unendlichkeit* is at bottom the *in itself,* the *ob-ject*——For me the infinity of Being that one can speak of is *operative,* militant finitude:
the openness of the *Umwelt*——I am against finitude in the
empirical sense, a factual existence that *has limits,* and this is
why I am for metaphysics. But it lies no more in infinity than in
the factual finitude

84. EDITOR: Bergson says that "living beings constitute 'centers
of indetermination' in the universe . . . ," and further he explains:
". . . if we consider any other given place in the universe we can
regard the action of all matter as passing through it without resistance and without loss, and the photograph of the whole as trans-
lucent: here there is wanting behind the plate the black screen on
which the image could be shown. Our 'zones of indetermination' play
in some sort the part of the screen." *Matière et mémoire* (10th ed.,
Paris, 1913), pp. 24, 26–27. [English translation by N. M. Paul and
W. Scott Palmer, *Matter and Memory* (London, 1912), pp. 28, 32.]

The philosophy of the sensible as literature

May, 1960

The scientific psychology thinks that there is nothing to say about quality as a phenomenon, that phenomenology is "at the limit impossible" (Bresson [85]) (and yet what are we talking about, even in scientific psychology, if not phenomena? The *facts* have no other role there than to awaken dormant phenomena)————The truth is that the *quale* appears opaque, inexpressible, as life inspires nothing to the man who is not a writer. Whereas the sensible is, like life, a treasury ever full of things to say for him who is a philosopher (that is, a writer). And just as each finds to be true and rediscovers in himself what the writer says of life and of the sentiments, so also the phenomenologists are understood and made use of by those who say that phenomenology is impossible. The root of the matter is that the sensible indeed offers nothing one could state if one is not a philosopher or a writer, but that this is not because it would be an ineffable in Itself, but because of the fact that one does not know how *to speak*. Problems of the "retrospective reality" of the true————It results from the fact that the world, Being, are polymorphism, mystery and nowise a layer of flat entities or of the in itself

"Visual picture" → "representation of the world"
Todo y Nada

May, 1960

Generalize the critique of the visual picture into a critique of "*Vorstellung*"————

For the critique of the visual picture is not a critique of realism or of idealism (synopsis) only————It is essentially a critique of the meaning of being given by both to the *thing* and to the *world*.

That is, the meaning of being In *Itself*—(in itself not re-

85. EDITOR: François Bresson, "Perception et indices perceptifs," in Bruner, Bresson, Morf, and Piaget, *Logique et perception* (Paris, 1958), p. 156. "The phenomenological description is at the limit unrealizable and interior experience ineffable. Consequently it is no longer the object of any communication and of any science, and it would suffice to admit the existence of this experience, without occupying oneself with it any further."

ferred to what alone gives it meaning: *distance,* divergence, transcendence, the flesh)

but if the critique of the "visual picture" is that, it generalizes itself into a critique of *Vorstellung:* for if our relation with the world is *Vorstellung,* the world "represented" has the In Itself as the meaning of its being. For example, the Other represents the world to himself, i.e. there is for him an internal object which *is* nowhere, which is *ideality,* and apart from which there exists the world itself.

What I want to do is restore the world as a meaning of Being absolutely different from the "represented," that is, as the vertical Being which none of the "representations" exhaust and which all "reach," the wild Being.

This is to be applied not only to perception, but to the Universe of predicative truths and significations as well. Here also it is necessary to conceive the signification (wild) as absolutely distinct from the In Itself and the "pure consciousness"—the (predicative-cultural) truth as this Individual (prior to the singular and the plural) upon which the acts of significations *cross* and of which they are cuttings.

Moreover the distinction between the two planes (natural and cultural) is abstract: everything is cultural in us (our Lebenswelt is "subjective") (our perception is cultural-historical) and everything is natural in us (even the cultural rests on the polymorphism of the wild Being).

The meaning of being to be disclosed: it is a question of showing that the ontic, the *"Erlebnisse,"* "sensations," "judgments"—(the ob-jects, the "represented," in short all idealizations of the Psyche and of Nature) all the bric-a-brac of those *positive* psychic so-called "realities" (and which are lacunar, "insular," without *Weltlichkeit* of their own) is in reality abstractly carved out from the ontological tissue, from the "body of the mind"——

Being is the "place" where the "modes of consciousness" are inscribed as structurations of Being (a way of thinking oneself within a society is implied in its social structure), and where the structurations of Being are modes of consciousness. The in itself-for itself integration takes place not in the absolute consciousness, but in the Being in promiscuity. The perception of the world is formed in the world, the test for truth takes place in Being.

254 / THE VISIBLE AND THE INVISIBLE

Sartre and classical ontology The historical Totalization which Sartre always assumes—is the reflection of his "nothingness"— since nothing, in order to "be in the world," must support itself on "all."

Touching—touching oneself
seeing—seeing oneself
the body, the flesh as *Self*

May, 1960

To touch and to touch oneself (to touch oneself = touched-touching) They do not coincide in the body: the touching is never exactly the touched. This does not mean that they coincide "in the mind" or at the level of "consciousness." Something else than the body is needed for the junction to be made: it takes place in the *untouchable*. That of the other which I will never touch. But what I will never touch, he does not touch either, no privilege of oneself over the other here, it is therefore not the *consciousness* that is the untouchable——"The consciousness" would be something positive, and with regard to it there would recommence, does recommence, the duality of the reflecting and the reflected, like that of the touching and the touched. The untouchable is not a touchable in fact inaccessible—the unconscious is not a representation in fact inaccessible. The negative here is not a *positive that is elsewhere* (a transcendent)——It is a true negative, i.e. an *Unverborgenheit* of the *Verborgenheit*, an *Urpräsentation* of the *Nichturpräsentierbar*, in other words, an original of the *elsewhere*, a *Selbst* that is an Other, a Hollow——Hence no sense in saying: the touched-touching junction is made by Thought or Consciousness: Thought or Consciousness is *Offenheit* of a corporeity to . . . World or Being

The untouchable (and also the invisible [86]: for the same analysis can be repeated for vision: what stands in the way of my seeing myself is first a *de facto* invisible (my eyes invisible for me), but, beyond this invisible (which lacuna is filled by the other and by my generality) a *de jure* invisible: I cannot see myself in movement, witness my own movement. But this *de*

86. EDITOR: The parenthesis opened here is not closed: the rest of the paragraph will deal with the invisible.

jure invisible signifies in reality that *Wahrnehmen* and *Sich bewegen* are synonymous: it is for this reason that the *Wahrnehmen* never rejoins the *Sich bewegen* it wishes to apprehend: it is another of the same. But, this failure, this invisible, precisely attests that *Wahrnehmen* is *Sich bewegen*, there is here a success in the failure. *Wahrnehmen* fails to apprehend *Sich bewegen* (and I am for myself a zero of movement even during movement, *I do not move away from myself*) precisely because they are homogeneous, and this failure is the proof of this homogeneity: *Wahrnehmen* and *Sich bewegen* emerge from one another. A sort of reflection by Ec-stasy, they are the same tuft.

To touch is to touch oneself. To be understood as: the things are the prolongation of my body and my body is the prolongation of the world, through it the world surrounds me——If I cannot touch my own movement, this movement is entirely woven out of contacts with me——The touching oneself and the touching have to be understood as each the reverse of the other——The negativity that inhabits the touch (and which I must not minimize: it is because of it that the body is not an empirical fact, that it has an ontological signification), the untouchable of the touch, the invisible of vision, the unconscious of consciousness (its central *punctum caecum*, that blindness that makes it consciousness i.e. an indirect and *inverted* grasp of all things) is the *other side* or the *reverse* (or the other dimensionality) of sensible Being; one cannot say that it is *there*, although there would assuredly be points where it *is not*——It is there with a presence by investment in another dimensionality, with a "double-bottomed" presence   the flesh, the *Leib*, is not a sum of *self-touchings* (of "tactile sensations"), but not a sum of tactile sensations plus "kinestheses" either, it is an "I can"——The corporeal schema would not be a *schema* if it were not this contact of *self* with *self* (which is rather *non-difference*) (common presentation to . . . X)

The flesh of the world (the "quale") is indivision of this sensible Being that I am and all the rest which feels itself (*se sent*) in me, pleasure-reality indivision——

The flesh *is a mirror phenomenon* and the mirror is an extension of my relation with my body. Mirror = realization of a *Bild* of the thing, and I-my shadow relation = realization of a (verbal) *Wesen*: extraction of the essence of the thing, of the pellicle of Being or of its "Appearance"——To touch oneself, to see oneself, is to obtain such a specular extract of oneself. I.e. fission of appearance and Being—a fission that already takes place in the touch (duality of the touching and the touched) and which, with the mirror (Narcissus) is only a more profound adhesion to Self. The visual *projection* of the world in me to be understood not as intra-objective things-my body relation. But as a shadow-body relation, a community of verbal *Wesen* and hence finally a "resemblance" phenomenon, transcendence.

The vision-touch divergence (not *superposable,* one of the universes overhangs the other) to be understood as the most striking case of the overhanging that exists within each sense and makes of it *"eine Art der Reflexion."*

This divergence, one will say, is simply a fact of our *organization,* of the presence of such receptors with such thresholds, etc. . . .

I do not say the contrary. What I say is that these *facts* have no *explicative power.* They express differently an ontological relief which they cannot efface by incorporating it to one unique plane of physical causality, since there is no physical explanation for the constitution of the "singular points" which are our bodies (cf. F. Meyer [87]) nor therefore our aesthesiology——

Phenomenology is here the recognition that the theoretically *complete,* full world of the physical explanation is not so, and that therefore it is necessary to consider as ultimate, inexplicable, and *hence as a world by itself* the whole of our experience of sensible being and of men. A world by itself: i.e. it is necessary to translate into *perceptual logic* what science and positive psychology treat as fragments of the In Itself *absque praemissis.*

$$\begin{cases} \text{touching—touching oneself} \\ \text{(the things} \\ \text{the lived body } [le\ corps\ propre]) \\ \text{seeing—seeing oneself} \\ \text{hearing—}hearing\ oneself \text{ (Radio)} \\ \text{understanding—speaking} \\ \text{hearing—singing} \end{cases}$$

$$\begin{cases} \text{Unity by } nervure \\ \text{pre-objective—} \end{cases}$$

The touch = movement that touches
and movement that is touched

87. EDITOR: *Problématique de l'évolution.*

To elucidate *Wahrnehmen* and *Sich bewegen,* show that no *Wahrnehmen perceives* except on condition of being a *Self of movement.*

One's own movement (*mouvement propre*), attestation of a *thing-subject:* a movement like that of the things, but movement *that I make——*

Start from there in order to understand language as the foundation of the I think: it is to the I think what movement is to perception. Show that the movement is *carnal——*It is in the carnal that there is a relation between the Movement and its "self" (the Self of the movement described by Michotte) with the *Wahrnehmen.*

Visible and invisible

May, 1960

The invisible is

1) what is not actually visible, but could be (hidden or inactual aspects of the thing—hidden things, situated "else-where"—"Here" and "elsewhere")

2) what, relative to the visible, could nevertheless not be seen as a thing (the existentials of the visible, its dimensions, its non-figurative inner framework)

3) what exists only as tactile or kinesthetically, etc.

4) the λέκτα, the Cogito

I am not uniting these 4 "layers" *logically* under the category of the *in*-visible——

That is impossible first for the simple reason that since the *visible* is not an *objective positive,* the *invisible* cannot be a negation in the logical sense——

It is a question of a negation-reference (zero of . . .) or separation (*écart*).

This negation-reference is common to all the *invisibles* because the visible has been defined as dimensionality of Being, i.e. as universal, and because therefore everything that is not a *part* of it is necessarily *enveloped in it* and is but a modality of the same transcendence.

. . . .

Visible invisible

May, 1960

The sensible, the visible, must be for me the occasion to say what nothingness is——

Nothingness is nothing more (nor less) than the invisible.

Start from an analysis of the total philosophical error which is to think that the visible is an *objective* presence (or the idea of this presence) (visual picture)

this entails the idea of the *quale* as in itself

Show that the *quale* is always a certain type of *latency*

Sartre saying that the image of Pierre who is in Africa is only a "manner of living" the very being of Pierre, his visible being, the only one there would be——

In reality this is something else than the free image: it is a sort of perception, a teleperception——

The sensible, the visible must be defined not as that with which I have in fact a relation by effective vision—but also as that of which I can subsequently have a teleperception——For the thing seen is the *Urstiftung* of these "images"——

Like the *Zeitpunkt* the *Raumpunkt* is the *Stiftung* once and for all of a Being-there

History, Transcendental geology,
Historical time, historical space | Philosophy

June 1, 1960

Oppose to a philosophy of history such as that of Sartre (which is finally a philosophy of the "individual praxis"—and in which history is the encounter of this praxis with the inertia of the "worked-over matter," of the authentic temporality with what *congeals* it), not, doubtlessly, a philosophy of geography (it would be as vain to take as axis the encounter of the individual praxis with the spatial in Itself as his encounter with the inert, the "relations between persons" mediatized by space as the relations between persons mediatized by time)—but a philosophy of structure which, as a matter of fact, will take form better on contact with geography than on contact with history. For history is too immediately bound to the individual praxis, to interiority, it hides too much its thickness and its flesh for it not to be easy to reintroduce into it the whole philosophy of the person. Whereas geography—or rather: the Earth as *Ur-Arche* brings to light the carnal *Urhistorie* (Husserl—*Umsturz* . . .[88]) In fact it is a question of grasping the *nexus*—neither "historical" nor "geographic" of history and transcendental geology, this very time that is space, this very space that is time, which I will have rediscovered by my analysis of the visible and the flesh, the simultaneous *Urstiftung* of time and space which makes there be a historical landscape and a quasi-geographical inscription of history. Fundamental problem: the sedimentation and the reactivation

Flesh—Mind

June, 1960

Define the mind as the *other side* of the body——We have no idea of a mind that would not be *doubled* with a body, that would not be established on this *ground*——

The "other side" means that the body, inasmuch as it has this other side, is not describable in *objective* terms, in terms of the in itself—that this other side is really the other side *of the body,* *overflows* into it (*Ueberschreiten*), encroaches upon it, is hidden in it—and at the same time needs it, terminates in it, is *anchored* in it. There is a body of the mind, and a mind of the body and a chiasm between them. The other side to be understood not, as in objective thought, in the sense of another projection of the same flat projection system, but in the sense of *Ueberstieg* of the body toward a depth, a dimensionality that is not that of extension, and a transdescendence of the negative toward the sensible.

The essential notion for such a philosophy is that of the flesh, which is not the objective body, nor the body thought by the soul as its own (Descartes), which is the sensible in the twofold sense of what one senses and what senses. What one senses = the sensible thing, the sensible world = the correlate of my active body, what "responds" to it——What senses = I cannot posit one sole sensible without positing it as torn from my flesh, lifted off my flesh, and my flesh itself is one of the sensi-

88. EDITOR: *Umsturz der Kopernikanischen Lehre: die Erde als ur-Arche bewegt sich nicht* (unpublished text).

bles in which an inscription of all the others is made, the sensible pivot in which all the others participate, the sensible-key, the dimensional sensible. My body is to the greatest extent what every thing is: a *dimensional this*. It is the universal thing——— But, while the things become dimensions only insofar as they are received in a *field*, my body is this field itself, i.e. a sensible that is dimensional *of itself*, universal measurant———The relation of my body as sensible with my body as sentient (the body I touch, the body that touches) = immersion of the being-touched in the touching being and of the touching being in the being-touched ———The sensoriality, its SICH-*bewegen* and its SICH-*wahrnehmen*, its coming to *self*———A self that has an environment, that is the reverse of this environment. In going into the details of the analysis, one would see that the essential is the *reflected in offset* (*refléchi en bougé*), where the touching is always *on the verge* of apprehending itself as tangible, misses its grasp, and completes it only in a *there is*———The *wahrnehmen-sich bewegen* implication is a thought-language implication———The flesh is this whole cycle and not only the inherence in a spatio-temporally individuated this. Moreover a spatio-temporally individuated this is an *Unselbständig*: there are only radiations of (verbal) essences, there are no spatio-temporal indivisibles. The sensible thing itself is borne by a transcendency.

Show that philosophy as interrogation (i.e. as disposition, around the this and the world which *is there*, of a hollow, of a questioning, where the this and the world must *themselves* say what they are—i.e. not as the search for an invariant of language, for a lexical essence, but as the search for an invariant of silence, for the structure) can consist only in showing how the world is articulated starting from a zero of being which is not nothingness, that is, in installing itself on the edge of being, neither in the for Itself, nor in the in Itself, at the joints, where the multiple *entries* of the world cross.

Visible-seer

November, 1960

In what sense exactly visible?———What I see of myself is never exactly the seer, in any case not the seer of the moment——But the seer is *of* the visible (is of it), is in the prolongation of the signs of the visible body, in dotted lines (visible for another)——To tell the truth even for the other is it properly speaking visible as a seer?——No in the sense that it is always *a little behind* what the other sees——To tell the truth neither behind, nor in front—nor *where* the other looks.

It is always *a little further* than the spot I look at, the other looks at, that the seer I am is.——*Posed* on the visible, like a bird, clinging to the visible, not *in* it. And yet in chiasm with it——

So also the touched-touching. This structure exists in one sole organ——The flesh of my fingers = each of them is phenomenal finger and objective finger, outside and inside of the finger in reciprocity, in chiasm, activity and passivity coupled. The one encroaches upon the other, they are in a relation of real opposition (Kant)——Local *self* of the finger: its space is felt-feeling.——

There is no coinciding of the seer with the visible. But each borrows from the other, takes from or encroaches upon the other, intersects with the other, is in chiasm with the other. In what sense are these multiple chiasms but one: not in the sense of synthesis, of the originally synthetic unity, but always in the sense of *Uebertragung*, encroachment, radiation of being therefore——

The things touch me as I touch them and touch myself: flesh of the world—distinct from my flesh: the double inscription outside and inside. The inside receives without flesh: not a "psychic state," but intra-corporeal, reverse of the outside that my body shows to the things.

In what sense it is *the same* who is seer and visible: the same not in the sense of ideality nor of real identity. The same in the structural sense: same inner framework, same *Gestalthafte*, the same in the sense of openness of another dimension of the "same" being.

The *antecedent* unity me-world, world and its parts, parts of my body, a unity before segregation, before the multiple dimensions—and so also the unity of time——Not an architecture of noeses-noemata, posed upon one another, relativizing one another without succeeding in unifying themselves: but there is first their underlying bond by *non-difference*——All this is *exhibited* in: the sensible, the visible. A sensible (even exterior) involves all that (this is what forms the so-called synopsis, the perceptual synthesis)———

Visible-seer = projection-introjection   They both must be abstracts from one sole tissue.

The visible-seer (for me, for the others) is moreover not a psychic something, nor a behavior of vision, but a perspective, *or better:* the world itself with a certain coherent deformation——— The chiasm truth of the pre-established harmony———Much more exact than it: for it is between local-individuated facts, and the chiasm binds as obverse and reverse ensembles unified in advance in process of differentiation

whence in sum a world that is neither *one* nor two in the objective sense—which is pre-individual, generality———

language and chiasm

· · · · · · · · · · · · · · · · · · · ·

Dream
Imaginary

November, 1960

Dream. The *other stage* of the dream———
Incomprehensible in a philosophy that *adds* the imaginary to the real—for then there will remain the problem of understanding how all that belongs to the same consciousness———
understand the dream starting from the body: as being in the world (*l'être au monde*) without a body, without "observation," or rather with an imaginary body without weight. Understand the imaginary sphere through the imaginary sphere of the body———And hence not as a *nihilation* that *counts as* observation but as the true *Stiftung* of Being of which the observation and the articulated body are special variants.
———what remains of the *chiasm* in the dream?
the dream is *inside* in the sense that the internal double of the external sensible is *inside,* it is on the side of the sensible wherever the world is not———this is that "stage," that "theater" of which Freud speaks, that place of our oneiric beliefs—and not "the consciousness" and its image-making folly.

The "subject" of the dream (and of anguish, and of all life) is the *one* [89]—i.e. the body as *enclosure* (*enceinte*)———
Enclosure which we leave since the body is *visible,* a "sort of reflection."

Chiasm———Reversibility

November 16, 1960

Speech does indeed have to enter the child as silence—break through to him through silence and as silence (i.e. as a thing simply perceived—difference between the word *Sinnvoll* and the word-perceived)———Silence = absence of the word due. It is this fecund negative that is instituted by the flesh, by its dehiscence ———the negative, nothingness, is the doubled-up, the two leaves of my body, the inside and the outside articulated over one another———Nothingness is rather the difference between the identicals———

Reversibility: the finger of the glove that is turned inside out ———There is no need of a spectator who would be *on each side.* It suffices that from one side I see the wrong side of the glove that is applied to the right side, that I touch the one *through* the other (double "representation" of a point or plane of the field) the chiasm is that: the reversibility———
It is through it alone that there is passage from the "For Itself" to the For the Other———In reality there is neither me nor the other as positive, positive subjectivities. There are two caverns, two opennesses, two stages where something will take place—and which both belong to the same world, to the stage of Being
There is not the For Itself and the For the Other   They are each the other side of the other. This is why they incorporate one another: projection-introjection———There is that line, that frontier surface at some distance before me, where occurs the veering I-Other Other-I———
The axis alone given———the end of the finger of the glove is nothingness—but a nothingness one can turn over, and where

89. TRANSLATOR: *On*—the indefinite pronoun.

then one sees *things*——The only "place" where the negative would really be is the fold, the application of the inside and the outside to one another, the turning point——

Chiasm   I—the world
            I—the other——

chiasm my body—the things, realized by the doubling up of my body into inside and outside—and the doubling up of the things (their inside and their outside)

It is because there are these 2 doublings-up that are possible: the insertion of the world between the two leaves of my body
the insertion of my body between the 2 leaves of each thing and of the world

This is not anthropologism: by studying the 2 leaves we ought to find the structure of being——

Start from this: there is not identity, nor non-identity, or non-coincidence, there is inside and outside turning about one another——

My "central" nothingness is like the point of the stroboscopic spiral, which is *who knows where*, which is "nobody"

The *I—my body chiasm*: I know this, that a body [*finalized?*] is *Wahrnehmungsbereit*, offers itself to . . . , opens upon . . . an imminent spectator, is a *charged field*——

Position, negation, negation of negation: this side, the other, the other than the other. What do I bring to the problem of the same and the other? This: that the same be the other than the other, and identity difference of difference——this 1) does not realize a surpassing, a dialectic in the Hegelian sense; 2) is realized on the spot, by encroachment, thickness, *spatiality*——

November, 1960

. . . .

Activity: passivity——Teleology

The chiasm, reversibility, is the idea that every perception is doubled with a counter-perception (Kant's real opposition), is an act with two faces, one no longer knows who speaks and who listens. Speaking-listening, seeing-being seen, perceiving-being perceived circularity (it is because of it that it seems to us that perception forms itself *in the things themselves*)——*Activity = passivity.*

This is obvious when one thinks of what nothingness is, that is, *nothing.* How would this nothing be active, efficacious? And if the subjectivity is not it, but it plus my body, how would the operation of the subjectivity not be borne by the teleology of the body?

What then is my situation with regard to *finalism?* I am not a finalist, because the interiority of the body (= the conformity of the internal leaf with the external leaf, their folding back on one another) is not something *made, fabricated,* by the assemblage of the two leaves: they have never been apart——

(I call the evolutionist perspective in question   I replace it with a cosmology of the visible in the sense that, considering endotime and endospace, for me it is no longer a question of origins, nor limits, nor of a series of events going to a first cause, but one sole explosion of Being which is forever. Describe the world of the "rays of the world" beyond every serial-eternitarian or ideal alternative——Posit the existential eternity—the eternal body)

I am not a finalist because there is dehiscence, and not positive production—through the finality of the body—of a man whose teleological organization our perception and our thought would prolong

Man is not the *end* of the body, nor the organized body the *end* of the components: but rather the subordinated each time slides into the void of a new dimension opened, the lower and the higher gravitate around one another, as *the high and the low* (variants of the side-other side relation)——Fundamentally I bring the high-low distinction into the vortex where it rejoins the side-other side distinction, where the two distinctions are integrated into a *universal dimensionality* which is Being (Heidegger)

There is no other meaning than carnal, figure and ground——Meaning = their dislocation, their gravitation (what I called "leakage" [*échappement*] in *Ph.P* [90])

90. EDITOR: *Phénoménologie de la perception*, p. 221. [Eng. trans., p. 189.]

Politics——Philosophy——Literature

November, 1960

. . . .
. . . the idea of *chiasm*, that is: every relation with being is *simultaneously* a taking and a being taken, the hold is held, it is *inscribed* and inscribed in the same being that it takes hold of.

Starting from there, elaborate an idea of philosophy: it cannot be total and active grasp, intellectual possession, since what there is to be grasped is a dispossession——It is not *above* life, overhanging. It is beneath. It is the simultaneous experience of the holding and the held in all orders. *What* it says, its *significations,* are not absolutely invisible: it shows by words. Like all literature. It does not install itself in the reverse of the visible: it is on both sides

No *absolute* difference, therefore, between philosophy or the transcendental and the empirical (it is better to say: the ontological and the ontic)——No absolutely pure philosophical word. No purely philosophical politics, for example, no philosophical rigorism, when it is a question of a Manifesto.

Yet philosophy is not immediately non-philosophy——It rejects from non-philosophy what is positivism in it, militant non-philosophy—which would reduce history to the visible, would deprive it precisely of its depth under the pretext of adhering to it better: irrationalism, *Lebensphilosophie,* fascism and communism, which do indeed have philosophical meaning, but hidden from themselves

The imaginary

November, 1960

For Sartre it is negation of negation, *an order in which nihilation is applied to itself,* and consequently counts as a positing of being although it would absolutely not be its equivalent, and although the least fragment of true, transcendent being immediately reduces the imaginary.

This assumes then a bipartite analysis: perception as observation, a close-woven fabric, without any gaps, locus of the simple or immediate nihilation
the imaginary as locus of the self-negation.

Being and the imaginary are for Sartre "objects," "entities"——

For me they are "elements" (in Bachelard's sense), that is, not objects, but fields, subdued being, non-thetic being, being before being—and moreover involving their auto-inscription their "subjective correlate" is a part of them. The *Rotempfindung* is part of the *Rotempfundene*—this is not a *coincidence*, but a dehiscence that knows itself as such

Nature

November, 1960

"Nature is at the first day": it is there today   This does not mean: myth of the original indivision and coincidence as *return*.

The *Urtümlich*, the *Ursprünglich* is not of long ago.

It is a question of finding in the present, the flesh of the world (and not in the past) an "ever new" and "always the same" ——A sort of time of sleep (which is Bergson's nascent duration, ever new and always the same). The sensible, Nature, transcend the past present distinction, realize from within a passage from one into the other   Existential eternity. The indestructible, the barbaric Principle
Do a psychoanalysis of Nature: it is the flesh, the mother.

A philosophy of the flesh is the condition without which psychoanalysis remains anthropology

In what sense the visible landscape under my eyes is not exterior to, and bound synthetically to . . . other moments of time and the past, but has them really *behind itself* in simultaneity, inside itself and not it and they side by side "in" time

Time and chiasm

November, 1960

The *Stiftung* of a point of time can be transmitted to the others without "continuity" without "conservation," without fictitious "support" in the psyche the moment that one understands time as chiasm

Then past and present are *Ineinander,* each enveloping-enveloped—and that itself is the flesh

November, 1960

. . . .
The very pulp of the sensible, what is indefinable in it, is nothing else than the union in it of the "inside" with the "outside," the contact in thickness of self with self——The absolute of the "sensible" is this stabilized explosion i.e. involving return

The relation between the circularities (my body-the sensible) does not present the difficulties that the relation between "layers" or linear orders presents (nor the immanence-transcendent alternative)

In *Ideen II,* Husserl, "disentangle" "unravel" what is entangled
The idea of chiasm and *Ineinander* is on the contrary the idea that every analysis that *disentangles* renders unintelligible——
This bound to the very meaning of *questioning* which is not to call for a response in the indicative——

It is a question of creating a new type of intelligibility (intelligibility through the world and Being as they are—"vertical" and not *horizontal*)

Silence of Perception
Silent speech, without express signification and yet rich in meaning——language——thing

November, 1960

Silence of perception = the object made of wires of which I could not say what it is, nor how many sides it has, etc. and which nonetheless is there (it is the very criterion of the observable according to Sartre that is here contradicted—and the criterion of the imaginary according to Alain that intervenes in perception)——

There is an analogous silence of language i.e. a language that no more involves acts of reactivated signification than does this perception—and which nonetheless functions, and inventively   it is it that is involved in the fabrication of a book——

"The other"

November, 1960

What is interesting is not an expedient to solve the "problem of the other"——

It is a transformation of the problem

If one starts from the visible and the vision, the sensible and the sensing, one acquires a wholly new idea of the "subjectivity": there are no longer "syntheses," there is a contact with being through its modulations, or its reliefs——

The other is no longer so much a freedom seen *from without* as destiny and fatality, a rival subject for a subject, but he is caught up in a circuit that connects him to the world, as we ourselves are, and consequently also in a circuit that connects him to us——And this world is *common* to us, is intermundane space——And there is transitivism by way of generality——And even freedom has its generality, is understood as generality: activity is no longer *the contrary* of passivity

Whence carnal relations, from below, no less than from above and the fine point   Entwining

Whence the essential problem = not to make common in the sense of creation *ex nihilo* of a common situation, of a common event plus engagement by reason of the past, but in the sense of uttering—language——

the other is a relief as I am, not absolute vertical existence

. . . .

Body and flesh——
Eros——
Philosophy of Freudianism

December, 1960

Superficial interpretation of Freudianism: he is a sculptor because he is anal, because the feces are already clay, molding, etc.

But the feces are not the *cause:* if they were, everybody would be sculptors

The feces give rise to a character (*Abscheu*) only if the subject lives them in such a way as to find in them a dimension of being——

It is not a question of renewing empiricism (feces imprinting a certain character on the child). It is a question of understanding that the relationship with feces is in the child a concrete ontology. Make not an existential psychoanalysis, but an *ontological* psychoanalysis

Overdetermination (= circularity, chiasm) = any entity can be *accentuated* as an emblem of Being (= character) → it is to be read as such

In other words to be anal *explains* nothing: for, to be so, it is necessary to have the ontological capacity (= capacity to take a being as representative of Being)——

Hence what Freud wants to indicate are not chains of causality; it is, on the basis of a polymorphism or amorphism, what is contact with the Being in promiscuity, in transitivism, the fixation of a "character" by investment of the openness to Being in an Entity—which, henceforth, takes place *through this Entity*

Hence the philosophy of Freud is not a philosophy of the body but of the flesh——

The Id, the unconscious—and the Ego (correlative) to be understood on the basis of the flesh

The whole architecture of the notions of the psycho-logy (perception, idea—affection, pleasure, desire, love, Eros) all that, all this bric-a-brac, is suddenly clarified when one ceases to think all these terms as *positive* (the more or less dense "spiritual") in order to think them not as negatives or negentities (for that brings back the same difficulties), but as *differentiations* of one sole and *massive* adhesion to Being which is the flesh (eventually as "lace-works")——Then problems such as those of Scheler (how to understand the relation of the intentional with the affective which it crosses transversally, a love being transversal to the oscillations of pleasure and pain → personalism) disappear: for there is no *hierarchy* of orders or layers or planes (always founded on the individual-essence distinction), there is dimensionality of every fact and facticity of every dimension——This in virtue of the "ontological difference"——

The body in the world.
The specular image——resemblance

December, 1960

My body *in* the visible. This does not simply mean: it is a particle of the visible, there there is the visible and here (as variant of the there) is my body. No. It is *surrounded* by the visible. This does not take place on a plane of which it would be an inlay, it is really surrounded, circumvented. This means: it sees itself, it is a visible—but it sees itself seeing, my look which finds it *there* knows that it is here, at its own side——Thus the body *stands* before the world and the world upright before it, and between them there is a relation that is one of embrace. And between these two vertical beings, there is not a frontier, but a contact surface——

The flesh = this fact that my body is passive-active (visible-seeing), mass in itself *and* gesture——

The flesh of the world = its *Horizonthaftigkeit* (interior and exterior horizon) surrounding the thin pellicle of the strict visible between these two horizons——

The flesh = the fact that the visible that I am is seer (look) or, what amounts to the same thing, has an *inside*, plus the fact that the exterior visible is also *seen*, i.e. has a prolongation, in the enclosure of my body, which is part of its being

The specular image, memory, resemblance: fundamental structures (resemblance between the thing and the thing-seen). For they are structures that are immediately derived from the body-world relation——the reflections resemble the reflected = the vision commences in the things, certain things or couples of things call for vision——Show that our whole expression and conceptualization of the mind is derived from these structures: for example *reflection*.

"Vertical" and existence

December, 1960

Sartre: the circle is not inexplicable, it is explicable by the rotation of a line around its end——But also the circle does not exist——Existence is inexplicable. . . .

What I call the *vertical* is what Sartre calls existence—but which for him immediately becomes the fulguration of nothingness which makes the world arise, the operation of the for itself.

In fact the circle exists and existence is not man. The circle exists, inexplicable, as soon as I take into account not only the circle-*object*, but this *visible* circle, this circular physiognomy which no intellectual genesis nor physical causality explains, and which *has* the very properties that I do not yet know

It is this whole field of the "vertical" that has to be awakened. Sartre's existence is not "vertical," not "upright": it certainly cuts across the plane of beings, it is transversal with respect to it, but precisely it is too distinct from it for one to be able to say that it is "upright." What is upright is the existence that is threatened by weight, that leaves the plane of objective being, but not without dragging with it all the adversity and favors it brought there.

The body always presents itself "from the same side"—(by principle: for this is apparently contrary to reversibility)

It is that *reversibility* is not an actual *identity* of the touching and the touched. It is their identity by principle (always abortive)——Yet it is not ideality, for the body is not simply a *de facto* visible among the visibles, it is visible-seeing, or look. In other words, the fabric of possibilities that closes the exterior visible in upon the seeing body maintains between them a certain *divergence* (*écart*). But this divergence is not a *void*, it is filled precisely by the flesh as the place of emergence of a vision, a passivity that bears an activity—and so also the divergence between the exterior visible and the body which forms the upholstering (*capitonnage*) of the world

It is wrong to describe by saying: the body presents itself always *from the same side* (or: we remain always on a certain side of the body—it has an inside and an outside). For this unilaterality is not simply *de facto* resistance of the phenomenon body: it has a reason for being: the unilateral presentation of the body condition for the body to be a seer i.e. that it not be a visible among visibles. It is not a truncated visible. It is a visible-archetype—and could not be so if it could be surveyed from above.

Descartes

March, 1961

. . . .
Study the pre-methodic Descartes, the *spontaneae fruges*, that natural thought "that always precedes the acquired thought" —and the post-methodic Descartes, that of after the VIth Meditation, who lives in the world after having methodically explored

it—the "vertical" Descartes soul and body, and not that of the *intuitus mentis*——And the way he chooses his models ("light," etc.) and the way that, in the end, he goes beyond them, the Descartes of before and after the order of reasons, the Descartes of the Cogito before the Cogito, who always knew that he thought, with a knowing that is ultimate and has no need of elucidation——ask what the evidence of this spontaneous thought consists of, *sui ipsius contemplatio reflexa,* what this refusal to constitute the Psyche means, this knowing more clear than all constitution and which he counts on

Descartes—*Intuitus mentis*

March, 1961

The definition of the *intuitus mentis,* founded on analogy with vision, itself understood as thought of a visual indivisible (the *details* that the artisans see)——The apprehension of "the sea" (as "element," not as individual thing) considered as imperfect vision, whence the ideal of *distinct* thought.

This analysis of vision is to be completely reconsidered (it presupposes what is in question: the thing itself)——It does not see that the vision is tele-vision, transcendence, crystallization of the impossible.

Consequently, the analysis of the *intuitus mentis* also has to be done over: there is no indivisible by thought, no simple nature ——the simple nature, the "natural" knowledge (the evidence of the I think, as clearer than anything one can add to it), which is apprehended totally or not at all, all these are "figures" of thought and the "ground" or "horizon" has not been taken into account——The "ground" or "horizon" is accessible only if one begins by an analysis of the *Sehen*——Like the *Sehen,* the *Denken* is not identity, but non-difference, not distinction, but clarity at first sight.

. . . .

Flesh

March, 1961

To say that the body is a seer is, curiously enough, not to say anything else than: it is visible. When I study what I mean in saying that it is the body that sees, I find nothing else than: it is "from somewhere" (from the point of view of the other—or: in the mirror for me, in the three-paneled mirror, for example) visible in the act of looking———

More exactly: when I say that my body is a seer, there is, in the experience I have of it, something that founds and announces the view that the other acquires of it or that the mirror gives of it. I.e.: it is visible for me in principle or at least it counts in the *Visible* of which *my* visible is a fragment. I.e. to this extent my visible turns back upon it in order to "understand" it———And how do I know that if not because my visible is nowise my "representation," but flesh? I.e. capable of embracing my body, of "seeing" it———It is through the world first that I am seen or thought.

My plan: I The visible
           II Nature
          III Logos

March, 1961

must be presented without any compromise with *humanism,* nor moreover with *naturalism,* nor finally with *theology*———Precisely what has to be done is to show that philosophy can no longer think according to this cleavage: God, man, creatures— which was Spinoza's division.

Hence we do not begin *ab homine* as Descartes (the 1st part is not "reflection") we do not take Nature in the sense of the Scholastics (the 2d part is not Nature in itself, a philosophy of Nature, but a description of the man-animality *intertwining*) and we do not take Logos and truth in the sense of the Word (the Part III is neither logic, nor teleology of consciousness, but a study of the language that has man)

The visible has to be described as something that is realized through man, but which is nowise anthropology (hence against Feuerbach-Marx 1844)

Nature as the other side of man (as flesh—nowise as "matter")

Logos also as what is realized in man, but nowise as his *property.*

So that the conception of history one will come to will be

nowise *ethical* like that of Sartre. It will be much closer to that of Marx: Capital as a *thing* (not as a partial object of a partial empirical inquiry as Sartre presents it), as *"mystery"* of history, expressing the "speculative mysteries" of the Hegelian logic. (The *"Geheimnis"* of merchandise as "fetish") (every historical object is a fetish)

Worked-over-matter–men = *chiasm*

Index

Chronological Index
to Working Notes

[279]

RRf: 168, 100-1,

reversal: 199, 83, 91, 98

Reduction: 171-2, 198, 98, 100-1,

rendering explicit: 97, 100-1,

Dialectic: 89-95